Bogota
Bin
Nov
2013

THE
INTELLIGENCERS

THE
INTELLIGENCERS

British Military Intelligence
from the
Middle Ages to 1929

Brigadier (Retd)
B.A.H. Parritt, CBE

Late Director of
The Intelligence Corps

Foreword by
Colonel A. H. Southwood MBE

Pen & Sword
MILITARY

First published in Great Britain in 2011 by
PEN & SWORD MILITARY
an imprint of
Pen & Sword Books Limited
47 Church Street
Barnsley
S. Yorkshire S70 2AS

ISBN 978 1 84884 414 8

A CIP catalogue record for this book
is available from the British Library

Typeset in Palatino by Chic Media Ltd

Printed and bound in England
by CPI

Pen & Sword Books Ltd incorporates the imprints of
Pen & Sword Aviation, Pen & Sword Maritime,
Pen & Sword Military,Wharncliffe Local History, Pen & Sword Select,
Pen & Sword Military Classics, Leo Cooper, Remember When,
Seaforth Publishing and Frontline Publishing

For a complete list of Pen & Sword titles please contact:
PEN & SWORD BOOKS LIMITED
47 Church Street, Barnsley, South Yorkshire, S70 2AS, England.
E-mail: enquiries@pen-and-sword.co.uk
Website: www.pen-and-sword.co.uk

Contents

Acknowledgements

M y thanks go to Nick Van de Bilj for acting as a catalyst to the concept of this revised edition of *The Intelligencers* and to his wife Penny, who voluntarily undertook the tedious task of typing out the original manuscript. I am also most grateful to the Staff of the Intelligence Corps Museum for their unfailing helpful attitude and positive help and above all to the remarkable Mr A.F. Judge (Fred) whose detailed research into the history of the Intelligence Corps during the First World War made the last chapters of this book possible. Finally to Colonel A.H. Southwood MBE for his professional and meticulous help in the production of the script and to my friend Michael Bowers for his wizardry with the computer.

Foreword

by

Colonel A. H. Southwood MBE

In today's world we are treated to a plethora of books and reports in the media describing the achievements of the National Intelligence and Security Agencies, MI5, MI6 and GCHQ.

They have indeed played an important role in protecting our country and its citizens from many threats. However their revelations, while absorbing and praiseworthy, often fail to make the point that much of their product is aimed at the Whitehall and political community. Little or nothing is revealed about the worker bees at the sharp end who provide the product from which the National Agencies high level assessments are made and who also provide the intelligence on the enemy forces' capabilities and intentions on which Service commanders in the field base their operational plans.

Brigadier Parritt, in providing a most absorbing and readable history of the development of Military Intelligence through the ages, tells a sorry tale of incompetence, unpreparedness and vested interests in high places; little or nothing was done to establish an intelligence organisation to support the forces sent to meet threats to British interests in various parts of the world so that it was necessary to build up an intelligence organisation locally on arrival in the theatre of operations. Then as soon as the campaign was successfully accomplished the intelligence organisation was swiftly disbanded.

It took many years for it to be accepted that a full time professional Military Intelligence organisation is a necessary integral part of any force sent to conduct campaigns around the world. Thankfully there is a happy ending as in the 1950s wise heads won the day and a regular Intelligence Corps became part of the Army's Order of Battle to provide professional intelligence support to military commanders in the field both before and during operations which has proved its worth.

CHAPTER ONE

The Scoutmaster General

The British Army has never liked or wanted professional intelligence officers. It has continually been held that the best man to help a commander assess the capabilities of enemy infantry is an infantryman, the best man to judge the potential threat of cavalry, is a cavalryman. To have an officer devote his military career to Intelligence was, in most Generals' opinion, a short sighted policy which would lead to the officer having a specialised and narrow outlook to problems which require a wide and practical background of military experience. It was not until 1957 that the gathering of intelligence and the employment of counter intelligence techniques was accepted by the British Army as a task worthy of continuous professional endeavour. In 1957 the Intelligence Corps became a regular corps, and a cadre of one hundred regular officers was formed.

The use of intelligence by the British Army, however, is as old as the Army itself. Even before the formation of the New Model Army in the middle of the 17th Century, regarded by many historians as the birth period of the British Army, there was a man appointed whose duty it was to 'Discover the whereabouts and intentions of the enemy'. He was called the Scoutmaster, one of the most senior titles in the Army. There was a Chief Engineer appointed by Edward II in 1347 at the Siege of Calais, and a Master of Ordnance established in the Tower of London during the middle of the Fifteenth Century. Then, following these two appointments came the post of Scoutmaster 'Chief reconnoitier of the army'. It was the Scoutmaster's responsibility to provide tactical military intelligence for his Commander, as described by King Henry the Eighth in 1518:

> It is the office of the Scoutmaster when he cometh to the field to set and appoint the scourage, he must appoint some to the high hills to view and see if they can discover anything. Also the said Scoutmaster must appoint one other company of scouragers to search, and view every valley thereabouts, that there be no enemies laid privily for the annoyance of the said camp, and if they do discover any, they are to advertise the Scoutmaster; and

he must either bring, or send word, to the high marshal of their advertisement, with speed.

A hundred years later the Scoutmaster still had these responsibilities, although sometimes there were failures in the system. In 1639 when King Charles the First was advancing into Scotland, he had just dismissed a review of his army and sent away the horses, when an excited Sir John Byron galloped into the camp with news that the enemy was upon them 'which alarm caused a confused riding and hurrying up and down the camp and seemed to strike an amazement into these spirits otherwise undaunted at other times, it coming so sudden and unexpected.' King Charles rode forward with his 'prospective glass' and saw to his surprise the whole Scots Army on this side of Dunce Hill at which many of the nobility and gentry being about the King said they could discern the colours flying for the advance, to which the King replied (with a Court oath) they were mistaken as the colours were still fixed upon the ground. On returning to camp, however, the King sent for the Earl of Arundel and complained that the Scoutmaster had not given adequate warning of the enemy's movements. The Scoutmaster was Roger Widdringon, chosen by Arundel as the most suitable man because he had been born in Northumberland, was familiar with the border districts and was notoriously known to be a 'Gentleman who ever bore a perfect hatred to the Scots'. Widdrington defended himself by blaming the soldiers who had been given to him as scouts and who had failed to provide timely intelligence 'but in the opinion of the court and the commanders, the Scoutmaster bore the blame and his crime was aggravated because he was a papist'.

On the outbreak of the Civil War both sides created their own Scoutmasters, and it was in this period that the duties became more complicated. Sir Samuel Luke was appointed Scoutmaster to the Earl of Essex and soon won a well-deserved reputation for the excellence of his intelligence 'This noble commander who watches the enemy so industriously that they eat, sleep, drink not, whisper not, but he can give us an account of their darkest proceedings'. Based on Eton College and then Newport Pagnell, Luke successfully ran a series of scouts and agents who provided detailed and accurate information about the Royalist Forces. He was given the very large salary of eight pounds a day (a Lieutenant General received only three pounds a day) but out of this had to pay his scouts and one pound a day spy allowance to employ 'Gentlemen and servants residing in the Royalist Court'.

In 1643 Luke was promoted to become Scoutmaster General and was made responsible for co-ordinating the intelligence gathering activities of several deputies and a far greater number of scouts and horsemen. These men would leave Newport Pagnell each day and bring back information from as far as Bristol and Gloucester and it is interesting to read that the reports covered not only military movements, but also details of every aspect of the enemy's logistics, morale, discipline and technical developments. On their return Luke would question them and then allot fresh tasks. He kept a detailed record of their activities and many of their reports subsequently proved extremely accurate. The following typical extracts from his journal must have been extremely useful to Essex as it provided confirmatory evidence that the enemy had left Oxford, were beginning an economic blockade of Aylesbury in preparation for an attack and hoped to be aided by a treacherous captain:

> James Carey returned this day and said that there are 1,000 of the Kings horse now at Bister, and a great number of horse and foot at Brill, and some at Buckingham, and that there are proclamations newly come out at Oxford to command all tenants that hold lands under the Parliament shall in future pay their rents to the King.' Christopher Goodwyn returned this day and said that the King, Queen, Prince Rupert and Prince Maurice dined yesterday in Wallingford and afterwards went to Harlington attended with 3 Colours of Horse. That there are not above 500 soldiers left in Oxford being all gone to Reading, Brill and Bister, and that there are about 1,000 in Wallingford, and that they press men daily in Oxford and Wallingford for the King's service. And he hears that the King's forces are very speedily to go against Aylesbury, and that a captain in the Town hath promised to betray it unto them.

But like all intelligence operations a hundred successes do not avert bitter comment if the enemy achieve surprise. Luke was heavily criticised for the lack of intelligence before Edgehill when the two armies, although only twenty miles apart, marched in the same direction for ten days with neither side discovering each other. But this type of criticism is perhaps a little unjustified. Luke was well aware of the clear distinction between close tactical reconnaissance, which has always been a unit commander's responsibility and his own responsibility for gaining strategic intelligence in depth. Luke was responsible for knowing all the enemy's activities, but he did not have executive power over the patrolling duties of forward units.

It is perhaps surprising that although Luke's scouts continually passed in and out of the Royalist lines 'On 16 May Samuel Brayne returned to Luke's Headquarters after spending two nights in the White Swan, Oxford and Richard Shawe returned from a barber's shop in Wallingford', only one was actually discovered and executed. Francis

Coles had crept out of Oxford on 24 December 1643 to report the affray in which the Governor of Oxford had been wounded and when returning to the City on Boxing Day was caught and hanged. Later however, both sides became more vindictive as is demonstrated in Major General Brown's letter to Abingdon, 19 December 1644, to Lord Digby:

> My Lord, you have hanged a spy (as you say) of mine, whom I know not; but that you may be balanced in this, this very morning I will cause to be hanged one of yours, condemned by our council of war six weeks ago, in accordance with an ordinance of Parliament, resolving never to be outdone by you, either in civility or justice.

The Royalists also had their Scoutmasters, but there appears to be no Scoutmaster General and there was no centralised control. Sir Charles Blunt was the Royalist Scoutmaster for the battle of Newbury and in June 1644 was Scoutmaster to the Earl of Brentford. The disaster of Naseby was in part due to the negligence of one of the King's Scoutmasters. Prince Rupert wished to know whether it were true that Fairfax was advancing to fight and sent Mr. Ruce, his Scoutmaster, to find out. 'He, in a short time returned with the lie in his mouth that he had been two or three miles forward and could neither discover or hear of the rebels.' Ruce, like many subsequent intelligence officers, must have found a satisfactory explanation to cover his negligence, for on 4 April 1646, ten months after Naseby he was honoured with a knighthood. Luke, on the other hand provided Cromwell with accurate reports of the Royalist movements from Market Drayton to Leicester and between Newport Pagnell and Naseby.

After this battle, which saved Newport Pagnell for the Parliamentarians, Luke's importance as Scoutmaster General gradually diminished and he was eventually 'paid off'. Although in a letter dated 6 June 1645 the Committee of both Kingdoms requested him 'to procure what active intelligence he is able, and communicate it to this Committee and Sir Thomas Fairfax, for the charge of which he shall be reimbursed.' Luke's successors were not necessarily soldiers; Leonard Watson was a Major, but Henry Jones who held the post in Ireland was Bishop of Clogher. The most famous, however, was undoubtedly George Downing, a twenty-six-year-old Puritan Minister who came to England from Salem, Massachusetts. Following the dissolution of Parliament in 1629, Downing's family had fled to New England but after the defeat of the royalists at Naseby, George Downing returned to become a padre, soldier and then Scoutmaster General in the New Model Army. Unlike Luke very little of George Downing's secret activities have survived, a fact which is no doubt due to his great care in destroying any incriminating evidence when the Restoration took place. In the two manuscript volumes in the British Museum containing George Downing's official papers 1644-1682, none give any clue as to the secret side of his Scoutmaster General duties. His account of the battle of Worcester however, is a model of 17th Century reporting as this extract taken from his letter to the Lord Mayor of London reveals:

Near Worcester
3 Sept 1651
Nine at night

While Lieutenant General Fleetword was still hot in dispute with the enemy at Powick bridge, then Captain Ingoldsby's and Captain Fairfax's regiment were drawn over Severn, then twenty horse; then the lifeguards, then my lord general's regiment of horse, and so, one party after another. The dispute was from hedge to hedge, and very hot; sometimes more with foot than with horse and foot. The lifeguard made a gallant charge, so did my lord general's regiment of horse; and, indeed, all who came to it did their parts gallantly, through the Lord's power in and upon them. The dispute continued to the evening all along with very great heat; and about sunset we had beaten into Worcester, and our men possessed of St. John's at the bridge end. While we were thus hot in debate, the enemy drew forth horse and foot on the other side the town towards our men who were left there; and after a while there was a very desperate charge on that side also, between them and ours, both horse and foot, where was Colonel Prise.

In conclusion, our men there also put them to the rout, and pursued them to the very town, possessed the great fort, and also that part of the city of Worcester. Truly our work is all wonders. I can inform your Lordship but little what is done, only that, so far as my eyes could on the hurry take up, there are more slain than were at Dunbar; as for prisoners, I cannot tell what number; (they being not yet brought together), nor who are taken. Of our side, I know none of note killed but Quarter Master General Moseley and, as far as yet I can judge, not a hundred of our private soldiery. Our word was 'The Lord of Hosts'. In the evening, we could see them fly out of the further side of Worcester, horse and foot. Night cuts off our pursuit but Major General Harrison is sent after them, and notice given to Colonel Lilburne and others. Captain Howard is wounded; Major General Lambert's horse shot. Your Lordship will, I hope, pardon my hasty scribbling.

We long for the appearance of the day, when we also look for the Lord's further appearance.

I am,
My Lord,
Your Lordship's most humble servant,
G. Downing.

Following the battle of Worcester the need for tactical military intelligence began to diminish and as a result the Scoutmaster's importance began to decline as well. The Government now became extremely anxious to reduce their defence expenditure. Then, as now, Parliament were prepared to vote vast sums for the unspecified use of covert 'Secret Service' but enjoyed fighting long and vociferously about relatively small amounts being spent on overt military intelligence. On 20 October 1649 they sent the following letter:

Council of State to the Lord General. Wishing to reduce the present great charge of the Commonwealth, and finding there is no action in the field, and no necessity for employing many scouts, and the Scoutmaster himself conceiving his allowance too much when there is no field service; we have thought fit and he is satisfied that henceforth and as long as there is no field service he shall receive only twenty shillings a day.

Six months later on 27 April 1650 when the son of the 'Martyr King', young Charles Stuart came marching south at the head of 16,000 avenging Scotsmen, they quickly raised the salary again to eighty shillings. But on 1 January 1653 following the prince's crushing defeats at Dunbar and Worcester, once more cut it back to forty shillings. The important intelligence targets now became political rather than military and were concentrated on the activities of the exiled Prince Charles and the imminent war with Spain. To deal with these problems in December 1652, Cromwell appointed a new man to be Secretary of State and to take charge of Intelligence, John Thurloe, a thirty-six year old lawyer. Thurloe lasted for seven years and in this time built an organization of military and political intelligence, which has never been equalled. Under Cromwell the country was divided into eleven districts, each commanded by a Major General. These men ruled with fervent puritanical ardour and encouraged a system of 'informing' wherein any man's economic, social or domestic activity was subject to report and the findings sent to Thurloe. The effect of a civil war based on religion and politics had left the country fragmented and the people suspicious of each other; an allegation that someone had conspired against the

Protector was sufficient to have the suspect incarcerated in the Tower of London 'So easy to get in, so hard to get out'.

Reports of real plots and real conspiracies abounded, but rumours of suspected plots and imaginary conspiracies were more numerous, all of which were channelled back to the Secretary of State. It was not only this flow of information however that made Thurloe so successful, there were two other important contributory factors – he had the confidence of his commander and unlimited money. Dictatorships are traditionally more generous to intelligence organizations than democracies and not since this period of Cromwell's rule has so much money, in comparative terms been granted by an English parliament for 'spying'. Thurloe spent £70,000 a year, a staggering sum for the 17th Century, which he used to establish a system of spies and informers spread not only through the United Kingdom, but also to all the capitals of Europe.

Having built his organization, Thurloe then briefed it thoroughly and paid it well. His average spy received ten pounds a month but this could be increased by good results. If the man managed to get himself admitted into close royalist circles, Thurloe was quite prepared to pay all the expenses of his clothes, home and even hunting. One spy who made friends with four Gentlemen of the Bedchamber wrote successfully for extra money. 'I thought it best to oblige them by an invitation, with some of the others of the Court to a tavern, where it cost me some five pounds, which I think not ill bestowed to effect my designs.' To George Downing, who in 1657 had given up his appointment as Scoutmaster General and become Resident in Holland he wrote:

> I desire you not to spare money for intelligence ... I pray you endeavour to lay a correspondence, and a good one, in Flanders in the Spanish court there, as also with Charles Stuart's party. I shall be at the charge thereof ... I would give some £1,000 so that it were near and intimate. I pray inform yourself what strength de Ruyter's ships are and whither bound, and when the rest of their fleet will be ready and what their number and strength will be. I pray be a little curious to know what the fleet bound for Spain carries, both the merchantmen and their convoy.

But for his generosity, Thurloe demanded a high standard in return. He insisted on weekly reports which had to contain information of significance. If a man failed to do this, he was abruptly struck off the payroll. On 26 October 1653 a man in Danzig wrote anxiously:

> Sir, Yours I received by yesterday's post, whereby you do actually discharge me from this employment because you find my letters to speak nothing of the business about which I was first sent here.

I grant the truth of what you say but there has been a great change of affairs since that time.

The man concluded by asking for a further chance, promising to do better in the future.

The result of this 'carrot and stick' policy adopted by Thurloe was that a continuous flow of information came to him from all over Europe. And as he guarded against error by always endeavouring to have more than one correspondent in each place, unknown to each other, so that the reports could be corroborated, the intelligence he produced was generally extremely accurate. Cromwell was kept up to date on the movements of fleets, the political intrigues on the Continent and the 'drinking, dancing and wenching' of the Royalist Court. In fact, very little that Charles Stuart did, failed to reach Thurloe. On one occasion a Cavalier who had sought permission to travel abroad was allowed to do so, on the condition that he did not visit the Prince. The man once abroad, however, under conditions of extreme secrecy and caution, met Charles one dark night in the presence of only three trusted courtiers. At the end of the interview the Cavalier was given a letter to take back to England that he sewed for safety in the crown of his hat. On his return he went to see Cromwell but after confirming vigorously that he had not broken his promise was suddenly asked by Cromwell:

Who put out the candles when you spoke to Charles Stuart?

In spite of the Cavalier's startled cries of innocence Cromwell then picked up his hat and extracted the letter. This denouncement, although dramatic and no doubt gratifying to Cromwell must have dismayed Thurloe, for the news eventually reached Charles who thus discovered that one of this three 'trusted' courtiers was in the Secretary's pay.

After Cromwell had decided to become 'Protector' and be appointed in Westminster Hall using the Scottish Coronation Chair, Thurloe's counter intelligence responsibilities increased. The threat of assassination now came not only from the Royalists but also from fanatical Puritans embittered by Cromwell's assumption of temporal powers. Thurloe was deluged with reports of impending disasters and his skill as an intelligence officer in selecting good from bad information was fully and continually tested. In 1657 Monsieur Stoupe, a Minister of the French Protestant Church in London received what he believed to be reliable information about a plot to kill the Protector by a man living in King Street. He offered the information to the Secretary of State but after hearing the story Thurloe decided to take no action and ignored the suggestion that he should send men to search King Street, replying, 'If we find no such person, how shall we be laughed at.' Stoupe in some pique complained to his friends who reported the matter to Cromwell. The Protector was annoyed at not being informed of the plot and a contemporary historian had described what happened:

> The Secretary of State was sent for immediately. Monsieur Stoupe repeated the story in his presence and Mr. Thurloe did not deny it, merely stating that he frequently received information of the same kind and had never yet found any of it to be true. The Protector said in his sternest manner that he should have been told this news, and have been left to judge for himself whether it was important or not.
>
> Thereupon Mr. Thurloe asked to be allowed to speak to Cromwell in private, and Monsieur Stoupe was dismissed. If he was disappointed at not being able to witness the expected scene between the two men, at least he went away satisfied that Mr Thurloe would be disgraced. But he was mistaken. Nobody knew what passed between the two men, but in the end Mr. Thurloe was forgiven.

As well as these counter intelligence responsibilities, Cromwell's expansionist aims, 'You cannot plant an oak tree in a flower pot', created a need once more for tactical military intelligence. The war against Holland had been mainly a naval affair, but after Admiral Blake's victory over Admiral Tromp, Cromwell sent 6,000 men to Flanders in support of France against Spain. Thurloe collected and collated military intelligence to help the Expedition. He asked his Agent in Flanders Colonel Marshall, about the strength of the enemy and the number of horse and foot in Dunkirk:

> This you may do with a little pain, but do it exactly, that I may certainly know how many effective men they are and how many Irish, English and Scots. If you will take pains, I will not fail to answer your desires, but a slight doing of this business will be of no use to me nor can it be expected to be of any great profit to you.

By 1657 the future of the New Model Army seemed so secure that Parliament, with traditional lack of foresight, confidently proposed to abolish the post of Deputy to the Scoutmaster General. At this time the Deputy was serving with the Army of Occupation in Scotland and General Monck replied vigorously, 'I must confess' he wrote 'That there has been as much good service done for the public by the intelligence I have gotten by the help of a Deputy Scoutmaster General, than hath been done by all the other forces in preventing of rising of parties; so that I think his Highness's affairs in these parts cannot well be carried on without such a man'. Monck, as a Service Head, was more successful than his 20th Century successors in resisting redundancies and the Deputy remained in post – although at a reduced salary.

After the death of Cromwell, Thurloe, who had served the Protector with outstanding loyalty, seemed to lose his interest for intelligence work and in 1659 made no objection when the previous incumbent Thomas Scott replaced him. As a good 'professional co-ordinator of intelligence' however, Thurloe refused to tell Scott the names of his agents 'Esteeming it treachery to reveal them without their consents.' In the abrupt reversal of fortunes that followed the return of the King, Thurloe successfully managed to retain his 'head' but was gradually deprived of all his possessions and died penniless in 1667. The place of Thurloe is unique in the story of British military and political intelligence. Although primarily a political appointee, the periods of Cromwell's totalitarian rule created the peculiar environment where one single man could control the spectrum of field, overt, covert and counter intelligence. It is from this time that the British people developed their inherent antipathy towards military rule; it is from this time that the Army developed its distrust of professional intelligence officers.

George Downing also lost his ardour for Puritanism on the demise of the Protector and began to make tentative offers to Charles. Although the King disliked him intensely he recognised, as Cromwell had done, Downing's ability to gain intelligence and so gave him employment. Downing henceforth employed all his talents to ingratiate himself with the King. He chose the best possible way, the capture of the Regicides, the killers of the King's father. He arranged with a Dutchman, who knew three of the men, to betray them, and later described with terrible vividness their capture. He and his armed escort approached,

> And on knocking at ye door, one of the house came to see who it was and the doors being open, the under scout and whole company rushed immediately into the house, and into the rooms where they were sitting by a fyere side with a pipe of tobacco and a cup of beere, immediately they started up to have got out at a back door but it was too late, the room was in a moment fulle. They made many excuses, one to have got liberty to have fetch his coat and another to go to privy, but all in vayne. Corbet did not lodge in that house but had that night supped with Barkstead so had we come a moment later he had been gone and before I could have disposed of the other two would in all probability have gotten the alarm, but fynding himself thus seized on, his body fell to purging upwards and downwards in a most strange manner.

After a brief imprisonment in the tower, Corbet, Okey and Barkstead were executed on Tyburn and the fact that Colonel Okey had been Downing's old commanding officer seems to have caused the ex-Scoutmaster General few qualms of conscience. The King was delighted with the affair, Downing became Sir George Downing and was given a succession of lucrative diplomatic and Governmental posts, including Secretary to the Treasury; he built himself a town house and settled down a staunch royalist. George Downing's treachery and double-dealing had paid handsome dividends and his house is still used by the Government – Number 10 Downing Street. But Charles the Second did not use him as Scoutmaster and in 1660 for the campaign in Ireland appointed Sir Theopilus Jones, the pay being '6s.8d a day and £100 a year besides'. Jones duties, like Luke's were quite distinct from the tactical reconnaissance tasks of the cavalry and forward infantry, and this was well described in 1671 by Sir James Turner:

> The English have a General officer whom they qualify with the title of Scoutmaster General. I have known none of them abroad, but I hear in some places of Italy they have something very like him, and that is Il Capitano di Spioni, i.e. the Captain of the Spies. I cannot believe that this Scoutmaster, has anything to do with that intelligence which I call publick and is obtained by parties whether of horse or foot; for the commanding of these, and the keeping of the lists of their turns or toures belongs properly to the Major Generals and the several Majors of Regiments both of the Cavalry and Infantry, none which I conceive will suffer the Scoutmaster to usurp their office. They must then only have the regulation of the private intelligence, wherein no doubt there may ease the General of the Army very much.

In the 1684 Nathan Brooks 'Army List', under General Officers, it gives second from bottom, senior only to the 'Chirurgeon General', Colonel James Halsey, the Scoutmaster General, but this is the last reference and in 1686 after the accession of James II the post of Quarter Master General was created and the duties formerly done by the Harbinger who was the officer responsible for provisioning the Army, the Provost Marshall and the Scoutmaster General were amalgamated. The effect of this unification was that for the next one hundred years Britain had neither an individual nor an organization primarily concerned with the collecting and collating of military intelligence. Instead the Commander himself assumed responsibilities of Head of Intelligence, and the first to do so was the greatest of British Captains, John Churchill, Duke of Marlborough.

CHAPTER TWO

John Churchill

he last battle fought between Englishmen on English soil was at Sedgemoor on 6 July 1685. Two factors enabled King James' Army to beat the Duke of Monmouth – the dogged courage of the King's regular soldiers, alarmed from their beds at 2 am to fight in the dark against an enemy having the advantage of surprise; and a gross failure by Monmouth's 'intelligence adviser', a bastard called Richard Godfrey. For three weeks after landing in England in his attempt to seize the throne Monmouth, who called himself the 'New Head and Captain General of the English Protestants' had been harried and pursued by Colonel John Churchill, Second in Command of the Royalist forces. Using the Household Cavalry and Kirk's Regiment of Foot (The Queens), Churchill had drawn a net around the unfortunate Duke and by a methodical series of advances had driven him back to Bridgwater in Somerset. On the morning of 5 July, Monmouth had decided to retreat once more and was moving northwards to Bristol but as he led his dispirited troops over the bridge he was halted by an excited young farmer who gave him the news that the Royalist forces were setting up camp only three miles from Bridgwater and seemed open to attack.That morning a Mr. Sparks who was a landowner in the village of Chedzoy had climbed the village church and with his 'perspective glass' had seen the King's army settle down to camp on the open ground around Weston Zoyland. Having sympathies with the rebel cause, but a prudence, which perhaps saved his life, Sparks did not go himself to alert Monmouth but sent his farm labourer. Richard Godfrey. Godfrey, who was illegitimate and sometimes known by his Mother's name of Newton, explained the position to Monmouth and then led him up the tower of Bridgwater Church to see for himself. For the Duke it was to be the most crucial decision of his life. Should he attack, or once more retreat? He hesitated then asked his Commanders for advice. They all urged attack – provided the Royalists had not constructed any defences.

For Godfrey also it was the moment of fate. The Duke turned to him and asked that he return to Weston and discover the exact positioning of the enemy. Willingly, but no doubt with great trepidation Godfrey did as he was asked then returned with a detailed description of the Royalist

Camp. It was extremely accurate, the guns under the guard of Colonel Churchill were on the left, the infantry were 150 yards away on the right facing the Moor and the cavalry were posted in Weston Zoyland itself. It was a creditable effort and well worth the reward of a guinea given to him by Monmouth, but it omitted the vital piece of intelligence that to the West and North sweeping round in a protecting arc was a wide, deep and flooded canal known to the Somerset farmers as the 'Bussex Rhine'. Some historians allege that Godfrey must have mentioned the obstacle to Monmouth, and that the Duke intended to incorporate it in his plan. But the evidence points the other way. Although it was July, the rainfall had been heavy and a few days earlier Lord Feversham the Royalist Commander had written complaining to his wife 'We have an abundance of rain which has very much tired our soldiers, which I think is ill, because it makes us not press the Duke of Monmouth as we should be.' Now, as the Duke viewed from his church tower observation post the ground no doubt looked green and clear, and in this he may be forgiven for even today with modern binoculars it is extremely difficult to distinguish existing rhines. Without sound advice even a commander's personal eye is not always sufficient as General Sir Garnet Wolseley subsequently wrote when describing this incident in detail.

> Godfrey's omission to report the existence of the Bussex Rhine in front of the Royal army was fatal to Monmouth. To come as he did, unawares and at night, upon such a formidable obstacle with undisciplined troops, was certain to occasion confusion, if not panic. History tells us of many military operations which, though apparently well planned, have failed entirely because the scheme of attack was based upon imperfect information. The civilian spy often does not understand the relative importance of obstacles. He gets over them himself with the greatest ease, and it does not occur to him that an army will have greater difficulty. The tactical importance of a wet ditch even as big as the Bussex Rhine is incomprehensible to the peasant or farmer who has been accustomed to cross it daily at a ford or a single plank.

Godfrey could also tell the Duke that the King's soldiers had been drinking appreciatively and copiously, of the Somerset cider and that throughout the camp he had heard the sound of carousing. It was this last piece of intelligence that decided the Duke; he would risk everything and try that most hazardous of all engagements, a night attack. A few hours later in a dark swirling mist Richard Godfrey led the rebel force out of Bridgwater across the unmarked Moor towards Weston. With so much at stake silence was essential and Monmouth had given explicit instructions that if anyone made a noise 'He was to be stabbed dead by his nearest comrade.' But in the excitement and fog poor Godfey lost his way, there were two other ditches to be crossed before they reached the Bussex Rhine and it was two a.m. before Monmouth's Horse and Foot were across the second. It was at this critical moment that the alarm was given, a shout; a pistol shot and Churchill's men came tumbling out of their quarters cursing and tense. The Duke's cavalry now spurred forward leaving Godfrey standing by the ditch but to their horror instead of being able to gallop into the half-awake soldiers they were pulled up short by the yearning gap of the Bussex Rhine. Like sheep at a stream they split left and right seeking a ford, and as they rode frantically up and down the west bank, the infantry of the east bank formed up by platoons and then issued their challenge:.

'Who are ye for?'
'The King.'
'Which King?'
'King Monmouth – and God with him.'
'Then take that with ye.'

And out of the darkness with a spluttering crackle a volley crashed into the Duke's Horse. It caused the untrained cavalry to disintegrate in panic. If Monmouth had been able to burst in on Feversham's sleeping army, success might well have been his. King James was never popular and a victory in the West would inevitably have brought more supporters to the Protestant cause. It is virtually certain that 1685 would not have marked the last battle on English soil. As it was, the original regiments of the British Army, the Grenadier Guards, the Coldstream Guards, the Royal Scots, the Kings Own and the Queens Royal Regiment regrouped, advanced and slaughtered their countrymen as they fled. Monmouth was caught and beheaded and his followers were hunted and hanged by the pitiless Judge Jeffreys. The revolution was crushed. Colonel John Churchill had been caught asleep. His spy in Bridgwater has warned him that Monmouth intended to leave the Town, and this information Churchill had passed to Clarendon:

I find by the enemy's warrant to the constables, that they have more mind to get horses and saddles than anything else, which looks as if he had a mind to break away with his horse to some other place and leave his foot entrenched at Bridgwater.

He did not appreciate however that Monmouth was going to attack that night. But he learnt his lesson. In all his subsequent campaigns, in all the great battles and marches between 1702-1711 he was never again surprised by the enemy. He never forgot how disciplined training had saved him in the alarm and confusion of a night attack and he never forgot the tragic fate of Monmouth who had accepted his intelligence from the enthusiastic but unskilled Richard Godfrey. The result was, that fifteen years later when he was appointed Commander of the Allied Armies in the Low Countries he carefully divided his intelligence organization into two distinct parts, close tactical military intelligence and deep strategic political intelligence. He then chose two men to supervise these separate aspects both of whom had his complete trust and both of whom showed an exceptional ability to 'Think with their Commander's mind'.

The man responsible for military intelligence was a large, wild, Irish extrovert called William Cadogan. Cadogan had fought as a boy cornet under King William at the battle of the Boyne and then with Marlborough at the sieges of Cork and Kinsale. At these sieges he had so impressed Marlborough, that when he left for the Hague in 1701 he took Cadogan with him to be his Quarter-Master General. This in spite of the fact that Cadogan was only a major and twenty-five years younger than the Duke. As Quarter-Master General, Cadogan revealed an exceptional ability to 'Make the wheels run smoothly'. The staffs were extremely small and Cadogan handled all the detail for moving, feeding and maintaining the polyglot Allied Force. But this logistic support provided by Cadogan was not his greatest contribution. His value to Marlborough lay in his role of 'Chief Reconnoitier'. In all ten campaigns of the War of the Spanish Succession, Cadogan was continually detailed to move ahead of the main force to recruit guides and to discover what was happening. Sometimes, with only with a small party, as on the march to the Danube when he pressed ahead of the 'Scarlet Caterpillar' to site the camps; sometimes with a larger force as at Ramillies when, with six hundred cavalry he first sighted the glinting splendour of Villeroy's army; and sometimes, as at Oudenarde, when in command of the Advance Guard with sixteen battalions, eight squadrons and thirty-two guns he first discovered that the French Army was still East of the River Scheldt and was able to dart forward and establish bridgeheads for Marlborough to cross with the main body of the army. He had his horse shot beneath him at Donauworth, was wounded at Blenheim and captured at Tournay. But his wild élan in battle was coupled with an ability to make calm, sound assessments of the enemy's forces and intentions. Marlborough learnt that he could trust the intelligence of his Quarter-master General and as a result Cadogan became a Colonel in 1703 and a Brigadier-General in 1709.

The other man responsible for co-ordinating intelligence reports was Adam de Cardonnel, Marlborough's Private Secretary. Over the years Marlborough had gradually built up a network of informers, agents and spies spread throughout Europe. It was an age when pre-knowledge of the enemy commander's intentions was perhaps even more important than it was in the Second World War, as there were no means of rapid transport, such as aeroplanes, trucks or trains to help a General re-concentrate at the critical point of danger if a false appreciation was made of the enemy's movements. What a priceless piece of intelligence it must have been for Marlborough to receive a letter during his march to the Danube, which gave him, the complete composition of the French Army, together with their battle plans.

The author of this report was a man called Robethon who held the knowledgeable position of Confidential Secretary to the Elector of Brunswick. Well paid by Marlborough, he used the money to filch and bribe from the cabinet of the War Minister in Paris the complete French plans and then sent them on a long circuitous route through France and Germany to arrive eventually at the Duke's tent. Small wonder that a French historian has commented acidly 'Chamillart had let himself be robbed of the secret of the campaign plan. Nothing is beyond the reach of gold, and it looks as if Marlborough, although blamed for avarice, knew how to spend money. As clever at piercing the hidden designs of his enemy, as in beating him on the field of battle, he united the cunning of the fox to the force of the lion.' But Robethon was not Marlborough's best agent, there was someone else, still unknown, who had a position of trust in the French Court itself. The Blenheim papers contain over four hundred letters from Paris dealing with the events of 1708 to 1710. The letters, written in French and unsigned, reveal that the writer must have been a man of influence and intelligence, accepted by the French Court as one of themselves. The letters, as well as including pieces of military and political intelligence that the spy himself must have collected, also contain 'tit-bits' from a multitude of various 'contacts'. It is not clear whether these sources were conscious or unconscious, i.e. knew that they were passing on information to the spy or were just guilty of 'careless talk', but from the wealth of intimate detail the letters provide about the private lives of King Louis XIV and Madame de Maintenon, one of them must have been a servant in very close contact with the Royal Household.

But agents and spies of this calibre cost money and there was no money allocated by the Government for this purpose. Marlborough therefore adopted a practice that his predecessors had done before him, he misappropriated money allotted for other purposes. A sensible thing to do – as long as one's friends remain in power – but when the wheel of fortune turned and Marlborough's political enemies took office he suddenly found himself accused of being little better than a common thief. The facts were simple, and overpowering. Marlborough was shown to have accepted over £63,000 from the contractors who supplied bread and wagons to the Army. A clear case of corruption. Worse, he had not accounted for some £280,000 given to him to pay foreign soldiers serving with the British Army. The Duke now found himself attacked both in and out of Parliament and after the publication of a very critical official report decided it was necessary to make the following eloquent defence:

> The first Article in the Report is founded upon the deposition of Sir Solomon de Medine, by which you are informed of a yearly sum paid by him and his predecessor, contractors for Bread and Bread-Wagons, to myself. This payment in my letter I have called a perquisite of the general or commander-in-chief in the Low Countries; and it has been constantly applied to one of the most important parts of the service there, I mean the procuring of intelligence, and other secret service. It will be necessary that I trouble the House with an account of the time and occasion whence this payment of 2½ per cent by the foreign troops commenced. During the last war, the allowances by parliament for the contingencies of the army, of which that of Secret Service is the principal, was £50,000 per annum. But this allowance fell so far short of the expense of that head, that upon the prospect of this war's breaking out, the late king assured me that this last part of the service never cost him less than £70,000 per annum. However, the allowance of parliament for the whole contingent service during this war has been but £10,000 per annum, £3,000 of which or thereabouts has generally gone for other contingencies than that of intelligence. The late king, being unwilling to come to parliament for more money, on that head of the Service, proposed this allowance from the foreign troops, as an expedient to assist that part of the Service, and commanded me to make the proposition to them; which I did accordingly, and it was readily consented to. By this means a new fund of about £15,000 per annum was provided for carrying on the Secret Service, without any expense to the public, or grievance to the troops from whom the allowance was made.
>
> I cannot suppose that I need to say how essential a part of the Service this is, that no war can be conducted successfully, without early and good intelligence, and that such advices cannot be had

but at a very great expense. Nobody can be ignorant of this that knows anything of secret correspondence or considers the numbers of persons that must be employed in it, the great hazard they undergo, the variety of places in which the correspondence must be kept, and the constant necessity where is of supporting and feeding this Service; not to mention some extraordinary expenses of a higher nature, which ought only to be hinted at. And I affirm, that whatever sums have been received on this account, have been constantly employed in procuring intelligence, in keeping correspondence, and other Secret Service ... And though the merit of our successes should be least of all attributed to the general, the many successful actions, such as have surpassed our own hopes, or the apprehensions of the enemy, in this present war in Flanders, to which our constant good intelligence has greatly contributed, must convince every gentleman, that such advices have been obtained and consequently that this money has been rightly applied.

The Duke finished his defence by resort to a stratagem, which has long proved successful against charges of waste. He showed the expense to be an economy – 'And I believe I may venture to affirm that I have in the article for Secret Services, saved the Government near four times the sum this deduction amount to – which I must reckon so much money saved to the public.' But it was of no avail and a motion condemning the Duke was passed in the House of Commons. The Attorney General was directed to prosecute and proceedings began. Marlborough, sick at heart, left for exile in Europe and accompanying him in disgrace went Cadogan.

For the British Intelligence Officer Marlborough's fate is a salutary lesson. To obtain good intelligence is not sufficient, the methods used must also be above reproach. Today this rule still applies, and whether it be the use of pressure during an interrogation, or the use of public monies to pay informers, the military intelligence officer must be ever careful that he never pursues his aim in such a manner, or to such a degree, that he cannot subsequently justify himself in open court-martial.

CHAPTER THREE

The Eighteenth Century

hroughout the eighteenth century the story of British Military Intelligence is linked with the story of successive Quarter-Master Generals. Continuing the precedent established by Marlborough, the Quarter-Master General was responsible not only for obtaining guides and siting the camps but also for gathering what intelligence he could by interviewing deserters, sending out spies and co-ordinating the scouts. Sometimes with tragic results. In 1745 when the Young Pretender landed in Scotland to challenge the Hanoverian King he appointed as his Adjutant General, his Quarter-Master General and his Chief Intelligence Officer the one man, John William O'Sullivan. O'Sullivan was an excitable Irish Adventurer who firmly believed that in times of stress the best antidote was to retire to bed, open a vein and drain off a quantity of blood. If there had been a Jacobite victory at Culloden no doubt O'Sullivan's name would have been better know. As it was, he underestimated the size of the Duke of Cumberland's army and he selected a flat site quite unsuitable for the courageous but undisciplined Highlanders to charge into battle. He also insisted that the Scots Army should form up in ranks six deep. This meant that when the cannon balls came 'Floating through the air like big black puddings' they not only slew the front men but also continued to mangle the five men behind. Historians have dealt harshly with O'Sullivan. Perhaps it was the constant blood letting which sapped his courage, but after ordering the troops to 'Pray march directly on the enemy', it was he who first smelt the terror of defeat and galloped back to the small Jacobite cavalry with the alarmed cry 'All is going to pot'. It was O'Sullivan who realised that the long jabbing bayonets wielded by the lines of English soldiers were proving a murderous riposte to the whirling slashing broadsword; it was he who took hold of the dazed, unhappy, Prince's bridle and led him into a lifetime of exile.

During the Seven Years War the Quarter-Master General was again the intelligence officer but this time, as in the Marlborough Wars, the Commander split the intelligence duties between the Quarter-Master General, Friedrich Von Bauer and his Private Secretary, Christian Von

Westphalen. The similarity of Bauer and Westphalen with Cadogan and Cardonnel is remarkable. Prince Ferdinand who commanded 'His Britannic Majesties Army in Germany' continually used Bauer to move ahead of the army, obtain tactical intelligence and be his 'eyes and ears'. Like Cadogan, Bauer understood his Commander's mind and on several occasions took command of a reserve battalion and led it into battle at the critical point. Prince Ferdinand's Secretary Westphalen, like Marlborough's Cardonnel, maintained an extensive correspondence with agents, spies and informers and then presented his deductions to the Prince. But neither was designated 'Head of Intelligence' and very probably would have considered themselves insulted if such a title had been suggested. The General himself was Head of Intelligence and this is demonstrated in what is surely the most dramatic British battle of the eighteenth century. Here the commander used neither Quarter-Master General, Private Secretary nor Head of Intelligence to help him. He interrogated deserters himself; he did his own reconnaissances and then made his own decisions. He successfully deceived both the enemy and his own brigadiers. It was a masterly example of good intelligence, brilliantly applied. The battle was Quebec, the General, James Wolfe.

By the beginning of September 1759 General Montcalm with his French Army in Montreal must have felt reasonably confident of success. The end of the campaigning season had practically arrived and already the bad weather was showing that the invading English army would soon have to attack, or retreat in shame. Three landings had already been repulsed and it was known that General Wolfe was continually sick and had 'fallen out' with his senior officers. Quebec, protected by the River St. Lawrence was as secure a fortress as anywhere on the Continent, the high natural defences having been skilfully strengthened by French Engineers. Time was on the French side, all they had to do was 'sit tight' and wait. General James Wolfe was only 32. The age that regular British Army officers are now promoted from captain to major. He had however, seen active service at Dettingen, Falkirk, Culloden and Louisburg and had risen in rank because of his exceptional ability to command men. As he lay on his sick bed he made his appreciation of the opportunities to give battle. His conclusion was, that to capture Quebec he must force Montcalm to leave the fortified City and meet him in open battle on the Plains of Abraham. But where could he cross the River? Each time he moved his Force, the French counter-marched on the other side and when he had made a river assault, the French had stoutly manned the overhanging entrenchments and put down such a rate of musket fire that the attacking force had been driven back with heavy casualties.

From his various intelligence reports however one spot began to isolate itself in Wolfe's mind, the beach at the Anse on Foulon. He knew four important facts: first that there was a path leading from this small beach to the summit, second that the regular French Regiment de la Reine which had been in the area had been posted to Montreal, third, that the man in charge of the path, a French Canadian called Feagor Duchambon, had recently been court-martialled for failing in his duties and fourth, that of the one hundred militiamen allotted to guard the path, half had been allowed to go home to help gather in the harvest. Four random snippets of information garnered from intercepted letters, spies, deserters, redskin scouts and locally enlisted Ranger units, unimportant items in themselves but if collated together, all pointing to one weak link in Montcalm's armour. Another piece of information gathered from the Navy was that a rowing boat, carried on the ebb tide, could move faster downstream than any body of horsemen riding along the bank.

The next step was to confirm the reports. He could have sent the Yankee Rangers, a guide and scout unit specially raised to carry out such tasks. 'They are better for ranging and scouting than either work, or sentry duty'. Instead, on 9 September Wolfe decided to carry out a lone reconnaissance. Wrapped in his cloak he had himself rowed to a point opposite the Anse on Foulon and with his telescope closely observed the path. He saw a furrow in the steep cliff face caused by a small rivulet and, by the side of this gully rising through the trees, a track, steep, difficult and blocked near the top with felled trees and shrubs. A dangerous climb, hazardous in the extreme if attempted at night, however, as reported, it did not seem heavily guarded with only 'Twelve or thirteen tents' clustered by the top and no other outpost visible within half a mile. Wolfe therefore concluded that an attack at the Anse on Foulon was possible. The path could be climbed by agile determined men – but if the enemy were at all forewarned, or even suspicious, fifty militiamen no matter how ill led could hold up a complete army. It was a case where counter-intelligence, i.e. the denying of information to the enemy, was as important as operational intelligence, i.e. obtaining of intelligence about the enemy.

The next day, the 10th, Wolfe went back down the River taking his Staff, including the Quarter-Master General with him. This time however, he did not land opposite the Anse on Foulon but a few hundred yards downstream. He insisted that the officers all wore soldier's greatcoats over their uniforms to cover their gold braid and had the party pace out the ground as if a new camp was to be sited. The French sentries saw the party, saw the gold braid beneath the flapping greatcoats – but took no significance in the matter. It was reported to their Headquarters but no deductions or action resulted. The strange fact is, that although Wolfe achieved the commander's ideal of showing his officers the site of the intended battle, discussing with them the problems of control and movement; amongst the ten officers included on the reconnaissance only three or four seem to have been aware of the exact point of landing. Throughout the following two days Wolfe supervised the implementation of his plan, 1,700 men in thirty five flat-bottomed boats to cast off in the dark and drift approximately thirteen miles downstream, past rocks and shoals to land on a small undistinguished, unmarked beach. Small wonder that on the afternoon preceding the assault his three Brigadiers wrote a joint letter to the General and complained 'As we do not think ourselves sufficiently informed of the several facts which may fall to our share in the execution of the descent you intend tomorrow, we must beg leave to request from you, distinct orders as to the plans, or place, we are to attack'. They had all been to the area, they had even discussed the path and its obstruction, but until seven hours before the assaulting boats cast off, only those actually responsible for guiding the fleet were aware of the exact landing site. It was a masterly example of good security, as Wolfe in his answering letter to the Brigadiers pointed out 'Its not the usual thing to point out in public orders the direct spot of an attack, nor for an inferior officer not charged with a particular duty, to ask instructions on that point'. Wolfe's crushing reply was justified, for on the same day a sergeant of the 60th Royal American Regiment deserted and although his report warned Montcalm that the troops were preparing to re-embark, the sergeant did not know the vital piece of intelligence, i.e. where the attack was to fall. How gratified Wolfe would have been to read in Montcalm's journal 'Deserters. Verbiage. Aucune Lumiere'.

One last danger remained, if the French sentries spotted the boats as they glided down the river, there was every chance that before they reached Foulon, Captain Duchambon would be alerted and ready to slaughter them on the beach. Again Wolfe took a snippet of intelligence and incorporated it in his plan. He knew that the French often sent provision boats down the River to Quebec, also that a fleet of such boats was preparing to sail. He therefore placed French-speaking officers in the leading boats and primed them with the story that they represented these provision boats and were members of a certain regiment. This foresight by Wolfe paid the ultimate dividend. As the English boats with their tense exposed cargos swirled downstream, out of the darkness came a sentry's startled cry:

'Qui Vive?'
'France – et Vive le Roi' replied Captain Fraser of the 78th
Highlanders
'A quel Regiment?'
'De la Reine' again replied Captain Fraser.

The man puzzled and unsure trotted along the bank 'Let them go, they are our provisions' called another sentry and in a moment the boats had disappeared into the darkness.

Captain James Chad of the Royal Navy was the man who guided the boats to Foulon. Any amateur yachtsman, who has tried to select a particular landing site against a heavily wooded slope in the dark, will sympathise with his problem. It was a battle where skill and daring achieved their just rewards. Chad got them to the exact spot, Captain De Laune, an Assistant Quarter-Master General, led the light infantry to the top of the cliff, and then Wolfe deployed his army and slew the flower of the French Army with three controlled musket volleys. Wolfe represents the acme of one man combining commander and intelligence officer. He had used his Quarter-Master General, Colonel Guy Carleton to seek intelligence as he reported in a letter to Pitt 'However, to divide the Enemy's Force and to draw their attention as high up the River as possible and to procure some Intelligence, I sent a detachment under command of Colonel Carleton, to land at the Point de Trampe to attack whatever he might find there, bring off some prisoners and all the useful papers he could get'. But Carleton was a commander in his own right, as was Cadogan and Bauer. At the battle of Quebec Carleton led the regiment of Louisbourg Grenadiers and was severely wounded. He was by no means a Head of Intelligence. It was Wolfe alone who read all intelligence reports, he personally questioned deserters and then sent the various scout units to gain collateral information. From all these sources Wolfe drew what he wanted and made his own plan. A perfectly secure plan, as he confided in nobody else.

General Wolfe showed that if one man is capable of assimilating all the information available, turning it into intelligence by relating it to other known facts and then incorporating it into a plan, then there is no need for a Head of Intelligence or indeed even an Intelligence Staff. But apart from General Wolfe's undoubted genius there was another factor that helped him succeed in his intelligence coup, it was the advantage of operating in the environment of an English speaking community. Only rarely in the eighteenth and nineteenth centuries did the British have this opportunity to mix easily with both friend and foe, using their own language and sharing the same habits of dress and social custom. During the wars in Canada and America those officers concerned with intelligence were presented with a wonderful chance to dabble in all sorts of sabotage and espionage activities not possible when fighting people of a different race or colour.

So great was this temptation that on 2 October 1780 in a small church converted into a temporary court-room was enacted one of the most poignant episodes in the story of British Military Intelligence. Standing in the 'dock' was a young handsome English officer who had been captured wearing civilian clothes by the rebel American Army under General Washington. The officer had proved his identity and had eloquently defended himself by explaining that he had taken off his uniform, against his will when under duress, but it had been to no avail and in a terrible silence the Court had pronounced the verdict.

> Major André, Adjutant General to the British Army, ought to be considered a spy from the enemy and that, agreeable to the law and usage of nations, it is their opinion that he that he ought to suffer death.

The following day André was taken outside and in front of a gawping crowd asked to climb upon a horse-drawn wagon. A rope was placed around his neck, the horse was struck and as it moved forward the Adjutant General, the 'Office in charge of Intelligence' swung to his death.

John André was a very accomplished man. As well as his ability to sketch fortifications and write good military English, he could sing ballads, write poetry and paint delightful cameos. He had been captured by the Americans under General Benedict Arnold in 1775 but had been released in a prisoner-of-war exchange and had then risen to the position of Aide-de-Camp to General Clinton, Commander of the British Army in New York. General Clinton was a man described at the time as 'Haughty, churlish, stupid and scarcely ever spoken with, rough as a bear – though as brave as a lion'. Like many other Generals whose advancement has been the result of prowess on the battlefield rather than through academic ability, Clinton found it satisfying and agreeable to have as his Aide a more refined, witty and cultured man. Although only seven years in the Army, John André so gained Clinton's confidence that to the undisguised disgust of more senior officers, he was promoted first to be Deputy Adjutant General and then Adjutant General. As well as the operational and administrative duties, which were the responsibility of the Adjutant General, André also became involved with intelligence work. During the period of his captivity he had made a conscious effort to memorise many details of the American forces and their dispositions, this gave him an advantage when the rebel forces were being discussed. He had also made many friends with the local loyal population, where his private income, his charm and his position made him a welcome visitor, especially to those homes with unmarried daughters. From all these contacts André drew information that he then passed onto General Clinton, until eventually he was nominated by Clinton to be the 'Officer in charge of intelligence'.

As well as collecting the reports of scout units and interviewing deserters André now spent more and more of his time with loyal refugees trying to establish a spy network behind the rebel lines. These men proposed that a 'Board of Intelligence should be formed composed of loyalist refugees from each state who would be empowered to gain information and prevent unrest by employing their own spies'. But although Clinton rejected this plan as he did not like the idea of civilians controlling an intelligence organization, he encouraged André to recruit spies for himself. It was a delicate and dangerous game and André was on several occasions completely deceived by men who proved to be acting as double agents. His scepticism can be imagined therefore when two men visited him late one night bringing a letter signed 'Augustus' and purporting to contain information from the celebrated American General, Benedict Arnold.

By 1779 Benedict Arnold had achieved an international reputation for his bravery and leadership. He had risen in rank because of an aggressive determination to lead his men into battle. Time and time again he had successfully inspired undisciplined and highly volatile militia to attack regular British soldiers. Unfortunately his military ambition was matched by a similar commercial ambition, and even in the comparatively loose atmosphere of the eighteenth century his constant ability to make money from his command appointments gave his enemies sufficient grounds to have him court-martialled and disgraced. André knew this, but still doubted if a man of Arnold's status would turn traitor. He therefore sent back to 'Augustus' a rather vague note offering to pay an unspecified sum for 'services rendered' and signed it John Anderson. He also sent a dictionary for use in any future correspondence so that the letters could be put into code using page number, line and word. So began a correspondence in which both sides stalked round each other like two dogs meeting in a narrow lane. Arnold was fearful for his life;, worried by his conscience but willing to send intelligence, provided suitable rewards could be guaranteed. André was delighted to have hooked such a large fish, but still not sure if he could land his catch – and at what expense.

Week after week, month after month, agents risked their lives to carry letters, but nothing definite emerged until Washington told Arnold that he was to take command of the new American Fortress at West Point. The Americans had no naval vessels so British ships were able to use the River Hudson as an unobstructed highway into the heartland of the rebel states. It was to seal this gap that the Americans had spent three years of labour and £3,000,000 to build a series of fortifications where the River was narrow and which they hoped would be impregnable against any attack. The capture of the site as well as being a great military victory would, in addition, be a great blow to American morale. After four years of fighting the rebel cause was at its lowest ebb. The whole of the South was lost and although in the North the British only held New York, there seemed no hope of ever dislodging them. The soldiers had not been paid and in many cases were short of food. The loss of West Point might well have meant the end of the war, as General Clinton suggested in a subsequent dispatch.

> General Arnold surrendering himself, the Forts and Garrisons, at this instant, would have given every advantage that could have been desired. Mr Washington must have instantly retired from King's Bridge and the French troops on Long Island would have been consequently unsupported, and probably would have fallen into our hands. The consequent advantage of so great an event I need not explain.

Benedict Arnold was prepared to surrender West Point for £20,000. He also wanted £10,000 for past intelligence and a £500 stipend for life. For André this letter must have represented an intelligence officer's dream – yet also a nightmare. As well as all the other advantages, the capture would be a personal triumph, for although he held the local rank of Major, his extreme youth precluded him promotion to substantive rank unless he could achieve some dramatic result. But how could he be sure that he was writing to Arnold and not some miserable pretender? The only answer was to meet Arnold in person and discover for himself what Arnold was like and by what means the capture of West Point could be arranged. A letter was therefore sent back to 'Augustus' allowing him £500 for past intelligence and agreeing to pay £20,000 for the surrender of West Point – 'provided 3,000 men and a great quantity of artillery and stores were captured as well'.

In any event, the letter continued, Arnold 'would have no cause to complain and essential services shall be even profusely rewarded, far beyond the stipulated indemnification'. But, the letter concluded, these matters could only be settled 'To mutual satisfaction' at a meeting which André 'Was willing himself to effect' either under a flag of truce 'Or in whatever manner at the time appear most eligible'. Again a series of disjointed and cryptic notes passed between the two until all was arranged for André, acting under a flag of truce and pretending to be John Anderson, a refugee who wished to work for the Americans, to meet Arnold secretly at a secluded spot between the American and British front lines. General Clinton was most reluctant to allow his young assistant to go on this dangerous mission, but he too was racked by the terrible fear that the whole plot might only be a hoax. He therefore yielded to André's pleas on condition that 'André did not place himself in the position of a spy by changing his uniform, he did not enter any enemy post and he did not carry any incriminating documents'.

André broke all these orders. The rendezvous with Arnold was successfully kept, the details of how to deliver up 3,086 men to the British discussed, but before the final points had been agreed dawn had broken and André, instead of being able to return to the boat that had brought him, was forced to seek refuge in an American house. At daylight rebel gunfire forced the boat to retire and André's only chance to escape now lay in using a safe conduct pass written by Arnold and to try and bluff his way back to the British lines.

Head Quarters Robinson House Sept 22nd 1780.

Permit Mr. John Anderson to pass the guards to the White Plains, or below, if he chooses, he being on Public Business by my direction.
B. Arnold
M. Gen

But to use this pass it was necessary to take off his red staff officer's coat and replace it with a civilian brown coat and 'gentleman's hat'. The noose was thus slipped quietly round poor André's neck. Then, with a stupidity that is hard to explain that wretched intelligence officer proceeded to hide six papers written by Arnold and giving details of the West Point defences, in his shoe. Next day, accompanied by a guide he set off back for safety. Twice his cover story prevented discovery, but then, when in sight of the British piquets he was stopped by three young militiamen who were lying in ambush. Had André produced his pass, West Point may still have fallen, but one of the young men was wearing a captured Hessian coat and André, believing himself safe, revealed that he was a British Officer. The noose was thus drawn tight. In spite of André's protestations and offers of financial rewards, he was searched, the papers found, and he was taken back to the nearest American outpost. Even at this stage General Arnold's pass might still have secured his release but the papers in his shoe, written in clear, not in code and in the same handwriting as the pass were sufficient grounds for the outpost commander to hold André until confirmation came from Washington of his true identity and mission.

General Clinton tried desperately to save his Aide but short of giving up Arnold, who had escaped on hearing of André's capture and had been made a Brigadier General in the British Army, there was nothing he could do. André asked only one favour, that he be shot not hanged, but as this would have implied a doubt as to the justice of his conviction and his status as a spy, Washington refused. André was hanged. Benedict Arnold escaped a traitor's death, but did not escape dishonour. He lived for a further twenty years a wanderer and outcast, then died unnoticed and unmarked. The three young militiamen were entertained by dinner by George Washington, presented with a medal and each given a farm valued at £500. In 1853, 50,000 people assembled in the streets of Tarry Town a suburb of New York to see the unveiling of a statue to their memory.

John André was also given permanent recognition. In 1821 his body was exhumed from a spy's grave at the foot of the gallows and brought back to England where it was reburied more ceremoniously, in Westminster Abbey. George the Third then ordered that a monument be erected to André that can be seen in the South side of the Nave. This rare distinction given to a junior military officer for his courage and bearing when facing death is well deserved, but to an intelligence officer, André's memorial is a reminder of poor staff work, rank disobedience and crass stupidity.

CHAPTER FOUR

The Corps of Guides
and The Depot of
Military Knowledge

In March 1784 a man aged twenty-four became Prime Minister of England. William Pitt, son of the great Chatham, was swept into power with a large majority to continue his Father's work of social and economic reform. This he did remarkably well. Under his direction Britain's commercial interests flourished and expanded but, in contrast, the Armed Forces contracted and withered. The Army shrank to some 17,000 men and the Militia fell into decay. From 1784 to 1793 Britain enjoyed nine years of peace but then once again, the growing militancy and strength of France, this time a new Revolutionary France, upset Westminster's idyllic dream of perpetual peace. When King Louis of France and his wife, Marie Antoinette were dragged through the streets of Paris and then publicly executed, a horrified British Government began to feel that money spent on defence might be a wise investment. With a change of heart that is traditional among British politicians, emergency measures were now rushed through to rectify past neglect. The Corps of Royal Engineers were reorganised, the first troops of Royal Horse Artillery to supplement the existing field Artillery were raised and men were for the first time housed in proper barracks rather than alehouses, but these and other improvements came too late. When an expeditionary force was sent to Flanders as part of an Allied Army to curb French aggression, it found itself outclassed, outmanoeuvred and outfought.

The English cavalry had received no training in scouting or outpost duty, and as those elementary tactics were considered rather beneath their dignity, had to be taught this aspect of their work by the Prussian Hussars. Lacking in knowledge of their opponents' strength, 40,000 men under the Duke of York were confronted by 150,000 enemy and, throughout the bitter winter of 1794 –1795 retreated across Holland and Hanover until they finally reached Bremen, where the dispirited remnants embarked for England.

On 5 March 1794 Pitt had made a dramatic speech in the House of Commons calling the country to arms. The defeat in Flanders now added weight and significance to his appeal. All over England gentlemen formed themselves into troops and regiments and while receiving no pay and with very little Government help, bought uniforms, supplied their own horses, gave allowances to their soldiers and drilled twice a week. It was a brave show of patriotic spirit and was surprisingly efficient. A contemporary account has described one exercise, 'The troop had a field day in a way which would have done credit to a regiment of the line. So correct were the firings that nearly a dozen balls were thrown into the bull's eye of the target at a distance of forty paces'. Although this range may seem short, troops were in fact ordered not to fire until they saw the whites of the enemy's eyes and at the battle of Quebec Wolfe, who continually practised fire discipline, had defeated Montcalm with his three well-aimed volleys delivered at this murderously short range.

The most successful of the new forms of volunteer service was undoubtedly the yeomanry. Famous regiments, which today continue in the Territorial and Volunteer Reserve Army, were raised and henceforth have formed an integral part of the British Army in war. England's position, however, grew desperate. With the advent of the 'Directorate' in Paris the European Coalition, which was sponsored by England, fell to pieces. Prussia and Spain withdrew, Holland was forced to become a French ally and Napoleon's successes in Italy brought to an end the opposition of Austria and Sardinia. The Dutch as well as the Spanish fleet now joined France and England, outnumbered by sea and land, was face to face with an ever growing danger of invasion. Her only possible safety lay in blockading the opposing fleets and preventing their concentration. If command of the Channel was lost, there was nothing to prevent the victorious French armies, which had overrun Germany, Holland and Italy, from landing in Kent or Sussex.

It was under this very real threat of invasion that the Deputy Lieutenant and Magistrates of East Kent met on 1 March 1798 in the Old Castle, Canterbury to consider defensive measures. After discussing the Government's directives concerning the formation of yeomanry and fencible units, it was suggested that in addition to these units a new corps should be raised – A Corps of Guides. A corps of men with local knowledge, country skills and scouting ability who could act as guides to the regular army if it were ever to be deployed in Kent. The motion was agreed and Lord Romney sent the proposal to Sir Henry Dundas, Secretary of State for War. On 6 March he received a reply – 'The King has been shown the letter and has expressed with great satisfaction both at the attention of the meeting to this important arrangement and with the zeal and public spirit of the Gentlemen who are ready to lend their assistance for carrying it into effect. The raising of a Corps of Guides is approved, it is to be a Captain, two Lieutenants and sixty men; with uniforms, and arming to be agreed between Lord Romsey, Sir Charles Grey and the commanding officer'.

The ready adoption of the title Corps of Guides was greatly influenced by the success and romance attaching to a similar unit in the French Army, called the Corps des Guides. After the battle of Borghetto on 29th May 1796, Bonaparte, Massena and his Aide, Murat had been lunching in a garden when they were surprised by a party of Austrian cavalry and had to escape by climbing over a wall. Bonaparte losing one of his boots in the process. A week after this episode Napoleon appointed a friend of Murat's, Captain Bessieres of the 22nd Chasseurs, to raise and command a 'Company of Guides of the Commander in Chief'. These Guides quickly achieved an international reputation for bravery and dash. At the Battle of Roveredo, Bessieres and six troopers captured two guns and at Arcola, victory was achieved mainly through the efforts of the Guides under their 'big black' Lieutenant Domingo, nicknamed 'Hercules'. The French Company was 136 strong and wore green coats with scarlet collars and cuffs, green waistcoats and breeches with red or green stripes down the side. They chose green as it was 'the colour of meadows in spring, signifying youth and renewal' – it was also Napoleon's favourite colour. But although the dress regulations laid down this uniform and the predominant colour of the Guides was green, the habit of trying to improve one's apparel by exchanging clothing with the dead of any regiment, enemy or friend, meant that in practice the Guides often appeared a very motley collection.

During the Italian Campaign the Guides emerged as Napoleon's own special unit and he concerned himself particularly with their pay and food. When he was appointed General in Chief of the Army of the East in 1798, he sent for them and it was a bandsman of the Guides who abandoned his bass drum and was first to scale the ramparts of Alexandria. After this battle, Bessieres was made Colonel of a Regiment of Guides, which included four companies of horse and three of foot, sixty horse gunners, twenty musicians and three companies of native auxiliaries. Thereafter the unit, although it continued to undertake special reconnaissance tasks, dabble in espionage and perform minor police duties, became more and more an elite force providing the personal bodyguards for Napoleon and the other Army General rather than a purely intelligence gathering organization. It thus established a precedent, which was followed very closely by the Indian Army Corps of Guides, raised fifty years later.

On 20 March 1798 encouraged by the success of this French Corps of Guides, a meeting was again called in the old Castle, Canterbury 'to take into consideration the arrangements to be made in case of an invasion, for nominating guides and other tasks'. Sir Charles Grey submitted the following questions to the Committee:

> First, what steps have been taken by the Commissioners relative to the road between Ashford and Tenterden, it having been reported to this Committee that the Government had acquiesced in allowing soldiers to be employed in repairing the road and to pay them for their labour. Second, whether the Guides have been procured for Kent, and whether the Lord Lieutenant has had a conference with the Duke of Portland upon the nominating and paying the officers.

The Minutes of the Meeting continue: 'Captain Hussey, having been selected by this meeting to the Corps of Guides has signified his Majesty's approbation to the appointment, and informed the Committee that he has procured thirty five men in part of his Corps of sixty, and has every reason to suppose he will be able to provide the remainder with the assistance of the Gentlemen of the County.' On 16 April 1798 Captain Hussey was able to report that he had procured the proposed number of guides, but that the final completion of the Company now rested with the Secretary of War, who had to decide the pay arrangements of officers. A letter from Dundas was already on the way however, and gave an allowance of twelve pounds per man to buy clothing and cavalry appointments, it also allowed officers the same rates as cavalry officers. This must have proved satisfactory for on 1 August 1798 when King George III held a review of the Kent Yeomanry and Volunteers in Mote Park, Maidstone, Captain Edward Hussey, 1st Lieutenant John Austin, and 2nd Lieutenant Brett led past the Kent Corps of Guides, believed to be dressed in green and composed mainly of game keepers.

The parade was a great success and that evening Sir Charles Grey wrote to the Lord Lieutenant to express his satisfaction:

> General Sir Charles Grey begs leave to return to his warmest thanks to Lord Romney, the Lord Warden of the Cinque Ports, and the Gentlemen, Yeomanry and Volunteer Corps of Kent, for the Honour conferred upon him by their unanimous request that he would take the command of them on this glorious and eventful day, a day on which happily for this Country, the House of Brunswick was seated on the Throne, and which is so conspicuously marked by the memorable victories of Minden and the Nile.

The King himself must have been impressed for on 7 September 1798, he wrote personally to the Duke of Richmond asking him to raise a Corps of Guides in Sussex on the same lines as the Kent Corps, also to consist of three officers and sixty men. His request was obeyed and on 29 March 1799 Captain Henry Shadwell, took command of a Sussex Corps of Guides and both Kent and Sussex Troops appear in the 1800 edition of the Militia, Yeomanry and Volunteers list as volunteer infantry.

From 1798 to 1802 the war with France continued in a desultory fashion in the West Indies, Holland, Malta, Minorca, Egypt, even in Britain itself when the French landed a small force in Pembrokeshire. Tradition holds that the French soldiers plundered local farms and stole geese and butter. After cooking one in the other the rich diet made them sick and in a weak state they mistook the red cloaks of Welsh women for soldiers and surrendered when called upon to do so. The Pembroke Yeomanry who captured the invasion force were awarded the battle honour of 'Fishguard' and this is still the only battle honour awarded to the British Army for service in the United Kingdom. But on 27 March 1802, the Treaty of Amiens was signed and the war, which had dragged on for eight years, now ended. Britain agreed to give up Egypt, Malta was to be handed over to the Knights of St. John and all the French Colonies taken in the war were to be given back, Britain received in exchange Ceylon and Trinidad.

Within days of the Treaty being signed the Government lost interest in home defence and together with many other yeomanry and fencible units, the troops of Guides were disbanded. However, Napoleon, now established as ruler of France, was not to be satisfied and from 1803-1805 began to concentrate at Boulogne preparing for the invasion of England. One hundred thousand men assembled in camps along the Channel, and Dover fishermen began to bring back alarming stories of French troops practising disembarkation drills from flat bottomed boats. Spy scares also flourished. As no commercial treaty existed between Great Britain and France, Napoleon had sent over a number of 'consuls' to establish trade relations. The suspicion that these men had more than one object in view was confirmed when a letter sent to the French representative in Hull was intercepted by the Post Office and found to contain a plan of Hull Harbour and the details of its approaches. News also reached London that the French had created a Corps of Guides consisting of one hundred and seventeen men who could read and write English. These Guides were mostly Irishmen or Frenchmen who had lived for many years in England and were to be used on 'liaison duties' after a landing.

All this activity alarmed the Government and once again they were forced to consider anti-invasion measures. With memories of Fishguard to spur them, it was decided to fortify the South Coast where a line between the Cliffs of Dover and the borders of Sussex was thought the most vulnerable. Seventy four gun towers, each of which held two howitzers and a swivel gun were built, and were named Martello Towers after the circular forts at Martella, Corsica, which had resisted the English fleet in 1794. In addition, as Romney Marsh was considered a likely invasion site, work was begun on a Royal Military Canal that would join Hythe and Rye and could be used to seal off the area.

One year and fifty days after pledging 'Perpetual peace with France' Britain declared war. Six weeks later the Government sent a letter to all counties in the South urging them to create a Corps of Guides:

> A Corps of Guides is to be drawn out in number, from three to six from each parish or district according to its extent. In the event of invasion, the knowledge of which must, at that instant be a matter of notoriety, the Corps is required to assemble at the headquarters of the army within the military district, or county (as may be agreed upon). Generals and staff officers will frequently have recourse to the local knowledge of the Guides when it is necessary to ascertain the exact state of the roads within their respective parishes. Sometimes, also, in regard to the nature of the country whether it is mountainous, open or enlaced, of a deep or light soil, what supply of water and where to be found, and other points which may be of great importance at the moment.

Kent and Sussex both responded and on 28 July 1803 their troops reformed, this time two other counties also decided to form a similar corps. A Cornwall troop was raised called the West Penwith Guides, the other, undoubtedly the most successful was the Devon Guides. This latter Corps was raised on 31 October 1803 when the Lord Lieutenant was informed 'His Majesty had been graciously pleased to accept the offer of Lord Boringdon to form a Devon Corps of Guides, subject to the provision of the Defence Act, and to be furnished with arms by the Government'.

The unit chose a dark green uniform with green facings together with white breeches and black boots. The hat was the current light cavalry helmet with a bearskin crest and hackle feather. The unit was supplied with sabres and pistols by the Government, but were not issued with the twelve carbines normally issued to yeomanry troops. This distinction with the yeomanry is significant and is shown in a letter from the Government to the Lord Lieutenant of Devon on 22 November 1803.

> On the subject of Guides, I have to acquaint your Lordship that a corps of that description should be officered and paid as

Yeomanry when called out on actual service, and that they should receive 20 shillings for clothing, with arms suitable to their service; but as they will not be required to be trained and exercised, no pay on this head will be allowed, nor will they be entitled to any exemption for the Militia or other Ballots.

Nor were the Guides a fencible unit, as the fencibles were required to train, and were committed to serve anywhere in the United Kingdom. The Guides were in fact a separate unit, the successors of the Scoutmaster General's horsemen, the men with local knowledge employed to get intelligence for the regular army when it was deployed in the field.

In addition to this realization of the need for tactical intelligence there was also a growing awareness of the need for strategic intelligence. There existed in London a grave lack of information available about Napoleon's strength and capabilities. The Duke of York and his Staff were constantly called upon to provide briefs about the military situation and found themselves embarrassed and unable to do so. On 26 March 1803, therefore, the Quarter-Master General, General Sir Robert Brownrigg submitted proposals to the Duke of York suggesting the establishment of a Repository, or Depot of Military Knowledge within his Branch of the Headquarters. The concept was to be modelled on the French Depot de la Guerre and was to have four distinct branches:

a.. A plans branch to examine plans and orders for the purpose of collecting military knowledge.
b. A movements branch to prepare and expedite routes for the movements of the Army.
c. A military library intended to expose the course of past events with a view to future utility – by showing the causes, which have led former military successes or may have occasioned their failure.
d. A topographical Branch, for the presentation and compilation of draft and manuscript maps.

The Duke of York was most enthusiastic about the idea and forwarded it to the Secretary of State for War adding, 'The most valuable books and maps concerning the enemy are printed by the enemy themselves and that the period of war is not favourable to their being collected.' The Secretary of State, in this hour of crisis was also enthusiastic and wrote back saying that he had consulted the Chancellor of the Exchequer and they both 'In view of the importance of the objects embraced by the arrangement, readily sanction what is proposed'. The Secretary 'Deemed it essential that a military deport should be formed, and a collection made of plans, manuscripts and maps under the direction and care of the Quarter-Master General with a view to preserving a knowledge of past events, and contributing useful information to the British Army hereafter employed on home or colonial defence or in other foreign military enterprises'.

On 3rd August 1805 the Duke of York wrote to the Prime Minster explaining that as '£700 had been spent on purchasing books and £178 on engraving a skeleton map of the country between Portsmouth, London and the Isle of Thanet, a further £2,000 was required to cover expenses'. The reply to the Duke's letter was startling. The Treasury immediately agreed to the request and promptly paid a cheque for £2,000 into General Brownrigg's own private account at Messrs Greenwood and Cox explaining 'That this was to help defray the cost of the Depot and asking him to submit estimates from time to time of further expenses'. General Brownrigg was thoroughly alarmed. He had no wish to have the responsibility of accounting for the money and pointed out that to give him, as Quarter-Master General, £2,000 was unprecedented. Anyway he said, 'The cost so far had only been £1,000'. But his efforts were in vain and after three unsuccessful attempts, he pleaded in desperation with the Duke of York to cancel the warrant and have the Depot paid as a normal War Office commitment. Eventually on 24 March 1806 the Commander himself had to beseech the Secretary 'Please may the Quarter-Master General be exonerated from the responsibility of becoming a public accountant and be authorised to repay into the Treasury the sum of £2,000'. The warrant was then transferred.

Of the four branches in the Depot of Military Knowledge it was the library section that made the most progress. In charge of this section was Colonel Lewis Lindenthal a colourful figure who had served for sixteen years in the Austrian Army finishing as a Major General. He had then transferred to the Queen's German Regiment of the British Army in Flanders and had received the rank of Major. After subsequent service in Majorca and Egypt he joined the Quarter-Master General's Department where he did so well that he eventually rose to become a Lieutenant-General. The present Ministry of Defence library is to a large extent his memorial and many books, even today, can be seen bearing his mark. One in particular, which is a literary treasure, being an early example of lithography printed from stone and ink. The list of books bought for the Duke's £700 however, do seem a little strange, they include 'History of the Early Roman Emperors', 'Penal laws in China' and Dauer's book on 'Christian Mythology' – however it was a start.

Topography was a traditional Quarter-Master General's task, all through the eighteenth century it had been his responsibility to supervise everything appertaining to marches, and maps were obviously part of the pre-march planning. Lieutenant Colonel John Brown, Royal Irish Engineers, was placed in charge of this Section but, as was to happen many times over the next one hundred and fifty years, in spite of all the good intentions expressed in Parliament and in spite of all the sound resolutions set down on paper, the clear aim of collecting intelligence about foreign armies was rapidly diffused because of the individual preferences and interests of the personality involved. Colonel Brown was an Engineer, and in addition to his intelligence duties had been given the task of constructing the Hythe Canal. It was to the latter project that he lent his efforts. His time in the Depot of Military Knowledge grew less and less and in 1810 the Financial Committee when reporting on the Topographical Department complained rather plaintively that 'Since 1804 the Department had done little but direct the activities of the Royal Military Canal in Kent and Sussex'. No intelligence data was produced about France, there was no help available for Wellington now fighting in the Peninsula – and it was a sign of the times that he didn't expect any.

In England interest in the Corps of Guides had also diminished. At Trafalgar in 1805, one fateful day had seen the threat of invasion removed and, following the defeat of their Navy the French soldiers who might have died at Bognor marched from Boulogne to die at Austerlitz. The Kent and Sussex Guides were again rapidly disbanded, and in Cornwall the Commanding Officer of the West Penwith Guides applied for permission to become yeomanry and on this being granted changed the title to the Mountsbay Troop of Yeomanry. The Devon Guides continued for a little longer, although, after Trafalgar parades were gradually relaxed and the unit appears to have become a haven for those who wished to avoid the heavier commitments of the yeomanry or militia. In 1812 efforts were made to improve the unit and it was placed on the footing of Volunteer Cavalry and became the Devon Guides Cavalry with corresponding pay and allowances. It was still not very successful however, and in 1813 Lieutenant Colonel Holdsworth of Widdecombe, who was Governor of Dartmouth Castle, was given permission to raise a troop of yeomanry in the Hundred of Coleridge on condition 'They served without any allowance whatsoever – and that he amalgamated with the Guide Troop'. This was accepted and Holdsworth became Lieutenant Colonel, Commandant of the South Devon Guides. In June 1821 the Guides did a six-day exercise at Dartmouth and in 1822 formally requested that their title be changed to the 'Dart and Erme Yeomanry Cavalry' but the change of name and lapse of original role was not successful and on 5th December the Corps expired without a struggle.

The French Corps of Guides were no more successful. They left Boulogne in 1806 and went to Prussia. On 30 June 1807 Napoleon changed their title to the Prince of Neufchatel's Corps of Guides and they were sent to Spain where they remained until November 1811. They then took part in the march to Moscow and were almost completely annihilated in the battle of Fere Champenoise on 25 March 1814 and the remnants were' Flung into the Furnace' at the Battle of Waterloo. By the end of the eighteenth Century both the French and British Armies had accepted that it was a good idea to group men with talents for guide work and scouting into one unit, but it was also accepted that such a task was not suitable for regular soldiers.

The title 'Corps of Guides' however continued, and for the next one hundred years it was used in to the Peninsula, India, Canada and South Africa. All through the nineteenth century, in the absence of any regular British Army units formed to gain intelligence in peace time, a Corps of Guides, or its equivalent, was raised to fill the gap but then disbanded as soon as the conflict ended.

CHAPTER FIVE

The Peninsular War

*O*n 1 April 1809 Sir George Murray, 3rd Foot Guards, who had been appointed to take charge of the Plans Branch of the Depot of Military Knowledge, was posted as Quarter-Master General to the War in the Peninsula. Murray, when an infant of only seven years, had been bought an ensign's commission and in his long military career had developed a keen appreciation of the value of intelligence. After Wellington's first battle against the French at Rolica, Murray realised the need to provide a pool of men capable of speaking the local language and who knew the local area; he decided therefore to raise a unit of men who had these special abilities. He called them the Corps of Guides. It may have been that this title was chosen in order to emulate the French Corps as the Kent Corps of Guides had been, it is more likely however, that Wellington himself selected the name because of his contact with a similar unit in the Mahratta Wars. In 1781 a small Madras Corps of Guides had been raised and these men accompanied Wellington during the savage war against the Mahrattas, Sir Jasper Nicoll who was also in the Force has described their duties. 'Here it may not be out of place to mention that on coming to our ground each day the neighbouring villagers are sent for, and the 'Captain of the Guides' after comparing their accounts, takes down all the necessary information relative to the roads, where and in what quantity water is procurable etc'.

The Peninsula Corps of Guides initially consisted of one sergeant, one corporal and sixteen men, mostly Spanish guerrillas and deserters from the French Army. They survived the hardships of the retreat to Corunna and were then evacuated to England. But Wellington had been impressed by their services and on 23 may 1809, when back in Lisbon, regrouped them and established them officially as part of the Army:

> The Quarter-Master General will forthwith furnish a Corps of Mounted Guides to be under the immediate superintendence of an officer of the QMG's Department. The Corps will receive the pay and allowances of cavalry, and the officers, NCOs and

privates will be mounted on horses and mules found by the public, the Corps to be composed of:

4 Lieutenants.
4 Cornets.
6 Sergeants.
6 Corporals
2 Farriers.
20 Privates.

The Deputy Assistant Quarter-Master General chosen to command the new Corps was Captain G.Scovell. Scovell was an old friend of Murray and they were among that select group of officers who could claim M.C.C. (Military College Certificate) after their names, the equivalent to our present P.S.C. (Passed Staff College), which showed that they had served for two years in the Senior Department of The Royal Military College then housed over the bar parlour of the Antelope Inn in High Wycombe. Under Scovell, the Guides soon achieved a high reputation and although initially recruited to provide intelligence for columns pushing into strange territory, their specialist qualifications eventually made them more useful as interrogators, agents and dispatch carriers, their place as guides being taken by local 'paysanos' who either volunteered or were pressed into service. Wellington recognised this development in their role and on 17 November 1810 increased their establishment to:

6 Lieutenants.
6 Cornets.
8 Sergeants.
2 Trumpets, and
50 privates.

He explained that it was necessary 'Not only to have a Corps whose particular duty it will be to make enquiries and to have a knowledge of roads, but to have a class of person in the Army who shall march with the heads of columns and interpret between the officers commanding them and the people of the country guiding them'. The men who replaced them as guides were merely guides and nothing else as this extract from the Quarter-master General's orders shows:

The Assistant Quarter-Master General must constantly provide guides when the division is in the field, and more especially if it is moving or acting separately from the body of the army; so that, in the event of any sudden movement, either during the day or night guides may be always at hand. Such should be selected, if possible, as are not only capable of showing the road from one place to another; but as are also men of intelligence, and who have a general acquaintance with the neighbouring country. These guides ought to be obtained through the Magistrates of the country and when permanently attached should have a fixed pay per diem. All guides who are detained for a day or more should have rations drawn for them. Guides taken from village to village, on ordinary marches, need not be paid.

This change in role of the original Guides typifies the evolution of field intelligence operations; from the basic qualification of being able to show the route or speak the local language, to a responsibility for providing a genuine intelligence service. Two examples of orders given to officers in the Guides demonstrate this development, the first to a Portuguese officer – 'You will proceed from Plasencia to Avila and have two objects in view, the one to gain information respecting the roads and the supplies in case it should be found expedient to move troops in that direction, the other to gain information respecting the force and movements of the enemy'. The next was given to Lieutenant Auberge who had originally been an officer in the French Army 'You will proceed to the outposts of Crawford's Division and endeavour to obtain information concerning the strength and the movements of the enemy in the country between Sierra de Gata and the River Douro, and respecting everything that may serve to indicate his intentions or influence his operations, including the composition of his formations and their commanders'.

As the war continued so the usefulness of the Guides became more apparent and on 6 September 1811 the unit was again increased to 80 privates under Major Scovell and six months later on 12 April 1812, to 150 privates under a rapidly promoted Lieutenant Colonel Scovell. The establishment now included a captain, sergeant major and quartermaster sergeant. The Corps was then split up and divided into the various Divisions in the same manner as the Wagon Train and other branches of the Staff and by 1813 was an accepted part of the Army. The Deputy Judge Advocate General, noticing them before the battle of Vittoria, wrote 'Seeing them in their scarlet jackets they look more regular than most of the Spanish regulars – not unlike some of our yeomanry cavalry and with an air of consequence that is amazing'. To the ordinary soldiers, however, they became heralds of trouble for inevitably when a Guide galloped into the camp, there followed the order for a move and action.

The Guides, like many subsequent intelligence units, were also used in a police role and the Duke of Wellington has described this and their courier duties in a letter to the Commander in Chief written on 24 February 1813. His Royal Highness had been perturbed by stories of crime coming from the Peninsula and had asked the Duke whether he favoured the formation of a Staff Corps of Cavalry under the Adjutant General 'for the purpose of police'. Wellington replied that he already had the Corps of Guides that he was using in this role, explaining that to speed up the carrying of dispatches he had placed a number of the Guides at points along the main routes to act as relay riders:

> As the nature of disorders committed by our troops were generally on their removal to, or return from, General Hospitals it suggested to me using the Guides in aid of the Police under the Provost on the roads where they are placed, and with this object I ordered an increase in their strength. I feel the Guides must still do this duty even if we create a Staff Corps of Cavalry because our English NCOs and soldiers are not fit to be trusted alone out of view of their officers, but the soldiers of the Guides are out for months together without occasioning any complaint.' In spite of this well-known low opinion by Wellington of his soldiers, he decided later in 1813 to form a Staff Corps of Cavalry and as Scovell had been so successful in forming the Corps of Guides, Wellington decided to transfer him across to be the new unit's first Commanding Officer. Some men from the Guides must have also transferred with Scovell, for the next commander of the Guides, Lieutenant Colonel Sturgeon had a reduced establishment of only 75 privates and 3 lieutenants. Unfortunately, however, Sturgeon lasted only a short time. He incurred Wellington's displeasure during the advance after the battle of Orthes, and evidently took his admonishment very much to heart for three weeks later, so it is alleged, he 'got himself deliberately killed at the outposts near Vic-en-Bigoire'. On the day following his death, 20 March 1814, Wellington appointed major Colquhoun Grant, 11th Foot to succeed him. Grant was one of a small group of officers who had been selected for their abilities as horsemen and linguists to ride deep into French occupied Spain, liase with the guerrillas, form contacts and arrange the supply of arms.

The activities of these men varied from 'stay behind' officers like Captain Somers-Cocks and Lieutenant Badcock who remained on the slopes of the Serra de Estrela to see which road General Massena would take, to the task of Lieutenant George Hillier who in June 1811 penetrated deep into Spain during the anxious days of the second siege of Badajos and, by establishing a successful spy network discovered that Wellington's fears that the French armies intended to concentrate were justified. However, as always, 'The pitcher that goes often to the well ends by being broken' and most of these gallant intelligence officers came to their day of ill-luck. Lieutenant Leith Hay, 29th foot, was captured near Toledo in April 1813 and Captain Cocks, 16th Light Dragoons, who after many adventures behind the lines was given a majority in the Cameron Highlanders, fell leading his men into the breach at Burgos. Colonel Waters who was on the Portuguese Staff had one escape when he was taken prisoner in Portugal and had as his escort a party of mounted gendarmes. He noticed that the only good horse among his guards was that of their leader and as he was still on his own good horse, he waited until the leader had dismounted, then spurred away. Chased by the gendarmes, swords drawn and in full voice, Waters galloped straight through a French column, emerging unscathed at the end. After three days in hiding he reached British Headquarters to find his kit ready and waiting as Wellington had brought it forward, observing, 'Waters would not be long away.'

As in World War Two, these men when on operations never stayed long in one place, committed few names to paper and unfortunately most of the documents concerning their activities have been destroyed. But Grant's brother in law Sir James McGregor, in his memoirs does tell of his relation's remarkable adventure. Colquhoun Grant made many sorties into Spain and gradually became completely accepted by the local population. He was a fluent Portuguese and Spanish speaker, knew Spanish literature, enjoyed Spanish wine and loved to join in the wild Spanish dances. With this local background he became an acknowledged expert not only on the location of each French Division in his area but on the personal habits of each battalion commander. On 10 April 1812 he was out with a Spanish guide watching Marmont's Army to see whether this General was intending to retreat to Salamanca or invest Ciudad Rodrigo, when a French officer leading a provision party spotted his red coat in the trees. The officer sent a party of dragoons to capture him and for some time it was a sharp game of hide and seek in the woods then, coming to a steep hill Grant and his friend abandoned their horses and took to the rocks. But a second French party, also out raiding for food, had been attracted by the noise of musket shots and climbing on foot shot the guide and captured Grant.

Marmont was highly intrigued at the presence of a British Staff Officer so far from the front but was delighted to find he had captured the almost legendary Grant. By this time many apocryphal feats had been ascribed to him, including that of spending a night in the French Headquarters in disguise. He treated Grant to dinner and afterwards gave him the choice of close confinement, or his word of honour not to escape. Wellington was very disappointed by his capture and told McGregor 'He was worth a brigade to me, I wish he had not given his parole for I would have offered a high reward for his rescue'. And when Grant, while still a prisoner, managed to get messages through to Wellington, the General was even more impressed. After reaching France and judging himself released from his parole, Grant escaped and assumed the role of Captain O'Reilley from a disbanded Irish battalion in the French service. Under this disguise he reached Paris and made contact with a Mr. McPherson, the descendant of an exiled Jacobite family who had been put in prison during the Reign of Terror and had little love for Napoleon. McPherson managed to get him an American passport and Grant then moved round Paris taking notes on the French army and their movements. It is almost incredible that, even at this stage, he managed to get a most important note to Wellington in Spain, telling him of the French Army's move to Russia, with its implication that further heavy reinforcements to the Peninsula would be unlikely.

Just when the French police were becoming suspicious of this mysterious 'American', Grant took the identity of another American who had recently died and travelled to Nantes hoping for a passage in a boat home, but war between America and Great Britain had now become certain and no American ships were sailing, so Grant became an 'out of work sailor' seeking a ship. Several times he attempted the dangerous task of persuading small boat owners to take him out to the blockading British Men-of-War, and his near escapes match those of his many successors in the 1914-1918 and 1939-1945 wars. Eventually a fisherman and his son agreed to take him out, but on their way a French coastguard cutter stopped them. The old fisherman placed Grant with his back to the mast and twisted the sail, which he had let down, twice around him so that he was invisible. The coastguards did not discover him but warned the fisherman of the presence of an 'English 74 lying in the offing'. When Grant eventually reached the ship and returned to England, he still felt a little guilty about his parole and arranged for a French officer of his own rank to be repatriated in his place. Later he learnt that, in spite of the 'protection' he had given them 'Commending them to the goodwill of all Naval officers', the old fisherman and his son had been put in Portchester Prison Camp. He therefore pleaded angrily on their behalf and after securing their release sent them back to France with enough money to buy a new boat.

Four months after his capture he was back in the Peninsula again doing intelligence work for Wellington. The activities of Grant and his colleagues were quite distinct from the normal reconnaissance duties carried out by ordinary cavalry patrols. The gaining of intelligence by forward troops has always been a fundamental responsibility of any cavalry force. But to supplement this information there has always grown an additional need for deeper penetration and more clandestine means. History has shown that many men, either because they have specialist qualifications, be it language, knowledge of a country or even exceptional self reliance and bravery often find themselves initially employed in a reconnaissance role and then in a more dangerous special role. During the nineteenth and twentieth centuries in the story of intelligence in the field, the distinction between 'conventional reconnaissance' and 'specialist intelligence' duty is very fine. But in each conflict there has emerged a group of men who have gradually become employed full time on the collection and analysis of information about the enemy, or on countering the enemy's intelligence effort. As these men must have the qualities needed for scouting and reconnaissance it is not surprising therefore that the link between such units and the intelligence organization has been so strong.

Colquhoun Grant typifies this link. Having proved himself to be a first class Intelligencer, on his return to the Peninsula Wellington selected him to command the Corps of Guides and appointed him 'Head Intelligence Officer'. At the beginning of the Hundred Days he was again selected by Wellington to be his Senior Intelligence Officer and become an Assistant Quarter-Master General and 'Head' of the newly created Intelligence Department. The Waterloo campaign was the first time the British Army had had an Intelligence Department, and there could have been no more suitable man selected to be its 'Head', than Colquhoun Grant.

Grant always maintained, with some justification, that the surprise of the British and Prussian armies by Napoleon before 15 June would never have taken place, but for the 'stupidity' of a cavalry brigadier who stopped one of his scouts bearing the news of the movement of the French army. Grant's messenger was detained by the Hanoverian General Dornberg whose cavalry was watching the frontier about Tournai and Mons and was not allowed to go on until the fighting had already begun around Charleroi. Grant could only deliver the message to Wellington a day later when the Battle of Quatre-Bras had actually begun. The loss of this twenty four hours was irreparable, for if Dornberg had not stopped this all important news Wellington could have concentrated a day earlier, and would certainly have co-operated with Blucher at Ligny, instead of being obliged to hold back Ney at

Quatre-Bras with detachments that kept arriving throughout the day.

The Corps of Guides was not reformed after the Waterloo campaign, although three days after the battle on 21 June Wellington, with a view to preserving order in the army, authorised Lieutenant Colonel Sir G. Scovell to recreate a Staff Corps of Cavalry. The Corps was to be formed from the 'Best and steadiest three men of every cavalry regiment, preferably those who can speak French and if possible from amongst those who had served previously with the Staff Corps'. This time the volunteers would get one franc a day extra pay.

Much to his disgust Grant was put on half pay after the Battle, but in 1821 went out to India in command of the 54th Foot. There he took part in the Burmese War of 1824 and was in charge of the brigade which overran the province of Arracan. Unfortunately he contracted a persistent malarial fever in the swamps of that unhealthy region and had to be invalided home. He never recovered his health, and died, aged only forty-nine at Aix-la-Chapelle on 20th October 1829 where his monument can still be seen in the Protestant Cemetery.

Before Waterloo, the Commander himself had been Head of Intelligence. Both Marlborough and Wellington had organised their spy and agent networks personally. They had received reports direct from the field without the aid of any cutting, abstracting or comment by an Intelligence Staff. This had its drawbacks, not least that Wellington often complained about the handwriting of various agents and when in May 1811 Wellington lost the keys of his dispatch boxes, the 'Intelligence Department' as such, may be said to have put up its shutters until they were found. Waterloo was the first time a British Commander had designated a Staff Officer to be specifically his Head of Intelligence and there was not to be another for 70 years..

From the abolition of the post of Scoutmaster General in 1688 until 1815, apart from the Commander, the responsibility for intelligence, particularly secret intelligence, had been a prize alternatively seized by the Adjutant General and Quarter-master General's Branch, depending on the personality of the respective 'Chief'. Logically the Adjutant General should have been responsible, as he controlled the conduct of operations, but in fact it had generally been the Quarter-Master General who had been successful, mainly because he was responsible for pre-march planning and by sending officers forward to discover routes and camp sites, he also obtained – almost as a side effect – intelligence about the enemy. In the Peninsular War it was again the Quarter-Master General's Branch which became 'The Branch most concerned with Intelligence'. Murray, like Cadogan, was a stronger character than the Adjutant General and gradually emerged as the most influential staff officer. He achieved this mainly by posting one of his own staff to each division and brigade and making sure that each of these Assistant Quarter-Master Generals and Deputy Assistant Quarter-Master Generals, in addition to their normal administrative duties, also had a responsibility for reporting direct to him:

> One of the first duties of the officers of the Quarter-Master General's Department is to acquire a knowledge of the country which is the theatre of the operation of the Army. This supposes not only an acquaintance with the natural and political division of the country and its principal features, but also detailed local information on the following points:

> What parts of it are mountainous or hilly, and what are level. Whether the hills are steep, or broken by rocks; or if they rise by gradual and easy slopes; or if the ground is undulated only in gentle swells. In what direction the ridges run, and which is their steepest side. What is the nature and extent of the valleys; and in like manner, what is the nature of the ravines, where they originate, in what direction they run, and whether they are of difficult access or to be easily passed. What are the sources of rivers, and the direction of their course; whether they are rapid or otherwise; their breadth and depth, and what variations they are subject to, at different seasons, the nature of their channels and of their banks whether rocky, gravely, sandy or muddy; of easy or of difficult access; the bridges across them, whether of stone or of wood; their breadth and length and whether accessible to artillery, and capable of bearing its weight.

The brief goes on to explain the need for sketches to accompany all reports, the care to be taken in putting the names of towns and villages in the same manner as by the natives of the country and how, when the spelling and pronunciation differ very much, the name should also be written in parentheses as it is pronounced. Murray also made it clear that although the reports could be seen by the local commander, all reports, whether done by order of the General Officer to whom they were attached, or upon any other occasion, belonged to the Quarter-Master General 'and are the property of the Public'. This could, and did, lead to disputes over sovereignty just as occurred in the South African War when officers from senior headquarters were attached to mobile columns and had the power to report over the head of their immediate commander. In both cases it was generally a matter of personalities and Murray on several occasions had to transfer officers from one division to another in order to avoid conflict.

Another task undertaken by the Quarter-master General's Branch, one which has become a traditional, and often onerous British Intelligence task ever since, was the provision of maps and sketches. Throughout the War there were always at least six officers employed at any one time making maps and sketches of the country and by the end of 1810 almost the whole of central Portugal had been mapped to a scale of four miles to the inch and copies distributed throughout the Army and back to the Depot of Military Knowledge in London. After the War Murray obtained permission for the mapping to continue and eventually in 1841 published an 'Atlas containing the principal battles, sieges and affairs of the Peninsula War' together with a text, written by himself, explaining movement orders issued at the time.

In London, however, even before the end of the Napoleonic War, interest in the Depot of Military Knowledge had begun to wane. One of the main reasons, and one which seriously handicapped the development of a central intelligence organization until well into the First World War, was that officers posted to the Depot and subsequently to the War Office Intelligence Department, continually used all their skill to get sent on active service. These officers claimed that their knowledge of the country and people would be of far more use to the commander in the field, than collating files in England. Until 1916-1917, and perhaps even later, postings were such a personal matter that inevitably if an ambitious officer did well in London, sitting as he was along the 'corridors of power' he soon managed to get himself posted away to the scene of action and possible promotion. This meant that the officers in the Depot were often of a very low standard.

Another factor in the decline of the Depot was the influence of the Duke of York's Mistress. In 1802 while taking the waters at Bath, the Duke had become enamoured with a vivacious and personable young wife called Mary Anne Clarke. Mrs Clarke had married at sixteen, but had quickly left her husband to live a life of freedom and ease. After meeting the Duke she moved to reside 'under his protection' in a fine house in Gloucester Place with carriages, servants and attendant luxuries. Eventually, however, the Duke, although anxious to enjoy her favours, became a little loath to pay cash for them, and so a tacit arrangement seems to have been made for the Duke to help commission whose who Anne recommended. In the early nineteenth century there were very few professions open to a 'Gentleman'. One son would succeed to the estate, one could go in the Church, but for the remaining sons, the choice was either to emigrate and seek a fortune, or enter the Army. The Army offered social status, the glamour of an elaborate uniform, an occasional taste of danger – but very little work. So it was that competition to purchase a commission was keen, and those with money were only too glad to pay Anne handsomely if she could intercede on their behalf. Unfortunately, her charges became higher and higher, until she was eventually demanding seven hundred guineas to assist someone wanting a majority, this sum being in addition to the amount the 'aspirant' had to pay the Government for his commission. The climax came when she 'helped' her footman obtain a commission to a Regiment in the West Indies, the scandal became public and the Duke was forced to resign. As in 1963 when Mr. Profumo, Secretary of State for War had to resign because of alleged immoral behaviour, speeches in Parliament ranged from pious vindictiveness to pragmatic support. In both cases the lady concerned sold her memoirs, but the effect on the British Intelligence Organization was quite different. In 1963 it resulted in an outcry for increased vigilance and the expansion of security measures. In 1809 it brought everything connected with Intelligence into disrepute, including the Depot of Military Knowledge.

It might have seemed logical that a nation like Great Britain with its unequalled world-wide influence and commitment, should have maintained a department charged with collecting topographic and military information about foreign countries and its own colonies; but logic has an unfortunate faculty of appearing illogical when the conclusion to which it points necessitates the expenditure of money. With the departure of the Duke and the prospects of peace reassuring, the Depot lost its sense of purpose and for the next forty years made no contribution whatsoever to Intelligence.

CHAPTER SIX

The Great Peace
1815–1854

*A*lthough for forty years after Waterloo Britain was at peace in Europe and interest in the Army and Intelligence practically non-existent, the British Army, far from being inactive, was in fact winning an Empire. In 1840 four fifths of the Army was abroad, fifty-nine battalions were in the Colonies, twenty-two were in India and China and twenty-two were stationed at home. The Period covers some of the most famous and stirring events in British history. The First and Second Burmese Wars, The First Afghan War, First Chinese War, First New Zealand War, First Kaffir War and the bloody campaigns against Punjabis, Mahrattas and Sikhs. It includes the battles of Ghuznee, Ava, Jellalabad, Kabul, Kandahar, Sobraon and Chilianwala, battles now emblazoned on the drums and colours of a score of infantry regiments. Battles whose stories are almost repetitious in the constant telling of outnumbered British soldiers who were dressed in outrageously uncomfortable clothing, marching, fighting and beating overwhelming numbers of various determined and brave men under the most atrocious of climatic conditions. They did not always have better weapons or discipline than their enemies, but always had the supreme factor – an unquestioning belief in their own superiority.

But the victories achieved throughout the Empire received scant recognition in England and although a medal for Waterloo was issued in 1816, apart from the Honourable East Indian Company's medal after Seringapatam, no medals were issued to European soldiers until the Ghuznee medal in 1842. Even the Peninsular War battles went unrecognised until 1848, when at last, the surviving junior officers and men received the first Military General Service Medal. Thus the veterans from the 57th Foot who made history by determining to 'die hard' at Albuera, had to wait thirty years for their official mark of appreciation.

It was during this period that the torch of field intelligence was carried not in Great Britain but in India. After the bloody battles of the Sutlej in 1846, Colonel Henry Lawrence, a Political Agent on the North

West Frontier recommended the formation of a small, specialised unit, composed of men with good local knowledge and a variety of languages to help him govern the area. He wrote:

> The necessity of having a small force, acquainted with localities, at the command of the Civil Authority in a new country, bordering on troubled districts, is too apparent to require comment. Ordinary Police Horse are usually very inefficient, and it often happens that the danger has passed and the mischief been accomplished before the prescribed forms of military routine have enabled the local Civil Officer to obtain assistance from the Military Authorities. It is desirable, that a European Officer should be attached to the Guides to direct their movements and record the information they obtain; he will generally be with me, but his attention will be almost entirely devoted to the object of quietly and unostentatiously obtaining information and recording it; and instructing his men in their duties as guides and intelligencers, so that, should occasion arise, men accustomed to the work may be at hand.

Colonel Lawrence suggested the force should be called the Frontier Legion but the Government preferred a more traditional title and on 14 December 1846 the Indian Corps of Guides was formed and a young Lieutenant of the 59th Bengal Native Infantry called Harry Lumsden made its commander. So began a unit, which for a hundred years brought glory and credit to the Indian and British Armies. There is no doubt that Colonel Lawrence's original concept of the unit was one similar to the Corps of Guides in the Peninsula, a small unit trained and employed to gain intelligence. But they chose the wrong commander. On several occasions Lumsden, having tracked down cattle thieves or wife-stealers to a particular village, instead of 'quietly and unostentatiously' reporting intelligence back to Colonel Lawrence formed up his Guides and then led a successful assault on the village with himself in the lead. Sadly, with each success the Corps of Guides moved further away from its planned intelligence-gathering role to become, like the French Corps of Guides another elite cavalry unit. Lumsden destroyed Lawrence's concept of a specialist intelligence-gathering unit, but he did create a magnificent fighting regiment.

Initially Lumsden's task in India was more difficult than Scovell's task in the Peninsula, as he had to recruit his own unit, horse, house, feed, clothe and pay them, all on 700 rupees a month. He was the first man to dress his men in khaki and discard the conspicuous scarlet of the old Indian Army. The type of man he recruited, however, was very similar to the Spanish guerrilla of 1809, one of the most famous being Dilawur Khan. Khan was a notorious bandit, hated and feared throughout the Province. He had been brought up by Mohammedan priests and was intended for the priesthood, but kidnapping bankers and rich traders was too attractive in adventure and remuneration and he forsook the sacred calling for a career of crime. Dilawur's equipment consisted of his sword, a piece of rope and a huge bullock's skin, which he would inflate and carry himself and his 'guests' to a secure hiding place across the River Indus. Once there, a message was sent to settle the sum the family would have to donate as ransom. Lumsden, who realised that Dilawur must have rare local knowledge and great courage to carry on such a dangerous trade, sent him an invitation to visit his camp, promising him also a safe return to the hills. The very novelty of the invitation took Dilawur's fancy, and to the astonishment of the Chiefs of the district he turned up. Lumsden received him with all courtesy and in the course of conversation pointed out that in a short time military posts would be so established throughout the country that his calling would become almost impossible and the risk of his hanging extremely high. He ended by offering to make Khan a Guide. Dilawur burst into laughter at the proposal and chuckling heartily took his departure across the border. Six week later, however, he returned to Lumsden's tent and asked to enlist, on condition that he be excused the degradation of doing foot drill. But Lumsden held out for the absolute necessity of his being taught the complete 'art of war' and finally had the satisfaction of seeing the most dreaded man on the Frontier patiently learning how to 'stand at ease' by numbers.

Many years later in 1869 Dilawur Khan was sent by the Government of India on a secret mission to Central Asia. In passing through Chitral he was taken prisoner and held captive for over two months. When released, he and some companions trekked home through the mountains, one died of cold, two others turned back and eventually the remainder took refuge for the night in a cave where Khan was found to be frostbitten and dangerously ill. His friends did what they could for him, but Dilawur Khan said to them 'I feel I am dying. It is quite true that I am Dilawur Khan of the Guides at Marden. I am a Khattack, a native of the village of Jenangira and I am on a secret mission for the English Government. If either of you live to return to Peshawar, go to the Commissioner and tell him Dilawur is dead. I have served the English faithfully, and I am happy to die in the service of the British Government'.

By 1852 The Corps of Guides had established itself as a permanent part of the Army, and in the Annual Inspection Report of that year the General wrote:

The Guides are an interesting and remarkable Corps. They are formed so that in the same body of men shall be united all the requisites of regular troops with the best qualities of guides and spies, thus combining intelligence and sagacity with courage, endurance and soldierly bearing, and a presence of mind which rarely fails in solitary danger and in trying situations. To ensure this combination of so many diverse qualities, the Corps has been composed of the most varied elements; there is scarcely a wild or warlike tribe in Upper India, which is not represented in its ranks. In raising this Corps, although soldierly qualities were chiefly regarded, the other qualifications were not overlooked. Men habituated from childhood to war and the chase, and inured to all the dangers of a wild and mountainous border, were freely admitted to its ranks. To whatever part of Upper India the Corps may be marched, it can furnish men conversant with the features of the country and the dialect of the people. It is calculated to be of the utmost assistance in the Quarter-Master General's Department as intelligencers, and most especially in the escort of reconnoitring officers.

During the Mutiny the whole Corps remained loyal and among the many distinguished awards made to the Guides was that of the Indian Order of Merit to a 'Bhisti' (Water carrier). The award was made as a result of a vote by the fighting troops and on their petition he was enlisted in the Corps as a sepoy – an unparalleled honour for a low caste 'follower'. The Bhisti rose to be an Officer and won a clasp to his Indian Order of Merit twenty years later in the fighting round Kabul. He was the original Gunga Din of Rudyard Kipling's poem.

Another reminder of the Corps of Guides is that article of military equipment worn by nearly every army in the world – the Sam Browne belt. Sir Guy Campbell, who was for some time on the General's personal staff, has stated that although Sir Sam Browne probably invented the belt while serving with the 2nd Punjab Cavalry, the Guides were the first Corps to take it into use:

Lieutenant General Sir Samuel Browne VC, KCB, who commanded the 1st Division Peshawar Valley Field Force was a very distinguished Indian Officer. I think it was in 1858 at an action at Sarpoorah that he commanded a mixed force with great success and was dangerously wounded in two places, losing his left arm in attacking single handed the enemy's guns, by which act of gallantry he won the VC. Continuing to serve, he found himself greatly handicapped by his loss and invented the 'Sam

Browne Belt', which was so highly thought of as practical military equipment that it was gradually adopted and approved for use by the Indian Army.

It is paradoxical that the period 1815–1854, a period that made Great Britain the most powerful country in the world, with the largest Empire, and which included the subjugation of the Continent of India should be described by British Historians as the period of the Great Peace. But as the residents of these Isles did not feel themselves threatened, the Government and the Public were united on a policy of reducing defence expenditure. Following the dictatorship of Cromwell's Major-Generals and the concentration of the Army outside London by King James in order to intimidate the inhabitants, there existed a strong resistance to the concept of a regular army and this, combined with the practical desirability of reducing taxation made a strong appeal. The Great Exhibition of 1851 was heralded a practical manifestation of universal peace. Not only did the politicians and people of the country feel money spent on defence was a waste, but the Duke of Wellington himself, now Commander in Chief, actively discouraged army reforms. Whatever his motives, it is indisputable that his reluctance to accept change, resulted in the Army of 1854 being quite unprepared for a European campaign. There were less than seventy field guns, most of a kind used at Waterloo, and 'Brown Bess', the Peninsular War smoothbore musket was still being issued. An advocate of the Minie rifle, which was then under trail at Enfield, offered to sit in a chair and be fired at for a whole day, provided the firers used Brown Bess and promised to aim at him carefully.

But as has happened so many times in the past, other countries were not willing to abide by the peace that Britain felt was satisfactory. Peace, just as much as war, requires two active participants and if one side becomes restless and believes that by the use of force they can successfully gain an advantage it becomes, at least initially, a disastrous and bloody affair for the unprepared contestant. After Russia had invaded Turkey and the Russian fleet based at Sebastopol had virtually destroyed the Turkish Navy, Britain and France felt they had to declare war in order to maintain the nebulous 'balance of power'. Their armies were dispatched first to Bulgaria and then following Turkish successes before Constantinople, diverted to the Crimean Peninsula. The British Army although only 26,000 strong was well drilled, confident and composed of long service troops. The strategic objective of Sebastopol was sound, as its capture would give the Allies command of the sea, and the Russian Fleet in the Black Sea would be at their mercy and could be destroyed at leisure. But two requisites for success were missing;

nothing was known of the country or its garrisons and there was no supreme commander to co-ordinate the work of the allied armies. The British Commander later complained bitterly, 'The Crimea was as completely an unknown country to the Chiefs of the Allied armies as it had been to Jason and his Argonauts when they journeyed to the same place in search of the Golden Fleece. I knew it contained a harbour', he wrote 'and a city with fortifications, but the nature, strength and resources of the enemy lay almost completely in the region of speculation.' And, strange to relate, the fact that the Commander did at least know that the City contained certain fortifications was only because a prematurely retired major of the Bombay Engineers had found a secret Russian map in a Belgian back street whilst on holiday.

CHAPTER SEVEN

Major Thomas Best Jervis

ajor Thomas Best Jervis did not have a very illustrious military career. Born at Jaffnapatam, Ceylon in 1796 his father died when he was one year old and his mother remarried and sent him, with his brothers George and John to a Mr. Delafosse's Classical School in Richmond. At Mr. Delafosse's he studied indefatigably and, so his biographer states 'Such was his eager thirst for knowledge that instead of wasting his youth in shirking lessons, he studied with the greatest earnestness taking great delight in Latin and Greek poetry.' After graduating, Thomas Jervis's Uncle managed to get him a cadetship to the Addiscombe Military Seminary and here Thomas worked for a year before enrolling as an ensign in the Bombay Engineer Corps. But before sailing to India he was sent to work for General Mudge, on the original Ordnance Survey of Worcestershire. This survey experience altered his whole career, for henceforth, cartography together with Christianity became the main elements of his life.

For thirty years he served in India, never taking part in any of the great campaigns but concerned almost wholly with topography and architecture. In 1821 he was at last promoted 'Owing to his great humility of disposition it had been seven and a half years before he rose to the rank of Lieutenant' and in this year saw his only active service when he was part of the force of 4,000 under Sir Lionel Smith who went to the Arabian Coast to help the Imam of Muscat in his fight against pirates. After a successful little campaign in which 1,097 prisoners were taken, the force was about to return to India when the European Officers discovered that the young boy prisoners were to be sold as slaves. This upset their Victorian morals so much that they protested indignantly to Sir Lionel who, after much negotiation with the Imam managed to secure the release of all those 'not truly of Bedouin race'. These the Imam decided could be given to the European Officers. Forty-nine were therefore distributed. Thomas received a young stripling whose father and brother had both been killed in the fight and his brother Captain John Jervis was given another. They took them back to India and put them in a missionary school. One eventually married happily in Bombay and settled as a bookbinder, the other was eaten by a tiger in Poona. As he travelled round India Thomas concerned himself more and more with the moral limitations of both the Indians and the Europeans. Of the Europeans he commented 'India was a touchstone to the newcomer who, if he gave way to his lower instincts, or if he took to drinking strong bottled beer or spirits in excess would be brought to the grave within six months ... even worse were those, who by adopting the native habits of life, yielded to the fascination of Eastern nations of lascivious gratification'. In 1836 he retired as a Major from the Army. He had expected to take over the appointment of Surveyor General of India, but when this was not offered he returned, rather sadly, to England.

For the next fifteen years he maintained his interest in cartography and tried at one stage to start his own lithography business but the expenses were too great and he was forced to sell out. In addition, this remarkable man busied himself with a dozen different causes. He was a leading figure in the Association for the Discouragement of Duelling and the English Section of the British Foreign Bible Society and was elected as a Fellow of the Royal Society for writing a paper on weights and measures. He took a leading part in the public debate on the advancement of Asiatic geography and the education of natives and had a particular soft spot for the protection of ladies, writing long papers on female education and their emancipation both at home and in India. He stirred public conscience with newspaper articles about the perils of girls emigrating to Australia and described how the morals of these girls were severely tried during the long voyage round the Cape. He attacked ships doctors who chose these girls to act as hospital assistants on the voyage, instead of more suitable elderly widows, the more so, as he alleged, the girls had been seen to drink beer which should have been reserved for the sick and feeble.

He bombarded the Government with letters on subjects as varied as the use of slate for roofing, the use of perforated zinc for windows, Britain's responsibility to Australian aborigines, postal orders in Asia and the value of penny receipt stamps in lieu of taxation. More significantly to our own story, in 1846 he wrote to Lord Aberdeen, Secretary of State for Foreign Affairs urging him to create a map depot in connection with the Foreign Office. He pointed out that Great Britain was the only world power that had no geographer attached to the Government and no one concerned with the maps of foreign countries. The Foreign Office acknowledge with thanks Major Jervis's plan for a map depot, assured him it would receive their best attention, and did nothing.

However, early in 1854 came Major Jervis's moment of glory, his chance of recognition and fame. Travelling on holiday in Belgium he came across a copy of a map of the Crimea compiled by the Russian General Staff, together with a copy of the great Austrian military map of Turkey in twenty one large sheets – all of immense strategic importance and virtually unprocurable. War had just broken out so Jervis returned excitedly to London and obtained an audience with the Secretary of State for War, the Duke of Newcastle. The Minister who 'looked in astonishment at the map of which no copies existed in the great public and military libraries' was urged by Jervis to authorise the reproduction of the maps to enable commanding officers on the eve of setting out for the East to have copies. The Minister agreed their value but replied that unfortunately 'As the Budget was marked out so categorically, he could not contemplate such an outlay, however, if Major Jervis would execute the maps at his own private cost, the Government would be willing to purchase from him as many copies as they might feel it desirable to obtain'. Undismayed by this lukewarm response Jervis took an office in Adephi Terrace and with a Royal Engineer officer and a clerk of the Sappers and Miners loaned by the Board of Ordnance began work. Within a few weeks he had produced an English edition of the Crimea map in ten sheets. It was printed in chromolithography and was the first instance in which a map was produced in England with the sea delineated in blue, the hill work in brown and the remainder in black. The Duke was pleased with the result and ordered a few copies but when these copies reached commanding officers the volume of demands rose so much that the Government was forced to order a great many more.

Following this success, throughout 1854 Jervis unceasingly pressed the Government to establish an intelligence organization similar to the Depot de la Guerre in France. A letter addressed to His Grace the Duke of Newcastle on 17 July 1854, contains the passage:

> The fact is palpable and notorious, that this great, intelligent, powerful commercial country, which may be said to impose laws on all civilised world, is entirely dependent for good maps on the Continent for German, French and other maps. What else we have are, in truth, but school atlases. We have an admirable hydrographical office for nautical surveys and charts, and another for the Tithe Commissions surveys, but for our Colonial, commercial, or war purposes we have no resource but foreign information.

Jervis's Crimean maps had also been given to Britain's Ally France and the French Emperor had been so delighted with them that he had invited Jervis to Paris, treated him most courteously and then presented him with a massive gold snuff box with the Imperial initials in brilliants. All these factors gradually swayed the Government and on 2 February 1855, the day after Queen Victoria had reviewed and bade farewell to her Guards at Buckingham Palace before they sailed to the Crimea, a new Government Department was sanctioned and Major Jervis appointed Director:

'Sir,

With reference to your letters of December 1 and January 9, I am directed by Lord Panmure to acquaint you that my Lords of the Treasury have given their sanction to the creation of a Statistical and Topographical Office in connection with the War Department, and the pay of a salary to the officer charged with its superintendence. Lord Panmure entirely concurs with the opinion recorded by His Grace the Duke of Newcastle that your varied attainments, science during many years, are valuable qualifications for the office in question, and I am directed to propose to you its acceptance.

In the event of this offer meeting your views, you will be charged with further arrangements for consolidating, as far as possible, in this department the various scattered collections of military plans, maps, books and documents that other departments of the public service hold in charge, so far as such consolidation is desirable for convenience of access and arrangement.

It is also Lord Panmure's intention to unite in the same establishment, as soon as it can be conveniently effected, the Topographical Department now under the Horse Guards. Temporary arrangements are now completed for the reception of the collection about to be formed. You are requested to transfer to it at your earliest convenience the maps and plans which Marshal Caillant and Admiral Ducos charged you to present to the Duke of Newcastle.

I am, Sir,
Your obedient servant,
'J. PEEL'.'

A few weeks later in a tumbledown building off Whitehall, hastily converted from a coach house and stable, the new Topographical and Statistical Department began work. Two officers, one military clerk and twenty-six civilian lithographers were engaged. But the 'offices' hardly

lent dignity to the new project and on 1 August 1856 they were moved
to a more suitable home at No. 4 News Street, Spring Gardens, a site now
occupied by the Admiralty Buildings. Here it remained until January
1874. During the first two years the Department produced a number of
excellent maps including:

> Map of the Principal Military Communications of the Caucasus and
> Contiguous Provinces, constructed in 1847 by the divisional staff of
> the Imperial Army of the Caucasus, and corrected to January 1, 1853.
>
> Two sheets in chromolithography.
>
> Map of Khiva, the Sea of Aral, and the Country between the Caspian
> and Heart, constructed by Lieutenant Colonel Jervis. One sheet in
> chromolithography.
>
> Administrative Map of Moldavia, from the original Rumanian map;
> the names translated by Lieutenant Colonel Jervis. One sheet in
> lithography.
>
> Plans of Sebastopol with the defences and siege operation.

The Department also produced several books the most notable being
the collected 'Despatches and Papers of the Campaign in Turkey and the
Crimea' which, as well as giving all the returns from the Commanders
in the field, contained excellent colour maps of the major battles.
Another 'side-line' of the Department was the production of lithographs
that were sold to the Public. The two most popular being 'View of the
Battle of Balaclava' and 'View of the Docks at Sebastopol'. In addition,
this irrepressible man continued to send endless memoranda to the
Duke. He urged that a limited number of officers and NCOs should be
sent to the Depot to be trained in military drawing, modelling and
intelligence, explaining that 'such instruction would involve no further
charge to the State than that of proper accommodation, books, drawing
materials, surveying instruments, precisely as limited at the Depot de la
Guerre in France'. Perhaps more important, he suggested in a very
detailed memorandum that as the best way of obtaining information
was to go and get it oneself, a number of small 'brigades' should be
formed to travel overseas and carry out geographic and statistical
research. These brigades should consist of seven men; four
draughtsmen, a geologist and someone who could sketch, all under the
command of an officer who had a 'flair for languages and a taste for
adventure'.

In 1856 Lord Panmure agreed to this idea and a party of civil
engineers, surveyors and draughtsmen with equipment supplied by the
Topographical and Statistical Depot under Lieutenant Colonel Geils, did

go to the Middle East and charted, for the first time, the entire upper course of the Euphrates River. This was Lieutenant Colonel Jervis's last achievement, for on 3 April 1857 racked by a disease brought from India, he died in his sleep. He was not a successful soldier, he was not a great geographer but as a simple religious man with a flood of creative ideas he saw before his contemporaries the need to establish a central store of intelligence in London, and above all he had the individuality and determination to strive and gain his ideals.

The concept of a 'Depot of Knowledge' had been started in 1801 but by 1854 it was almost extinct. Thomas Best Jervis picked up the threads again and from the makeshift Topographical and Statistical Department formed in cramped and dirty stables off Whitehall to the enormous Joint Service Intelligence Staff Department in the present Ministry of Defence there is an unbroken line of Majors, Colonels, Brigadiers, Major-Generals and now Admirals and Air Marshals. Hampden Gordon in his book 'The War Office' claims it was in fact the first step towards the creation of a British General Staff.

CHAPTER EIGHT

The Crimean War

The Crimean War is surely the most shameful in British history. Never have so many British soldiers been sacrificed through such complete lack of forethought. Casualties caused by logistical mistakes exceeded by ten times and more the casualties caused by enemy action. Lack of transport, lack of medical services, lack of suitable clothing and lack of ammunition all go along with lack of an intelligence service. Apart from Colonel Jervis's map, the only sources of information concerning the Russian military situation were the various British Consuls and the Minister in Moscow. The accuracy of their reports differed widely and of course ended as soon as war was declared. In Lord Raglan's dispatch to the Duke of Newcastle confirming his, and Marshall St. Arnaud's agreement that the Crimea should be invaded he concludes:

> The fact must not be concealed, that neither the English nor the French Admirals have been able to obtain any intelligence on which they can rely with respect to the army which the Russians may destine for operations in the field, or to the number of troops allotted for the defence of Sebastopol; Marshal St. Arnaud and myself are equally deficient in information upon these all important questions, and there would seem to be no chance of our acquiring it.

But although as the war progressed, the British people became more and more shocked at the revelations that lack of planning had produced and there were positive steps to rectify mistakes, particularly those exposed by Florence Nightingale's activities, no adequate measures were ever made to satisfy this lack of intelligence. The gaining of intelligence had disappeared as a function of the Army. War was declared on 29th march 1854 and it was only on 20 March that General Freeth, the Quarter-Master General had published a guide to the duties of his officers in the gaining of information – it was in fact an exact reproduction of General George Murray's directive written in the Peninsula. Thus Assistant Quarter-Master Generals going to Russia were told how to pay for goods with Spanish Rials and Portuguese Reas and warned to visit the billets of their soldiers at eight each evening to see 'If there are any complaints by the landlords and that the men are in their quarters instead of marauding in search of plunder'. But even this advice was better than nothing, for, by 1854 there were virtually no trained staff officers. As a result of patronage and favouritism, the staff qualification M.C.C. had become a handicap, rather than an aid to staff employment. Of the 216 officers who had obtained certificates between 1836 and 1854, only twenty had ever been employed on the staff, and two months after the outbreak of war out of 291 officers on army staffs, only fifteen were qualified. Lord de Ros, who was appointed Quarter-Master General for the Crimea, was described at the time as 'An extremely curious fellow, very eccentric both in his habits and dress and although fond of sunbathing is completely lacking in Staff experience and does not seem at least anxious to acquire any'.

In the Peninsular War the cavalry had been the 'eyes and ears' of the Commander but after forty years of play and reviews in Hyde Park, cavalry officers had very distinct ideas of their own status in life and their own role in battle. This role did not include 'dashing about in an undignified manner looking for the enemy'. Three days after the battle of the Alma, the first battle of the Crimean War, there occurred the incident where the Commander in Chief Lord Raglan himself, was the leading scout. It had been decided to make a flank march around Sebastopol and attack from the South, the Army therefore set off guided by a Major Weatherall of the Quarter-Master General's Staff. Major Weatherall's orders were to reconnoitre with the cavalry and a battalion of the Rifle Brigade, as far as a group of building marked on the map as 'Mackenzies Farm'. This farm had once been the home of a Scottish Admiral who had supervised the construction of naval defences at Sebastopol in the eighteenth century, and was surrounded by the thick brushwood of a dense oak forest. In the middle of the forest the track forked, and after a moment's hesitation Major Weatherall led the cavalry up the right fork. The track became more and more indistinct, and eventually petered out altogether. Major Weatherall was lost. The Artillery by this time had arrived at the fork and were told by a lone Hussar which way the cavalry had gone. The Gunners were very sceptical at the news and had stopped to discuss it when Lord Raglan and his staff galloped up, annoyed at what they thought was an 'unauthorised rest'. When shown the track the cavalry had taken however Lord Raglan agreed with the Artillery officers and took the lead up the other track. A little way beyond the fork General Airey, now Quarter-Master General on the return to England of de Ros, came up to him and talking softly they jogged down the track then, seeing a gap in the trees Airey galloped forward and suddenly found himself face to face with a column of Russians moving north from Sebastopol. Lord Raglan joined him, and some Russian soldiers lying on the verge of the wood must have failed to believe their eyes, for although they dashed away, presumably to report the presence of two British Generals alone in the wood, the Russian column continued its slow unconcerned march. In spite of the entreaties of his Staff Lord Raglan then remained at the head of his army while the Horse Artillery not waiting for the cavalry galloped out into the road, wheeled into action and began 'Blasting round shot down the hill.'

On the eve of the battle at Balaclava a Turk came into General Campbell's headquarters with the news that a large Russian force under General Liprandi was about to launch an attack. Campbell and Lucan questioned him and decided to send his news to Lord Raglan. General Airey received the letter and although the Commander-in-Chief was in conference with the French General felt it necessary to break in on their conversation. The Commanders were not impressed by the information however, and an Aide was sent back with the curt acknowledgement 'very well'. No action was taken and only dawn revealed the truth of the report. This lack of Intelligence applied not only at army level but had implications down to the most mundane of tactical tasks. After the charge of the Heavy Brigade at Balaclava, Lord Lucan did not have one scout posted, he took no steps to find out what was happening beyond the mounds and hillocks which surrounded him, and when the breathless and excited Captain Nolan reined up with the brief, critical message 'Attack and prevent the enemy carrying away the guns', Lord Lucan could only reply, 'Attack Sir! Attack what? What guns Sir?'

The third great battle of the war at Inkerman also began as a surprise to British Headquarters. Again a mass of contradictory messages had been pouring in to the Commander in chief who had no staff to analyse or digest them. On the evening of Saturday, 4 November, General Pennefather concerned by the appearance of large numbers of Russians gathering before his lines sent two officers Captain Carmichael and Major Grant down into the valley to see if they could discover anything of the enemy's intentions, but Major Grant was evidently not of the same calibre as his peninsular namesake for, after a careful watch the two officers returned to report that the Russian army appeared to be static. A little before dawn next morning Captain Ewart an officer on General Airey's staff rode through a thick early morning mist to collect the reports of the front divisions. At each headquarters everything was quiet and at the headquarters of the 2nd Division the men had already been dismissed from the dawn stand-to and were busy collecting wood for their breakfast fires. Ewart was half way back to Army Headquarters when he heard a crackle of fire from the outposts and then a sustained fire all along the line. He wheeled his horse and on galloping back met General Pennefather who ordered him to 'ride for all he was worth to Lord Raglan and tell him that the army was under attack'. So began, on Guy Fawkes Day 1854 the 'soldiers battle' one of the most bloody in British history where, in the initial stage, 4,000 British soldiers beat back 15,000 Russians from the slopes of Inkerman. Lord Raglan found himself committed to an unexpected engagement against dense Russian columns, far superior to his own and with no time to arrange his forces. The result was that British units were pushed piece-meal into the fight, confronting massive hostile columns as they loomed out of the fog. Only the determination of the British infantry and the Russian's lack of initiative saved the day.

Strange to relate there was a man at Lord Raglan's headquarters known at the 'Head of Intelligence'. Born at St. Petersburg of English parents, Charles Cattley had been educated in England and had then returned to be British Vice Consul at Kertch. He was thirty-six years of age and spoke fluent Russian, French and Italian. In May 1854 the Russians had ordered him to leave Kertch and in London he wrote a report describing his journey and the situation in the Crimea. This was presented to Lord Raglan on 29 July 1854 and proved to be the best information available to the General before he sailed. 'There are eight guns mounted along the coast between Kertch and Kaffa but only one man in a company is armed with a rifle, there is plenty of anthracite for steamers in Kertch at 50 shillings a ton and I strongly recommend that Kertch should be blockaded and the Sea of Asoff occupied, otherwise the Russians can continue to pour supplies of troop and provisions to the Crimea'.

Mr Cattley also made two other points, he estimated that there were 40,000 troops in Sebastopol, in fact Prince Menshikov had 50,000 men exclusive of sailors and marines, and suggested that use should be made of the Tartar population of the Crimea. 'These men have a strong anti-Russian feeling and would join the Allies if they could be assured that the country would not be given up again to the Russians'. He recommended that they should be approached 'Through their Moolahs or Priests and could be extremely useful as they are tough fighters, require little pay and know the locations of all stores of hay and cattle herds.'

Lord Raglan was impressed by this report and as a result on 3 August 1854 the following letter was sent:

Her majesty's Government having determined upon sending out to Turkey for the purpose of assisting Lord Raglan by this knowledge of Russia and its language Mr. Charles Cattley, late Consul at Kertch, I am directed by the Duke of Newcastle to request you will move the Lord Commissioners of the Treasury to issue pay to this gentleman at the rate of £1.1.0d per diem plus a reasonable allowance for living, plus £100 in advance to cover expenses.

On 13 September 1854 the huge armada arrived at the port of Eupatoria. There were no Russian forces there apart from a few convalescent soldiers, and the governor of the port was evidently a civil servant of the classic mould. Two colonels were sent ashore, with Mr Cattley acting as interpreter, to deliver a 'summons'. The governor, serene in his knowledge of local health regulations insisted on the fumigation of the note before he accepted it and then, placidly viewing the massed invasion fleet at anchor in the little bay, explained that it would be necessary for any landing troops to consider themselves initially in strict quarantine.

On his arrival in the Crimea Mr. Cattley decided, for security reasons, to change his name and henceforth was known by the alias of Mr. Calvert. His first task was to interrogate two Polish sailors who had been musicians in the naval band and had used an opportunity while playing near the front line to desert. Their story was typical of deserters – unrest in Sebastopol, shortage of food and the crime rate soaring because convicts had been released from gaol to serve the guns. Calvert's second interrogation was of a young Russian soldier captured after the battle of Alma, he said the Russians had had 13,000 killed, wounded and missing, (the actual figure proved to be about 9,000) and felt the British had won because their guns were heavier calibre and the infantry were better at bayonet fighting. The soldier catalogued with great detail the enormous quantities of ammunition and powder stored in Sebastopol ready to use against the invaders and so much was it that Mr. Calvert felt bound to conclude his report with his first interrogator's comment – 'My personal opinion is that this young man is not to be altogether trusted'.

Very soon after landing Lord Raglan had sent back to London a letter written by Mr. Calvert warning of the bad Crimean winter which might be expected 'Bleak, windy, heavy rain, sleet, snow and bitter cold, and once in every few years a fortnight of Russian cold.' By this Mr. Calvert meant a cold so intense that 'if a man touched metal with his uncovered hand, the skin would adhere to the metal'. But the Duke of Newcastle's reaction to this accurate forecast was to send out a book describing the Crimean climate as one of the mildest and finest in the world, adding that he thought Lord Raglan may have been 'Greatly misinformed'. At this early stage Mr. Calvert is referred to consistently as Lord Raglan's interpreter, there is no indication that he was originally intended to be 'Head of Intelligence', or indeed anything to do with military intelligence at all. He assumed the appointment in default of anybody else doing any intelligence work. General Airey, as Quarter-Master General was responsible for information and when Deputy Assistant Quarter-Master Generals were posted as liaison officers with the French, their reports were sent direct to him. But the winter of 1854 was proving the greatest administrative scandal in British Army history and General Airey was working up to twenty hours a day trying to feed, clothe and keep warm a hungry, cold and very vocal army. Any intelligence reports he received were filed at random next to 'fodder for oxen', 'repair of pickaxes' and 'issue of brandy to the sick'. There was no military officer or staff employed on collating or distributing intelligence and the embryonic Intelligence Department started at Waterloo had been forgotten. It was in this absence of a regular organization that Mr. Calvert, in what was to become traditional manner, gradually assumed responsibility for all intelligence duties. He had the two qualities that made him the logical choice, language and local knowledge. He worked in the Quarter-Master General's Department and is shown on the Quarter-Master Generals' medal roll for the award of the Crimean medal with clasp for Alma, Balaclava and Inkerman, but he reported not to General Airey but direct to the Commander in Chief. In fact he reported direct to London, for Lord Raglan forwarded his reports to the Secretary at War, Lord Panmure. In his dispatch of 17 March 1855 Lord Raglan says:

> A deserter is just come in who is not under examination – there is not time for Mr. Cattley to prepare his report for to-day's mail, but he has sent me word that the man reports that he is one of 8,000, who entered the Crimea two months ago; that of these 8,000, 2800 died on the road, the greater portion being frozen to death, 1,700 were sent back to reform and the remainder only reached Sebastopol. The man represents that there is much dissatisfaction in the camp, the soldiers are badly fed, and the old ones complain that those who are sent to them as reinforcements are mere boys and not equal to the duty assigned to them. There would seem also to be a good deal of discussion amongst them as to the consequences to follow Nicholas' death, and the question is agitated whether Constantine will succeed to the Kingdom of Poland.

Initially Lord Raglan allowed the reports to go back unedited, and without comment, but later he began to add his own thoughts. 'I enclose

Mr. Cattley's report of this day. The information it contains would lead to the supposition that Balaclava is to be attacked, if not tonight, at least on some very early day or night; but there is certainly nothing visible to confirm this intelligence, and Sir Colin Campbell, who is now in this house, is under no apprehension'. On 21 April – 'I send you Mr. Cattley's report of this day – it contains nothing very material'. With this paucity of intelligence it is not surprising that Lord Raglan was himself disconcerted when accused of withholding information from his French Allies.

> I am very much surprised at what you tell me of the suspicions of the Emperor, that I withhold from General Canrobert reports which reach me of the movements of the Russians. In general I should say that the French consider themselves better informed that we are; but it is our constant habit to send over the M. Lausky, who is at the head of the Bureau des Renseigments Militaires any deserters who can give any important intelligence.

Mr Calvert as well as his interrogation duties took over the task of controlling the Turkish spies. Soon after the Army had arrived in Sebastopol a Turkish agent had arrived on the British lines giving warning of an imminent attack. Lord Raglan had believed his story and circulated the following alarming, if uninformative, dispatch to all Divisional Commanders:

> From information received there is reason to believe that the enemy is desirous of making before long some attempt upon the Allies, but it is very uncertain with what directions and with what definite view. The present strength of the Allied force and the nature of the ground lead to little cause for apprehension but it is desirable that the officers should be instructed to keep their post thoroughly on the alert and have directions how to act, and that Generals of Divisions should be prepared with the best measures for the security of the ground immediately to their respective front'.

The Generals acted on the report and as a result men stood by their horses heads all night, many dying from the bitter cold. Another, report gave correct intelligence of the Battle of Balaclava but was not believed. Mr. Calvert was therefore appointed 'Head of Secret Intelligence' and charged with co-ordinating all 'spy' reports. He also developed his own spy network by using contacts made while acting as Vice Consul in Kertch. On 25 February 1855 one of his reports, after describing Russian troop movements ended with a warning from one of his agents that 'Greeks evacuated by us from Balaclava have been sent back by the Russians disguised as Tartars to act as spies'. This report was subsequently proved to be true, for in October, Greek soldiers in Britain's employ recognised another Greek masquerading as a Tartar and arrested him. The culprit was tried by Court martial and sentenced to death, General Simpson however, showed compassion and, while agreeing that the 'Laws of War demanded his death' allowed him to be sent to England as a prisoner of war, on condition he should not be considered in any prisoner exchange.

Another report, which was evidently correct, was on 30th April 'A tartar spy sent by me some days ago to the North side of the City returned yesterday and informed me that two regiments of Infantry had arrived there on Thursday from Skadousk and were part of 2 Corps Reserve. I hear also that a deserter who came into the French yesterday, also stated that two regiments arrived four days ago from the same place'. But this use of spies was regarded with grave suspicion. The nineteenth century British Army officer went to war with a rigid concept of how he should behave in battle. The number of officers killed in the various attacks on Sebastopol reveals clearly their acceptance of the need to lead their men from the front. The same feeling of honour however, created a sense of vocation and dedication in the officer that made him extremely loath to become involved with the type of men who acted as spies and traitors. The Official History of the Crimean War proudly, not apologetically, states 'The gathering of knowledge by clandestine means were repulsive to the feelings of an English Gentleman'. The Russians, on the other hand, had no such scruples and continually employed spies. On one occasion a friendly looking man wearing civilian clothes walked into a gun battery saying he was a surgeon, he asked several questions and then enquired the best way to the forward trenches. A little later he was seen running headlong back to the Russian lines. Other Russian officers were caught either wearing French uniforms inspecting British lines, or in English uniforms inspecting the French.

By the spring of 1855 Calvert's position had been officially designated 'Head of Intelligence'. He was now required to produce papers giving estimates of Russian strengths, the Russian order of battle, and the ammunition and morale state inside Sebastopol. He was also required to send Intelligence Reports to Divisional Generals, 'If he felt something would be of interest to them'. On Lord Raglan's death General Simpson asked him to continue as Head of Intelligence, and Calvert used this opportunity for writing a letter asking for better accommodation. He complained that he had to share a small room with a Captain and 'Although they had built a temporary wall to divide them, lack of space made it necessary to interrogate prisoners and brief spies outside'.

Another aspect of Calvert's work that gradually developed was the control of interpreters and guides. There was a great shortage of these men and letters were sent to Constantinople asking for more interpreters to be recruited. They were to be given an 'outfit' allowance of ten pounds plus five pounds or three pounds depending on their linguistic ability and were to be allowed to remit their pay back to Constantinople. When they began to arrive it was decided that they must be co-ordinated centrally in order to prevent waste and so, once more, after a lapse of forty years a field intelligence unit was created and given the title of Corps of Guides. Not under a military officer this time, but under this junior official in the Foreign Office:

GENERAL ORDER 23 JUNE 1855

A Corps of Guides will be formed under the direction of Mr. Calvert. It will consist of one headman and eight privates. The headman will receive 2s 6d a day, the privates 1s 6d a day, with free rations. The Director General of the Land Transport Corps will find a Horse for each man. They will be encamped at Headquarters, to be employed under the Quarter-Master General. Major Willis will be so good as to take charge of these men, and see that their Horses are properly looked after. Third Class Interpreter Chodlicks will be employed with these men.

But Mr. Calvert did not live long to direct the Corps. Three weeks later he died of cholera, as General Simpson described in his dispatch to Lord Panmure:

July 10 – Cholera broke in upon my family yesterday, and seized two valuable members of it – Colonel Vico, the French officer attached to our Army, and Mr. Calvert, the Chief of our Intelligence Department. Vico is still alive, but fast sinking; Calvert died this morning. Both are cases of spasmodic cholera. As for Mr. Calvert – his loss is irreparable. I have not a chance or any hope of finding a successor, and the want of such an officer in our Army will produce many evils. I sincerely trust your Lordship may be able to send some trustworthy man in his place.

General Simpson then went through a very bad period, weighted down with gout and dysentery and with practically his whole staff ill, he found himself working from 'four in the morning to six at night' on paper work. Calvert had been not only the Head of Intelligence, he was the Intelligence Department itself. He had no assistants apart from the Turkish Interpreters and had to write out all his reports himself in long hand. All this now fell on the General, and to add to his troubles came the installation of the new telegraphic system, a device that since that time has meant that politicians in Whitehall could cast their influence almost hourly over the decisions of commanders in the field. General Simpson's letter of 17 July 1855 must surely count as the supreme example of a Commander in Chief's tongue in cheek, tolerance when on active service:

> I think, my Lord, that some telegraphic messages reach us that cannot be sent under due authority and are perhaps unknown to you, although under protection of your lordship's name. For instance, I was called up last night, a dragoon with a telegraphic message in these words, 'Lord Panmure to General Simpson – Captain Jervis has been bitten by a centipede. How is he now?' This seems rather too trifling an affair to call for a dragoon to ride a couple of miles in the dark, that he may knock up the Commander of the Army out of the very small allowance of sleep permitted him! Then, upon sending in the morning another mounted dragoon to inquire after Captain Jervis, four miles off, it is found that he never has been bitten at all, but has had a boil from which he is fast recovering. I venture to mention this message because there have been two others equally trifling, causing inconvenience, and worse may come out of such practice with the wires.'

Lord Panmure's half-apologetic reply explained that the inquiry after Captain Jervis was made at the earnest request of his father, The Lord Chief Justice and in future the Commander-in-Chief should have an Aide to answer telegraphic messages. For two months, while Lord Panmure tried to find a replacement for Mr. Calvert the British Army in the Crimea had no Intelligence Department. On 23 July 1855 his Lordship's dispatch reported his progress and also revealed his conception of the duties of the 'Head of Intelligence'. 'I think in a short time I shall be able to find you a head of your Intelligence Department. I can send you out a clerk from the Foreign Office, a gentleman and man of information, who could act as your private secretary, write and keep your foreign correspondence, and be of service to you in many ways in your transactions with the French. What say you to this?'

Eventually a Mr. Lauder arrived to act as official interpreter and on 21 August Mr. Jackson, the clerk, arrived to become Head of Intelligence. It was Mr. Lauder who wrote the reports and there can be no clear indication that Lord Panmure was unhappy with the flow of intelligence for on several occasions he urged General Simpson to spend more money acquiring it. 'It is as well to remind you that if you can aid Mr. Jackson by the judicious application of money you may do so, because intelligence is of such infinite value in every way that it ought to be had, and I suspect Lord Raglan did not pay for it'. But the war was nearing its climax. A few weeks later on 8 September the Allies made their final assault on Sebastopol, and as French soldiers planted the tricolour on the Malakoff fortress, the Russians moved out of the City to the North and the year-long siege was over. It was in fact the end of the war and no further serious fighting took place, peace being concluded early in 1856.

Another aspect of intelligence that had been exposed in the Crimea was the absence of any counter intelligence organization. Security of information was a term that not only did not exist, but most people felt should not exist. The same had been true in the Peninsula where Wellington, although continually complaining about 'croaking' as he called it, did not consider it necessary or desirable to impose any system of censorship. In a letter to General Craufurd he wrote 'as soon as an accident happens, every man who can write and who has a friend who can read, sits down to write his account of what he does not know and his comments on what he does not understand'. On 10 August 1810 Wellington had published in Army Orders extracts of a letter from the Vice Consul at Oporto which showed the alarm in that City because of reports sent privately by senior British Officers. After making several acid comments on some of the statements made by the officers, Wellington had concluded ' That if they choose to communicate facts to their correspondents, regarding the positions of the army, its numbers etc., they will urge their correspondents not to publish their letters to the newspapers until it shall be certain that the publication of the intelligence will not be injurious to the army … it may be very right to give the British public this information, but if they choose to have it, they ought to know the price they pay for it and the advantage it gives to the enemy'. Extracts from Napoleon's letters confirm the extent to which he relied on British newspapers as a source of military information.

In the Crimean War this security threat was increased a hundred-fold by the appearance on the battlefield for the first time of a multitude of newspaper correspondents. Although William Howard Russell would say that he was writing only for The Times, and it was for the editor in London to decide what ought to be made public and what ought to be suppressed, a large amount of information of value to the enemy was regularly published. On 23 October 1854 The Times printed an article describing the conditions and dispositions of the Army, explaining the number of its guns, the location of various regiments, the shortages of round shot, bagions and fascines and giving the exact location of a powder mill, which some time later was the target of a very heavy cannonade. In February 1855 Lord Panmure wrote to Lord Raglan 'the villainous Times has outdone itself today in an article on the 63rd one Royal Fusilier officer wrote home advocating that 'that blackguard Mr. Russell ought to be hung – the Russians had left off shooting at our camp, but when he published that the balls were, in fact, reaching our tents, on the day The Times arrived in Sebastopol they began again, just as we were at dinner; Russell taking precious care to live about a mile out of range'.

But the press correspondents not only continued to send home graphic descriptions of the horrors of the winter, and details of past events, and by mixing with the officers were able to make very accurate forecasts of future operations. 'We have no need of spies' the Czar was reported as saying, 'We have the Times' adding 'that the best means of communicating the outcome of events from Sebastopol to Moscow was via London. Lord Raglan was very much aware of the leakages and commented bitterly 'the enemy need spend nothing under the heading of Secret Service as I am doubtful whether a British Army can long be maintained in presence of a powerful enemy, that enemy having at his command through the English press and from London to His Headquarters by telegraph, every detail that can be required of the numbers, conditions and equipment of his opponent's force'. He urged that the Deputy Judge Advocate should call a meeting of newspaper correspondents and press upon them 'The inconvenience of their writings and the need for great prudence in future'. He also persuaded the Duke of Newcastle to write to the Editor of The Times requesting restraint:

War Department 6 December 1854

'Sir,

I take the liberty of sending to you an extract from a private letter which I have lately received from Lord Raglan. Many complaints have reached me from the army of the advantage conferred upon the enemy by the publication of intelligence from the seat of War, not only in letters from correspondents of the English newspapers, but in letters written by officers to their friends at home in the spirit of confidential intimacy, and which those friends send to newspapers, from feelings, no doubt, of pardonable variety, but without consideration of the evil consequences to the army, and the public interests. I feel assured that I have only to appeal to your patriotism to ensure a rigid supervision of all such letters, and an endeavour to prevent the mischief of which Lord Raglan so reasonably complains.

I am, etc.,
NEWCASTLE'

And although on the following day, 7 December 1854, The Times did admit they had 'gone to the verge of prudence', for the whole war the press continued to publish facts and figures which undoubtedly provided both encouragement and guidance to the Russians, one Russian officer after reading the Times description of the Army, firmly believed the English Army to be inferior to the Turkish Army and was amazed at Balaclava to see the dress, discipline and morale of the English. Private letters, uncensored, also continued to reveal all aspects of life and conditions in the Crimean Army. We get a glimpse of this in the fascinating letters of the remarkable Mrs Fanny Duberly. Wife of the 8th Hussars paymaster, she was the only officer's wife to last the terrible winter of 1854-1855 in the Crimea, and throughout the campaign wrote continually to her sister Selina.

The letters reveal how much information was given to her, which would today be regarded as 'careless talk'. On 15 October the handsome Captain Nolan, Lord Raglan's most trusted Aide, visited Mrs Duberly in her cabin and had lunch with her. Before leaving he advised her 'on no account to miss being early at the front on the day after tomorrow as the greatest bombardment in history would open on Sebastopol'. On 17 October at 6.30 a.m. just as he predicted, the guns opened fire.

Another constant visitor to Fanny was Captain Stephen Lushington R.N., who, after one call, revealed the secrets of the first 'limpet mine'. A gunner's mate from H.M.S. Agamemnon had slipped into Sebastopol Harbour one dark night in a dinghy and attached a mine of his own invention to the hull of a Russian Warship. The ship had subsequently blown up to the great mystification of the Russians. Lushington, evidently one of the few naval officers in the secret, drew diagrams for Fanny explaining how the mine worked. Subsequently Fanny, who had sent on the details to Selina had pangs of conscience for she wrote home to warn Selina not to tell anyone and certainly not Lushington, who had been promoted Admiral and was planning to visit Selina on his return to England.

This feeling of conscience on Mrs. Duberly part came from purely personal reasons and not through fear of any official reaction; no one felt that private letters should be subject to official jurisdiction. Fanny at one stage not only drew and sent a map showing the British, French and Turkish positions in blue, red and yellow crayons to Selina, but also sent a similar map to Queen Victoria herself. The maps are well done, accurate and pinpoint each gun battery. They would undoubtedly have been of great use to the Russians but the 'Authorities' were more concerned at the 'unfeminine behaviour of a Lady' rather than any security risk. It was not to be until the siege of Ladysmith, over half a century later that press and letter censorship was to become the specific responsibility of a military intelligence officer.

So it was, that in all aspects of Intelligence, the British Army had been found wanting. Strategical, tactical and counter intelligence were at the beginning of the war non-existent and by the end of the war just developing. The only consolation was that these weaknesses had been exposed to public opinion, and the public demanded improvement.

CHAPTER NINE

The Recriminations

*O*n spite of the gallantry of individuals, and units, Britain's military prestige had been lowered in the eyes of the world. The glory, which had surrounded British arms since Waterloo, was exposed as a façade covering serious weaknesses in administration. It was an age when personal attacks on political and military leaders were still published in great detail and the Government, Lord Raglan, and his Staff were now all made the subjects of continued savage attack and ridicule, much justified, but much showing little understanding of the real cause of failure. Mr. John Arthur Roebuck, QC, the Radical member for Sheffield, caught the mood with a damning speech in the House of Commons. He suffered from a nervousness of delivery and a paralytic disorder which obliged him to falter, choke and lean heavily on the bench, but on this occasion it lent dramatic weight to his criticism, and well after midnight on 29 January 1855 the House divided on his bitter motion 'that a Select Committee be appointed to inquire into the conditions of our Army before Sebastopol, and into the conduct of those Departments of the Government whose duty it has been to minister to the wants of that Army'.

Sydney Herbert as Secretary of War replied for the Government with devastating logic, but in a manner that hardly can have raised Lord Raglan's morale in the Crimea:

> ... the responsibility lies with that collection of regiments which calls itself the British Army and not with the Government. When you come to the Staff, how can you expect men who have not only never seen an army in the field but have never even seen two regiments brigaded together, to exhibit an acquaintance with the organization of an army?

But the House was not impressed at this attempt to shuffle the blame and a two-thirds majority carried the motion. The Government then fell with 'such a whack' as Gladstone put it, that 'you could hear their heads thump as they struck the ground'. Not the first or last time that failure to prepare in peace has resulted in the downfall of a Government in war. The Roebuck' Committee then sat for several months delving into the causes of administrative failure. Three large blue books containing

21,421 queries and answers were produced and although individual errors were apportioned the final verdict blamed the complete unpreparedness of the authorities, both political and military to wage a sustained European war. But an anonymous book, called 'Whom shall we Hang?' and published at the same time in support of the Government, does perhaps suggest the real culprits:

> Then let every Government that has ever swayed the destinies of our Empire share the blame. Let the nation share it also. If the Duke of Newcastle, or Mr. Sidney Herbert, or Dr. Andrew Smith are liable to censure, because shirts were not washed or the dinners were badly cooked at Scutari, then Mr. Roebuck, every Member of Parliament and every elector in Britain are equally censurable; for the causes of the evils which have been so exaggerated and denounced, are to be found in the nature and constitution of our military service, and in the duties which it is called upon to perform.

The mood of the country was one of pride, shame and resentment and a long tradition of the Victorian type of pacifism gave way to a fierce determination never to be caught unawares again. Lord Palmerston speaking in 1857 reflected current feeling '... our army must be more than a domestic police. We have colonies to strengthen, possessions to maintain; and you must bear in mind that peace, however, long it may continue is not merely dependant on ourselves, but on the conduct of other Powers. We must look forward to having a force sufficient at least to protect us in the outset from insult or attack. Depend upon it, for a country great and rich to leave itself without the means of defence is not a method to preserve peace in the long run'. A sentiment one feels which is as valid today as it was in 1857.

A rash of other committees now followed the main committee, all examining various aspects of military life, the Government thus began a long tradition of 'committee-forming' which has proved such a successful method of taking the heat out of embarrassing situations. In the twelve years following the Crimean War there were seventeen Royal Commissions, eighteen Select Committees, nineteen Committees of Officers within the War Office and thirty-five Special Committees of Military Officers to Consider Points of Military Policy. By the time of the Esher Committee in 1904 there had been five hundred and sixty seven and although until the outbreak of the South African War forty years later the impetus for army reform had wilted as memories of the Crimean debacle faded, the continuing reports from these many committees did help to maintain governmental and public interest.

Not surprisingly, one of the departments examined was the Topographical and Statistical Department created by Colonel Jervis. Hardly had that Christian officer been laid to rest in the quiet Devon churchyard of St. Johns in the Wilderness, that Lord Panmure, feeling uneasy about the cost and efficiency of the 'T & S Department', formed a committee to examine its workings. The report was produced on 18 July 1857 and proved very critical of the Colonel. The members of the Committee, who admitted a lack of technical cartographical knowledge, asked for a preliminary report from Captain Cameron, RE, who was temporarily in charge. Captain Cameron earned their commendation for, since he had taken charge of the Depot he had 'cut the establishment by half and its expenditure to within reasonable limits'. The Committee felt that Colonel Jervis had acted in good faith over the expenses of the Department but stated 'Written authority for his expenditure was non-existent as regards almost the whole. However, we are informed, and see no reason to doubt, that Colonel Jervis received verbal instructions of a character sufficiently comprehensive to cover such expenditure as he thought absolutely necessary, though it was not always, in our opinion, judiciously directed'. They continued, 'The Department was organised in a hurry and under severe pressure, new men were hastily collected and had no traditions to guide them. No very definite instructions appear to have been given to Colonel Jervis with respect to the objects in view and the mode of pursuing them. But they added, 'Concerning much of that which seems at first sight to require explanation, it is very possible that if Colonel Jervis were alive such explanation might be satisfactorily given'. They note that in spite of Lord Panmure's recommendations a centralised Depot had not been formed and that three different organizations were still dealing with maps and records.

a. The Survey Department under the Inspector General of Fortifications	£81,500 per annum
b. The Topographical Department	£3,000 per annum
c. The Military Depot in the QMG's Department	£1,225 per annum

The committee repeated Colonel Jervis' previous points concerning the advantages of training officers at the Depot and that teams of military surveyors should be sent to record foreign parts – but do not acknowledge them as Colonel Jervis's thoughts. They concluded by recommending, once again, the centralization of the three units and suggested, 'It should be an independent branch of the War Office working directly to the Secretary of State, for him to employ at his discretion.' It condemned all concerned – but in the nicest possible way. One interesting point raised in the Report was its continual emphasis that neither the Head of the Department nor the Staff need necessarily be Royal Engineer officers. It explained with some deliberateness, that in no other country is it so and commented that in fact it was 'Originally Royal Artillery officers who did the work and it was not until 1821 that Royal Engineers took over.' One feels that there must have been a 'Gunner' on the committee, for when discussing the Head of Department, they concluded, 'We recognise that the field selection should be as wide as possible and although we want men who have a special aptitude for strategy, geography and statistical science, these men are not very common anywhere, not more so probably amongst the Royal Engineers. Therefore the Head of the Department ought not to be limited to officers of a single corps, but could be taken from the Army as a whole including the Indian Army and Civil life'.

But in spite of this very heavy hint, for the next one hundred years the evolution of military intelligence did continue to depend on 'sapper' officers. Jervis, Cameron, Charles Wilson and the Director of Military Intelligence during the South African War, General Ardagh, all received their training for intelligence appointments at the School of Military Engineering, Chatham and not at a School of Military Intelligence.

CHAPTER TEN

The Topographical
and Statistical Department

*L*ord Panmure reacted quickly to this latest Report and on 26 October wrote to Lieutenant Colonel Henry James RE, appointing him Director of a re-Organised Topographical and Statistical Branch which was to include the Ordnance Survey and be a separate department of the War Office. The letter allowed the Director the broadest possible charter and was generous both in policy and finance. His Lordship felt that 'He best consult the interest of the Public Service by conveying to Colonel James his general views and intentions and leaving it to him to adopt the best means of carrying them into effect, subject to such approval on the part of the Secretary of State as may from time to time appear necessary'.

Colonel James was to have four officers placed at his disposal, one from each arm of the service i.e. cavalry, artillery, engineers and infantry 'Who could be used in any way he thought fit, either in the General Office or on the Survey or on other duties'. The four were to receive 'Twice and one half the regimental pay of their rank and after one year's probation could be appointed for a further three years, at the end of which time they should return to regimental duty or revert to their position as unattached officers so as to ensure the training of a succession of officers in the T & S Branch'. Panmure added the promise that he was 'Fully aware of the necessity of providing better accommodation for the Department than New Street and that he had the subject under consideration'. Sad to relate, the great opportunities offered by this broad charter were not taken up. Colonel James was a 'Survey Man' and deeply involved in the new art of using photography to copy maps. He was also an enthusiastic author and was busy writing a series of books covering such diverse subjects as 'Notes on the Pyramids', 'Notes on the Pictish Towers' and 'The Tin Trade of the Phoenicians with Cornwall'. He was not interested in Intelligence. He felt far more 'at home' with the established Ordnance Survey Department in Southampton where he lived, rather than in the struggling Topographical and Statistical Department in London.

When Thomas Best Jervis had created his new Department it had been launched on the impetus of finding and reproducing a map. For this reason it had been called the Topographical and Statistical Department. To the 1857 Committee, the topographical responsibilities were clear, but the statistical or intelligence responsibilities were an unassessed innovation; and some of the Members felt it to be unnecessary now that the war had ended. It seemed therefore, a logical and economic measure to unite two departments, both of which were concerned with maps, i.e. the Topographical and Statistical Department and the Ordnance Survey. It seemed even more sensible when such a union was supported by the majority of the officers in the 'T & S' – who were themselves ex members of the Ordnance Survey.

Intelligence and maps are a natural combination, but the Ordnance Survey was to prove an 'Old Man of the Sea' to British Military Intelligence. The decision to join the two Departments is a good example of a policy, still practised today by establishment committees, of discovering two completely different organizations which are called approximately by the same name – and then amalgamating them. If the Survey had remained in London perhaps it would have been different, but on 30 October 1841 the Tower of London where the Survey Offices were housed, had caught fire. A sentinel on duty saw the blaze and fired his musket to give the alarm but although nine engines arrived the Thames tide was out and there was a shortage of water. Not unnaturally every effort was made to rescue the regalia, crowns and sceptres and as a result the map office was gutted. Lacking suitable accommodation the Survey then moved to Southampton to the Duke of York's Royal Military School.

It had been in October 1783 that the French Ambassador in London had sent Mr. Fox at that time Foreign Secretary, a paper showing the great benefit which would accrue to astronomy, by carrying a series of triangles from London to Dover, and connecting them with those already done in France, thus determining accurately the relative positions of the Observatories of Greenwich and Paris. As a first step it was necessary to determine an accurate base line, so General Roy of the Royal Engineers, a section of his soldiers and a military working party supplied by the 12th Foot began work. They chose a five mile stretch of Hounslow Heath and measured it three times using different instruments. Each night a plumb line was left suspended to mark the point with the plummet vibrating over a bronze cup filled with water sunk in the ground. The operation had proved so successful that in 1791 the Duke of Richmond ordered the preparation of a map covering the whole of the United Kingdom, and thus the Ordnance Survey of Great

Britain was begun. But the result of this commitment to map the country meant that the army organization began to drift away from purely military work, towards civilian surveys – and in the process dragged successive Directors with it, including Colonel James. He remained in Southampton and in London, where the Intelligence aspect of the 'T & S' Department should have been done, the officer in charge, called the Executive Officer was another sapper, Major Howard Elphinstone V.C.

Elphinstone had just returned from the Crimean War a well-known and much decorated officer. During the bloody but unsuccessful battle for the Redan on 18 June 1855 he had volunteered to lead a party back to retrieve the wounded and had done this with great gallantry. In the final assault on the City on 8 September he had been severely wounded, lost an eye, and was then evacuated to England with a brevet majority, the newly instituted Victoria Cross, the Legion of Honour, the Turkish Order of Medjidea, two mentions in dispatches and the Crimean War Medal. But Elphinstone, like his commanding officer, had no interest in intelligence work and spent his whole tour on the purely parochial task of compiling 'A Journal of Operations Conducted by the Corps of Royal Engineers in the Crimea'. His successor Major A. C. Cooke, another sapper, was also a brave and talented officer but his speciality was map design. Under his influence the Topographical and Statistical Department became renowned throughout the Army for its 'Original and artistic cartographic masterpieces'. 237,519 maps were produced, but virtually nothing concerning the 'Composition and characteristics of foreign armies'.

In 1863 the Commander-in-Chief ordered that the Department should produce the illustrations for a new edition of Dress Regulations, and in 1864 they published a 'Series of illustrations depicting army equipment relating to the Royal Artillery'. By August 1865 the concept that the Department should act as a centre for intelligence had been submerged so completely, that when a War Office Committee under Sir Richard Airey sat to review the progress of the Department their only criticism was to register surprise that the Department had thought fit to buy 782 maps of Delhi. They therefore recommended that in future, demands for maps should 'Pass through the Quarter-Master General, who after receiving the opinion of the Field Marshal commanding-in-Chief as to their desirability or necessity, should forward them for the approval of the Secretary of State for War together with an estimate of expense'.

The Secretary of State approved this extremely bureaucratic measure and, using the opportunity to increase his own authority added a clause reserving to himself the right to order any service from the Department without reference to the Commander-in-Chief. But there was little to control. There were only two officers in the Department, one was employed illustrating pamphlets on British Army equipment and the other was on safari in Abyssinia. By 1869, only twelve years after its triumphant and much publicised beginning, the Topographical and Statistical Department had reverted back to the insignificant role occupied by its predecessors before the Crimean War. There was, once again, no one in Britain employed on Military Intelligence.

CHAPTER ELEVEN

Major Charles Wilson
and the Formative Years of the
Intelligence Department

y 1870 the very existence of the Topographical and Statistical Department was in jeopardy. Money had been cut, staff reduced and the intelligence value to the General Staff was nil. Then once again the curve of interest in intelligence began to rise. This time not because of the direct involvement of Great Britain but through fear of Prussia. After the Crimean War Paris had become the hub of European civilization. In 1867 thousands of visitors from Britain had gone to see the breathtaking Universal Exhibition. Music, art and military splendour all centred on the French capital, yet now, only three years later, almost beyond belief, Paris was under siege. Initially sentiment in England favoured the Germans but the quick successes of the Prussian advance made the Government look to their defences. A spirit of reform swept through the War Office and Mr. Edward Cardwell, as Secretary of State for War, proved the right man to translate this spirit into action. 'To all appearances one of the coldest and least warlike of men he brought to his office an original and analytical mind with great courage and tenacity of purpose'. As Germany had revealed herself to be the most efficient army in the world, her methods of mobilization, tactics and even dress became the model for a receptive British Army.

As Prussia won victory after victory, Disraeli began to press for current assessments on the Prussian armies. In the War Office was a Department whose terms of reference included 'The duty of procuring and making available for military purposes all possible information of a topographical and statistical nature concerning foreign countries'. But no one remembered it, no one dreamed of using it, the 'T & S' Department was busily engaged producing lithographs of Westmoreland and drawing illustrations for dress regulations. It was into this situation that the right man came to the right place, at the right time. Captain Charles Wilson RE arrived to be the Executive Officer of the Topographical Department. Wilson had successfully passed the open competition to the Royal Engineers and had obtained a direct commission without first having to go through the Royal Military Academy. He had done a short tour in Shorncliffe Camp and then had spent four years delimiting the unmarked boundary between Canada and the United States. A testing and strenuous four years for a young officer which took him from Semiahmoo Bay opposite Vancouver Island, through swamps and forests to the summit of the Rocky Mountains. On his return in 1863 he heard by chance of a request by Miss Burdett Coutts for help in surveying Jerusalem. The philanthropic Miss Coutts wished to provide a water supply for the City and having learned that it was first necessary to attain an accurate survey she offered Sir Henry James, by now Director General of the Ordnance Survey, the sum of £500 to undertake the task. The War Office agreed to supply an officer – provided it cost no more than the £500, that the officer received no extra pay and that he paid all his own expenses. Several officers, perhaps not unnaturally, turned down the offer but Charles Wilson 'Jumped at the chance'. He then spent a year in Jerusalem not only surveying the City, but also making large scale plans of the Mohammedan sacred area of Haram, the Church of the Holy Sepulchre and other important buildings connected with the two Religions.

It was after these experiences of independent adventure overseas that Wilson came to the 'T & S' Department, and this perhaps explains why he felt so dismayed by what he found. After only a few months in post he submitted a strongly worded memorandum describing the unsatisfactory state of the Department, complaining that the 1857 Committee recommendations had not been implemented, that maps from the other Departments of the War Office had not been centralised and that the working of the Department was seriously hampered by insufficient funds. The memorandum had its desired effect, for Cardwell, who had already set Army circles afire with his new measures, authorised a strong committee under his Under Secretary of State for War, Lord Northbrook, to examine the Topographical Department once more. Captain Wilson was to be secretary and was to draft the report. His terms of reference were 'To recommend the best measures of bringing the Topographical Department to the greatest account'.

On 30th April 1870 Wilson presented his paper, and although only two pages long it marks a significant point in the development of British Military Intelligence as Cardwell adopted it almost in entirety. The first major change was that the Ordnance Survey with Sir Henry James in Southampton should be split from the Topographic Department and, recognising at last, that the Survey was not employed in making military maps, but on cadastral calculations for civil purposes, it should be a charge upon the Civil and not upon the Army vote. The next was that the Department should be divided into two sections: a Topographical Section, and a Statistical Section. The Topographical Section should collect and produce maps and the collection should be formed of:

The best map extent of Great Britain and Colonies and all foreign countries.
The best plans of foreign fortresses.
Maps and plans illustrative of campaigns, battles and sieges.
Photographs of the colonies and foreign countries
The Statistical Section should be divided into three sections, 'with the task of collecting and classifying information, rendering such information generally useful, and translating such foreign works as may be deemed advisable:
Section 'A'.Austria, Russia, Sweden, Norway, Turkey, Greece, Asia.
Section 'B'Prussia, Germany, Italy, Switzerland, Spain, Denmark.
Section 'C' France, Great Britain, Belgium, The Netherlands, America.'

The report also made a number of further recommendations.

1. A sum of money, say £250 should be inserted in the Estimates each year for the purchases of foreign newspapers, books, etc.
2. All Parliamentary reports on army matters, confidential and other War Office reports, the printed orders and circulars of all departments of the Army should be sent to the Topographical Department as a matter of course.
3. The present method of obtaining information from the military attachés is very bad. All their reports, whether confidential or otherwise, should be sent to the Topographical Department, and the officers of the Department should be allowed to communicate with them in a semi-official manner. The attachés should send, every quarter, notices of new books and maps published, and collect all army circulars and orders relating to equipment and organization.

The attachés should be encouraged to criticise the working of the foreign systems, and they should, as far as possible be selected from officers who have passed through either the Topographical Department or Staff College, or who belong to the Artillery or Engineers.

The Officers of the Topographical Department should be encouraged to travel. They should attend the autumn manoeuvres on the continent, and occasionally field days in England. A sum of £200 or £50 each to be taken for this in the estimates. No journey to be undertaken without the sanction of the Secretary of State, and payment to be made on condition that the officer worked and made a useful report.

The information collected by the sections should be made useful not only to the Secretary of State but to the whole Army by publishing quarterly a small sheet containing a list of all maps and books added to the Library during the quarter, and translation of interesting articles on military matters in foreign periodicals. The sheet not to exceed eight or twelve pages and be circulated to Heads of Departments, etc. Secondly, a series of pamphlets, descriptive of foreign armies, similar to those prepared by the Prussian Topographical Department, should be prepared, and sold to officers of the Army for a small fixed sum. The pamphlets not to be the medium of expressing any opinions of the author.

On receipt of this report Lord Cardwell set up yet another committee under Lord Northbrook, which published its findings in January 1871. Captain Wilson's recommendations were again accepted almost without change but an important proviso was added, that the statistical information kept in the Department should be divided so that internal British Army Statistics should become the responsibility of a Statistical Branch of the War Office and that the 'T & S' Department should concentrate on foreign armies. The Committee also strongly advocated a change in the method of procuring maps, explaining with heavy detail the current system:

Captain Wilson prepares a minute requesting that a map may be purchased. This passes to the Chief Clerk, who, after approving it, forwards the request to 'C' Division in which a demand on the Stationery Office is made out. The Stationery Office order the map from the map seller, who sends it to 'C' Division who forward it to the Chief Clerk who passes it to Captain Wilson.

The report concluded by recommending that 'soldiers should be encouraged to obtain plans of foreign fortresses and that sailors should be encouraged to do sketches of foreign ports' – practical advice, but advice which caused many embarrassing incidents in the next thirty five years.

So was laid the foundation of the Ministry of Defence Intelligence Organization as it is known today. The Ordnance Survey was transferred to the Office of Works and Captain Wilson was promoted to be Director of the reorganised Topographical and Statistical Department and given three officers to help him. Their charter was to 'Collect and classify all possible information relating to the strength, organization and equipment of foreign armies, to keep themselves acquainted with the progress made by foreign countries in military art and science and to preserve the information in such a form that it can readily be consulted and made available for any purpose for which it may be required' – a charter almost identical to the one in current use.

But Wilson was still not satisfied and after a year's experience he felt that sufficient had not yet been done to meet the requirements, so in 1872 he submitted another report to Mr. Cardwell emphasising the need to have an officer of General rank representing the intelligence contribution. He suggested that this officer should be relieved of command duties, and should be free to study the military defence of the Empire and the preparation of the Forces for war. It is the first time we have the suggestion that Intelligence and Operations are complementary. It marks the birth of the concept of G (Intelligence) i.e. the intelligence chain of command of the present General Staff system. Cardwell again accepted his views and, in a speech in the House of Commons on 24 February 1873 announced 'The intention of the Government is to establish an Intelligence Department with a Deputy Adjutant General and to amalgamate with it the Topographical Department under that most excellent officer Captain Wilson'. As a result, on April Fools Day 1873 Major General Sir Patrick Macdougal was appointed Chief of a new organization which was to be called the Intelligence Branch and was to include not only the Topographical Department with its responsibilities regarding foreign armies 'But in addition was made responsible for the strategic application of information available, and the consideration in time of peace of the measures to be taken for home defence in order to prevent delay and confusion on the outbreak of war'. The strength was to be one Deputy Adjutant General (Major General), one Assistant Adjutant General (Major) and five Deputy Assistant Adjutant Generals (Captain), one attached officer, nine military and ten civilian clerks.

So it was, that two hundred and thirteen years after the accepted birth of the regular British Army, Intelligence was recognised as a separate branch of the Staff, in its own right, and having a function in peacetime. The progress of the Branch has subsequently fluctuated between periods of intense activity and dull insignificance, but 1 April 1873 is a memorable day in the history of the British Military

Intelligence. Since this day an organization for intelligence assessment has existed in London, Captain Wilson was promoted Major and appointed Assistant Adjutant General and then, in January 1874 seventeen years after Lord Panmure had assured Sir Henry James that he had the matter under consideration, the Branch moved from New Street to Adair House, St. James Square (now the Junior Carlton Club). At this stage Major Wilson proposed a further enlargement of the organization bringing back the Ordnance Survey as follows:

Director's Department

Ordnance Survey	Three Geographical Sections	Home and Colonies Section	Railways and Telegraphs Section	Military History Section

But this time his ideas were not accepted and the plan was rejected. Not dismayed however this remarkable Intelligencer in April 1875 submitted a new memorandum summing up his recommendations on the way he felt the Intelligence Branch should function:

- To compile for publication a complete and accurate account of the strength, organization, equipment, tactics etc., of each foreign army.
- To collect all possible information from newspapers etc. and arrange it in a classified form.
- To prepare and periodically revise an 'Ordre de Bataille' for each country.
- Short biographies of foreign Generals.
- Geographical and statistical accounts of coast districts.
- Notes on maps of foreign countries.
- Special questions, such as the best mode of rendering assistance to Belgium, Holland, etc., in case of their independence being threatened, and the best course to pursue in the event of a war with Russia under various conditions.'

Major Wilson pointed out that newspaper cuttings and scraps of information should be collected then placed in large envelopes or pigeonholes, under their proper headings and a précis made once every twelve months, or more frequently if necessary.

For the next ten years the new Department now surged ahead. General Macdougal, an ex-Commandant of the Staff College, Camberley, was very keen that regimental officers should be attached to the Intelligence Branch, not only to give them knowledge of intelligence requirements but also as a means of testing the officers' suitability for subsequent employment on the Staff. He therefore arranged that each year four officers, not over the rank of Captain, were to be selected from those who had qualified at the Staff College to be attached to the Intelligence Branch for three months, and in the same way, eight officers, who had not passed the Staff College, were to be selected from the Army in general and attached for six months.

The officers chosen proved of high calibre and included Major Henry Brackenbury RA, Captain R. Home RE, Lieutenant J. Ardagh R.E.and as an attached officer Captain Hozier, later father-in-law to Sir Winston Churchill. The Intelligence Branch now went through a stage in its development that has never been repeated. Under its energetic Head and his enterprising Second in Command, the Intelligence Branch suddenly emerged as the most important department in the War Office. The line of thought behind this phenomenon was one of devastating logic. 'A branch that exits for the collection of military information and statistics about foreign armies, must necessarily be able to make an important contribution to any discussions or problems concerning our own British Army administration and organization'. This argument resulted in the Intelligence Branch finding itself inundated with a multitude of extra tasks, which had nothing to do with foreign intelligence! Between 1875 and 1879 among many projects, it was required to submit detailed reports on:

'1. The war establishment of a battalion, a cavalry regiment, a gun battery, a company of engineers, the Army Service Corps, the Medical Department and the Army Postal Corps.
The examination of the lines of communication system to include, railways, military telegraphs, field post offices, pay and remount depots.
The advantages and disadvantages of the bastion over the caponier system of fortification (This report discussed the different methods of bringing fire to bear on an enemy attempting to cross a ditch)
The preparations for summer and autumn manoeuvres by selecting camping grounds, water supplies and arranging transport.
The production of 'Rules for the Conduct of War Games'.
The preparation of a detailed mobilization plan to cover both home defence and the contingency of an expeditionary force of two Corps.'

This last task was a formidable commitment, requiring a vast amount of effort as it involved a plan being drawn up for mobilising a home force of eight Corps with places of concentration, allotment of tasks and a monthly record being maintained of units and personnel. In addition, a major reconnaissance was initiated around the English coast to discover the most likely places for an enemy invasion and to determine the best sites to select as defensive positions to cover these vulnerable points. The officer chosen to examine the coast between the Bristol Channel and Ilfracombe was Captain A. B. Tulloch who, whilst an instructor in survey at the Royal Military Academy Sandhurst, had been asked to take a 'fishing trip' in Belgium and a 'shooting trip' in Egypt, on behalf of the Intelligence Branch. Having made a success of these excursions he was then appointed as an 'Attached Officer' to the Branch. Captain Tulloch made his headquarters in a hotel at Weston-Super-Mare from where he set out on foot each day to cover his coastline. After examining a beach he would write a report, take a photograph and then send it back to London marked whether or not it was suitable for the disembarkation of cavalry and artillery. Foreign Intelligence Services were also doing similar work and when a surprised Captain Tulloch, at the end of his survey was told that a German Officer had done exactly the same beach survey a year before, and had stayed at the same hotel, he felt most disappointed. 'We might have done it together' he remarked.

During this summer Tulloch walked over three hundred miles and found to his interest that, without any previous knowledge, his conclusions often led to a selection of areas which proved to be the scenes of both Danish invasion sites and Civil War actions. In the winter he returned to London to write up his notes but, as with the remainder of the Intelligence Staff, he found himself employed on a variety of non-intelligence tasks one of which was a major work required by the Adjutant General on the commutation of officers' pensions. With all this work going on it is surprising that any foreign intelligence effort was achieved, and yet a great deal of work was done and published, concerning other armies. Books now held in the Ministry of Defence Library show the almost staggering detail obtained by the Victorian Staff Officer. France, Norway, Sweden, Denmark, Russia, Holland and Italy are all described with a meticulous attention to minor points not shown in today's pamphlets. But at this stage the Intelligence Branch was still a very novel organization and in February 1875 when Major Brackenbury gave a lecture on 'Intelligence Staffs' at the Royal United Services Institution, with the Duke of Cambridge in the chair, he felt obliged to start by explaining that by intelligence he did not mean merely information, and 'That afflicted relatives should not write to the Intelligence Branch to discover why their sons had ceased to write home!'

He went on to give the following significant figures:

Country	Square Miles of Territory	Population	Intelligence Staffs
Germany	212,000	41,000,000	61
Austro Hungary	240,000	36,000,000	68
France with Colonies	926.000	43,000,000	69
Great Britain and Colonies	5,4000,000	290,000,000	11 (7 permanent) (4 attached)

Adding that the foreign staffs were employed on purely intelligence and mobilization tasks, rather than general staff work. His words on the desirability of intelligence in peacetime, even though couched in 1875 language still have a powerful appeal today:

Do you remember that the cry for perpetual peace was far stronger before the Crimean War than it is now? At that time public consent had gone so far that an ill-advised person could write a pamphlet proposing that, if England were invaded, we should receive our guests with open arms and win them by tenderness to offer us an indemnity instead of exacting one. Since then, we do not seem to have come much nearer the Millennium, and may fairly say – 'scratch civilization and you find men and women with all their hopes and fears, pride and passion'. But there is no need for argument. Mr. Disraeli in his place in the House of Commons, Mr. Gladstone in his late writings, and that great exponent of public education opinion, The Times, have lately told us that England can no longer count on exemption from the common lot of mankind and of nations, a struggle for life, and, let me add, gentlemen – the survival of the fittest. Should such a struggle be forced upon us the country will turn to its soldiers and ask – 'are you ready?'

Brackenbury pleaded for a larger Intelligence Staff asking, 'What would it be if a rich man of indifferent eyesight, knowing that he would shortly be placed in a jungle of savage animals should grudge the money to buy a pair of spectacles?' His Royal Highness in his summing up speech agreed with Major Brackenbury's theme but felt bound to add a cold note of realism which still has a familiar ring, 'I must also point out that the Estimates form a very large item in the every-day consideration of Englishmen, and that everything that is spent on the Army is always scanned with the greatest care and not very favourable eye. Under these circumstances it may be very easily understood that however desirable it may be to add to the General staff of the Army for the purposes so very ably brought forward by Major Brackenbury, I must candidly state that it is not very easy to convince others that such is the case'.

An additional handicap in the Branch was the continual change of personnel. As always, the intelligence officers used all their ingenuity to get away from their offices and serve in the field. It was therefore decided that the method of attaching officers for temporary duty to the Branch should stop. The Duke of Cambridge decreed that in future officers of proved ability should be appointed for twelve months; at the same time he decided that the Intelligence Branch should revert back to the Quarter-Master General. On the formation of the Intelligence Branch, General Macdougal had been placed under the Adjutant General, almost certainly because of the influence of the head of that department, Sir Richard Airey. Airey was the man who had written the brief but confusing note to Nolan that had resulted in the charge of the Light Brigade and on his return to England, he had for many years, as with the remainder of the Crimean Staffs, been associated in the public mind with incompetence. But as Adjutant General he became the leading personality at the War Office. The Quarter-Master General on the other hand was a man who had served all his life in India and was not so powerful. When these two personalities changed, the question of controlling intelligence was resurrected and as a result in July 1874 the Intelligence Branch was transferred back to the Quarter-Master General's Department with its traditional responsibility for 'Reconnaissance and cognate duties'. General Macdougal therefore changed his title and became Deputy Quarter-Master General and Major Wilson Assistant Quarter-Master General.

In March 1876 the effervescent Major Wilson came to the end of his tour. It had been a great success for him and he had seen great changes. In the civilian field he had received the Diploma of the International Geographical Congress, had been elected a Member of Council of the Royal Geographical Society and the Society of Biblical Archaeology; he had been made a Fellow of the Royal Society and was President of the Geographical Section of the British Association. In the military field he had seen the Topographical and Statistical Department grow from one officer, one military clerk and thirteen civilians to seventeen officers, including a General, eleven military clerks, and fourteen civilians. He had the satisfaction of knowing that the Intelligence Branch was now established as a recognised and important part of the War Office, and as he left to take up his new appointment as Head of the Ordnance Survey in Ireland he had the more tangible pleasure of being created a Companion of the Bath for his services to Intelligence. Only a historian with his Kismetic ability to see round the next bend, can foresee that Charles Wilson's next chance for distinction and glory will be on the sand of the Sudan, where, on the death of his commander in action he is obliged to take charge of the vanguard attempting to relieve General Gordon trapped in Khartoum – and will fail.

CHAPTER TWELVE

Intelligence in the Field

*D*uring the twenty five year period following the Crimean War British soldiers fought in Persia, China, India, New Zealand, Sikkim, Bhootan, Jamaica, Canada, British Honduras, Abyssinia and the North West Frontier. In these campaigns, just as the Intelligence Branch was being accepted as part of the War Office in London, so it was becoming accepted that headquarters, when in the field, should also have a recognised Intelligence Department. It was, however, a very slow and gradual acceptance. Although the Intelligence Branch in London was raised to the status of an Intelligence Division in 1888 and only became the Intelligence Department in 1901, many records, including contemporary records, continuously refer to the London Office as the Intelligence Department throughout the whole periods. In this book the official dates will be used but in line with common practice, overseas organizations will be called Intelligence Departments.

In India, it had long been realised that only with a sound and efficient intelligence organization could this vast Continent be controlled by a small number of white soldiers. The Quarter-master General's Department had therefore been officially made responsible for military intelligence, but until 1876 no particular branch or section in the Department was allotted to this specialised task nor were any military intelligence officers appointed in peacetime. If a campaign was to be launched, regimental officers were selected at random from the Army as a whole and then grouped arbitrarily on the staff of the commanding General to form his Intelligence Staff. Paradoxically it was the success of this very 'ad hoc' system in the Persian Campaign, which added to the complacency of the Indian Army Authorities before the Mutiny.

In 1856, just one year before the Mutiny, the Quarter-Master General's Department had carried out its intelligence duties extremely well. The Shah of Persia, who had been growing restless at what he considered too much interference by Britain in his own internal affairs, had begun a series of verbal and economic attacks against 'British interests'. He had also 'Grossly insulted' the British Resident in Tehran by calling him 'Stupid, ignorant and insane'. Even worse he had publicly alleged that the Resident was 'Carrying on an intrigue' with the wife of the Persian First Secretary and to 'Stop the scandal' had put the lady into prison. This unromantic act was the climax to a series of incidents and on 26 October 1856 it was decided to send an Expeditionary Force commanded by General Outram to Persia to settle the matter – and release the Secretary's wife. Before letting the Persians know of the intended invasion however, the Quarter-master General, with a great deal of foresight and an equal amount of audacity despatched an intelligence officer to 'spy out the land'. This officer landed quite openly at Bushire and in front of the populace surveyed the fortifications using compasses and measuring chains. The Persian Authorities not unnaturally resented this activity and impressed upon the British Resident in Bushire, that the officer and his helpers should depart. This they did, although the Resident remained in Bushire until the Expeditionary Fleet arrived and then went on board to watch the bombardment of the Town. The cannonade proved most effective and the troops then landed with very little opposition to capture 2,000 Persians, all armed with British rifles given to the Shah some years before in order to strengthen his defences against Russia.

The Intelligence officer of the Force was Lieutenant J. Ballard, known as 'Superintendent of the Intelligence Department'. Ballard quickly began to organise a small spy network and, to increase his sources of information decided to follow the example of Harry Lumsden in India and raise his own Corps of Guides. The unit was most successful and before the final and crucial battle of the campaign, Ballard was able to present General Outram with a complete outline of the Persian dispositions and their plans for the engagement. Helped by this information Outram won a complete victory and three months after landing, a satisfactory Peace Treaty was signed and the Force then returned to India where they received the Indian General Service medal with clasp 'Persia'.

Unfortunately for Ballard, the success of his Corps of Guides led him into a bureaucratic whirlwind. On his return it was discovered that Army Headquarters in Simla had agreed to his request to raise the Persian Corps of Guides, but had only given permission for a small number of men to be recruited. This directive had, however, been lost at sea, and Ballard had enlisted far more men than he was officially allowed. A long and acrimonious 'paper-war' then began which culminated in a letter from Simla accusing General Outram of being 'Vague'. Jacub acting on Outram's behalf then sent a sharp but exceedingly clear letter back:

General Outram wishes to bring to notice the annoyance to which he is subject by the Military Department in connection with the Order about interpreters and guides, and points out that this order was lost in transit by a foreign vessel. The General points out that it is not for him to defend against the charge of vagueness the orders of the General under whom he was serving, and explains that the establishment in question was found to be absolutely necessary to enable the operations of the force to proceed. Also, that as he had authority from Her Majesty's Government to entertain any number of irregular troops, the charge of vagueness must rest on the orders of Her Majesty's Ministry if anywhere. Finally requests that in consideration of his Services, the Governor in Council may be moved to relieve him from the continued annoyance which the Military Secretary inflicts on him.

The file was then closed.

The events of the Indian Mutiny and the story of military intelligence in the Indian Army do not form part of this book. It is interesting however that before the Mutiny, just as before the South African War of 1899, it was not that the authorities had received no warnings of possible troubles and bloodshed from their intelligence agencies, but rather that having received such warnings they steadfastly, relentlessly and successfully convinced themselves that a policy of placid non-activity would result in the troubles going away. In other respects the story of intelligence in the Indian Army also matches that of the British Army.

For twenty years after the Mutiny, although warfare was practically continuous on the North West Frontier, the punitive and sometimes barbaric measures taken by Britain to punish and subjugate the rebellious Sepoys meant that India as a whole was extremely tranquil. The inevitable result of this tranquillity was the traditional a loss of enthusiasm for intelligence and eventually the complete disappearance of any intelligence activity within the Quarter-Master General's Department. This situation continued until 1876 when a young and ambitious Artilleryman, Captain Collen, submitted a paper to the Quarter-Master General, Major General F. Roberts, VC, complaining of lack of intelligence research being carried out and suggesting that an Intelligence Branch should be formed in India, just as Major Wilson and General Macdougall were doing in England. General Roberts gave his approval in principle, and allowed Collen to extend his leave in England in order to examine the British organization. Collen therefore attached himself to the Intelligence Branch in London and made an extremely detailed examination of how it operated. Working very closely with Charles Wilson and the other British intelligence staff officers, Collen very rapidly caught the fever of enthusiasm and thrust that pervaded in the British intelligence Branch at that time. He became even more determined that India should have a similar organization and in 1878 produced his report. It proved a most comprehensive and farsighted document.

The main problem the Report highlighted, concerned the division of intelligence gathering responsibility between India and the Horse Guards. Duplication was obviously wasteful and could lead to confusion yet, neither Headquarters wished to lose executive control over the limited intelligence resources available. After a great deal of 'backroom' work a compromise solution was eventually agreed, whereby London would retain responsibility for Russia, Turkey, Egypt, Africa and China and Simla would collate on Arabia and all those countries bordering India. In the Report, Collen repeated the suggestion made by Colonel Henry Lawrence thirty years previously, that the Intelligence Staff should have certain field units working specifically for them in war and that these field units should train for intelligence duties in peace. He pointed out that the Bengal Corps of Guides had been recruited 'Not only to provide a band of picked men for frontier services but to supply a body of men thoroughly acquainted with the countries in which hostilities were likely to arise. Trained in time of peace, to acquire during war, that accurate intelligence of the resources strength, position and movements of an enemy, the want of which has been so constantly deplored in the campaigns of the armies of India'. 'Now' Collen said, 'The special functions of the Corps, the formation of which had been Sir Henry Lawrence's dream to accomplish, were lost sight of. Neither officers nor men were trained to the special work, and for many years only one solitary instance was on record of a Guide, sketching or mapping the Frontier'. He concluded 'It may be said that the Bengal Corps has become too exclusively military and the Bombay and Madras Corps somewhat too civilian, though as reconnoitrers and intelligencers these latter two modest Corps have done work immeasurably more valuable than the large and expensive Bengal Corps of Guides'. Collen's Report with its painfully modest proposals was however, too revolutionary for its time. General Roberts gave limited approval to the idea of having an intelligence staff and wrote, 'The recommendation that there should be an Intelligence Branch for all India seems wise and the personnel proposed viz three officers, three draughtsmen and a Persian Monshee (Interpreter) seems all that is necessary at present.' He did not however, like the idea of changing the role of the Corps of Guides and in his final recommendation, while agreeing that the original aim had been altered, decreed 'The Queens Own Guides should retain its present character of an essentially fighting regiment, trusting to the esprit de Corps of that distinguished regiment and to its officers, to maintain its reputation as a most useful intelligence corps as well'.

Three officers, three draughtsmen and a persian moonshee does not seem a lavish establishment for an Intelligence Branch to cover the Continent of India, but the General's decision that the Guides could carry out the specialised tasks of an intelligence corps in addition to those of a normal fighting regiment is even more depressing. Throughout the story of the British Army, commanders have consistently exhibited a blind spot over the question of gathering intelligence. There can surely be no other aspect of the military art where so much lip service is paid to the need for establishing a reliable system in peacetime and yet so little is done in practical terms, to achieve such a system.

Thus the Indian Intelligence Branch was created in 1878, but the concept suggested by Collen of an Intelligence Corps trained in peace time and ready for field intelligence duties in war had to wait another fifty years before coming to fruition. In the meantime, the practice, when a campaign was planned, was to raise intelligence-gathering units in the country concerned from locally enlisted men. A good example of this is the Ashanti Campaign.

In 1824 the West African tribe from Ashanti defeated and killed the British Commission Sir Charles MacCarthy, and thereafter used his skull as a drinking bowl. They were a savage warlike race, practising human sacrifice and slavery. Their ferocity terrified all the neighbouring tribes, and for forty-five years they had successfully resisted all British attempts at control. In 1863-1864 a British force had been sent inland 'To teach them a lesson' but was wiped out by disease – 'an enemy was never seen nor a grain of powder expended'. Now, in 1873, under their bloodthirsty King 'Coffee' Kalkali, an Ashanti Army had advanced across the River Prah and was threatening the Gold Coast. Descriptions of terrible massacres, coupled with the effect on Britain's commercial interests decided the Government that a further expeditionary force would have to be sent. They planned however, not to send any British troops, only thirty British officers who would raise a native army on arrival in Africa. The man chosen to command was Major-General Sir Garnet Wolseley, and he was allowed to select the officers he wished to take with him. This group of men, who subsequently lived together for nearly a year in the hard isolation of a West African jungle, formed a bond between themselves, which was to last for the next thirty years. Field Marshall Montgomery, Victor of Alemein, has often said that the greatest tribute you can pay to a man's character is that you are prepared 'To go into the jungle with him'. Wolseley did just this, and he never forgot the men who went with him. As he rose in rank, so did they. They became known as Wolseleys 'Ring', Lieutenant Colonel Evelyn Wood, Major Colley, Captains Buller, Brackenbury, McNeill, Russell, Butler, Colonel Greaves and Lieutenant Frederick Maurice, all of whom later became Generals.

Many of these officers had previously served with Wolseley in Canada, where for eight arduous months using boat, train, sleigh and canoe they had pursued the rebellious French Canadian, Louis Riel. One such officer was the young and dashing Redvers Buller, of the Rifle Brigade and it was Buller that Wolseley appointed to be 'Head of Intelligence' for the Ashanti campaign. Buller, fired with enthusiasm, went hopefully to the newly formed Intelligence Branch in London, now six months old and rapidly developing under Major Charles Wilson – but found nothing. He did not want for advice however, for in the daily press and by a flood of letters he received a wealth of information from those who had previously served in the Gold Coast. It was all depressing and practically all erroneous. 'White troops cannot exist, never mind fight in the pestilent jungle. The jungle is so thick that an army can only advance on a two-man front and this exposes it to continued ambushes from the savage Ashantis. The country as far as the Prah is thirty miles of unbroken flat swamp'. (In fact it turned out to be an area full of ravines and gullies). All this information Captain Buller collated, and together with his colleagues, studied on the long sea voyage to Cape Coast Castle.

Wolseley had been charged by the Government with organising an army from the local population and forcing King 'Coffee' into submission. After his arrival however, it soon became clear that the local natives were incapable of tackling the Ashantis, such was their fear of this warlike tribe that they were often too terrified to approach even a dead Ashanti. Wolseley therefore decided to send home for a British Expeditionary Force and asked that instead of regular battalions, the force should be made up of one hundred good volunteers selected from each of the available battalions. The Government agreed to send British troops but the War Office decided against forming a special force. They assigned instead the first three battalions on the Foreign Service roster i.e., the 2nd Battalion Royal Welsh Fusiliers, 3rd Battalion Rifle Brigade and the Black Watch. In the Second World War General Wingate made a similar request and was successful. His first Chindit operation was composed of selected men from the whole army in India. Later General

Slim objected to this concentration of the alleged 'Better soldier' and on this experience it would appear that the War Office were correct in refusing Wolseley's request in the Ashanti Campaign. Comparison between the First and Second Chindit operations show it is a very doubtful advantage to break up the organization of several existing battalions in order to create one 'Superior unit.

The European force landed on 5 January 1875 where, for the preceding three months, Buller had been employed finding out as much as possible of the location and strength of the enemy. He had started with a clean sheet - 'even the Administrator himself could not lay his finger on the map and say with any certainty here is Mampon or here is Joogual. Two officers came back after a reconnaissance, one having visited Hamakind the other Jarsah and it took a deal of effort to discover it was the same place, the officers having written their own phonetic translation of Myaikin!'

Buller built his Intelligence Department by collecting a number of interpreters, having officers attached to native kings and by bribes, promises and threats gradually persuading people to bring him information. He also recruited a number of spies from the Elminas and Assins, as these were the only people capable of speaking Ashanti without betraying themselves. Most important of all he formed a Corps of Scouts, about 250 strong who, under the command of Lieutenant Lord Gifford, became an integral part of the Force and one which had more casualties than any other unit, as it was continually required to lead the advance. Buller also interviewed all prisoners. One was an 18 year old girl who revealed the vital piece of news that the Ashantis had broken camp and moved back across the Prah River. Captain Brackenbury has described her interrogation - 'Sitting on the floor, scantily clothed in a worn thin robe, whence, from time to time she delicately removed the insects that long dwelling in the Ashanti camp had fostered, she gave her evidence in the most straightforward and intelligent way. She was not without a certain coquetry of manner that never left her in our long subsequent acquaintance. When our march up country began, Major Baker hired her as a carrier, and she grew sleek and fat almost beyond recognition. She was always merry and good natured, and fond of her master, though much surprised on the first day's march that she was not to play Ruth to his Boaz, and lie at her master's feet. What has become of her now? When last the writer inquired he heard she was 'living with no. 1 Company'.

On the arrival of the three British battalions and a Naval Brigade Wolseley decided to march 150 miles north into the jungle and attack the capital, Kumasi. Preceded by Gifford and his scouts, the whole force moved through dense vegetation, often stretched over two to three miles of track. Eventually Buller, on 16 January located the Ashanti force near the village of Amoaful and gave it as his opinion that the decisive action would be at that spot. Brackenbury warned him against prophesying, but Buller felt so certain of his opinion that he insisted on its inclusion in his daily intelligence report. He was justified in his faith, for here, on 31 January the main battle of the campaign was fought. The commander of the leading British column Brigadier General Sir Archibald Alison was ambushed by hundreds of Ashantis lying hidden in the undergrowth. It was a savage battle fought for twelve hours against an invisible enemy who concentrated, fired, faded away and then re-concentrated against another part of the column. All Alison's reserves were committed and by nightfall there were two hundred British casualties, over half being men of the Black Watch. Young Lieutenant Frederick Maurice, who had distinguished himself by walking up and down in front of the native troops getting them to rest their rifles on his shoulder in order they should fire low, was among the wounded.

On the following day Wolseley sent a column to burn the village of Bakwai about a mile to the East. As usual, Gifford led the way and on encountering opposition he dashed fearlessly into the village shooting and slashing at the startled Ashantis, his chief scout was shot dead, and seventeen others wounded, but the Naval Brigade formed and charged and the village was taken. For this action Gifford received a Victoria Cross. The force then moved on in three columns with Sapper officers in front clearing the track. Major Home led the centre, Captain Buckle the left and Lieutenant Bell the right. Buckle was shot through the heart, but Bell kept his natives working in a manner which earned him the Victoria Cross for 'By example, he made these men do what no European working party was ever required to do in wartime – namely to work under fire in the face of the enemy without a covering party.' Finally on 3 February 'Their pipes playing, their officers to the front' the Black Watch broke through into Kumasi and the campaign was virtually over. Buller, as Intelligence Officer, was appointed Head Prize Agent and spent the night ransacking the King's treasure trove; gold masks, silver plate and nuggets, coral ornaments, silks and jewelled swords were all were listed and taken away. 'A thousand things which world be worth fabulous sums in cabinets at home were left'. Major Home and Lieutenant Bell then destroyed the town.

Buller, weak from fever began the long march back, his last action was to help Brackenbury and Maurice release many of the prisoners held 'In log'. These wretched men had had their wrists fettered to a large log by an iron staple, the pressure of which often cut the skin causing the flesh to fester. As the log was too heavy for the man to lift himself, he could only walk when it was put on his shoulders. Before he left, Buller also helped destroy the Fetish House where the King had slain an average of three bound men a day for many years, culminating with 2,000 in the few weeks before the final attack on his Capital.

The Expedition was judged to be a success. Wolseley, with the minimum of soldiers had pre-planned his campaign carefully, confined it to the winter when the climate was most suitable to Europeans, had defeated the 'undefeatable' King Coffee, preserved peace in the Gold Coast and brought home rich treasure. His reputation was made and, sharing the credit was his Head of Intelligence, Redvers Buller, who received a brevet majority and the Companionship of the Bath. Major Home, Commander Royal Engineers during the campaign was also promoted and became Assistant Quarter-Master General of the Intelligence Branch in London. But he died during his tour, and Colonel East 57th Regiment was appointed his successor.

Soon after taking up this appointment however the Transvaal Campaign began and Colonel East was posted to Zululand to join Sir Garnet Wolseley, though not in an intelligence appointment. In the Zululand Campaign, Intelligence did not do so well. The only member of the 'Ring ' initially in Zululand was Redvers Buller. He had served four years at the Horse Guards and in 1878, although most people believed that war with Russia was inevitable, Buller, who had been following the troubled events in Natal decided that this was where 'The path to promotion' lay. When therefore he was given the opportunity to go to Africa he readily accepted. Soon after his arrival he was given command of his own regiment, the Frontier Light Horse, a miscellaneous collection of 'Britons, Boers and Aliens' with poor morale and in very low state of training, described at the time as a 'Terror to everyone but the enemy'. However, throughout 1878 during the ten months campaign against the Kaffirs, Buller gradually raised their standard and eventually turned his mixed command into a first class reconnaissance unit.

Britain's recently acquired control of the Transvaal, as well as involving the nation in a fight against the Kaffirs, also resulted in a direct conflict with the Zulus under their proud and capable ruler King Cetewayo. At the end of 1878, after a long period of tension, an ultimatum was sent to Cetewayo ordering him to disband his Army, hand over a number of 'criminals' and allow a British Resident and missionaries to be installed in his Capital. To no-one's surprise these terms were rejected and on 11 January 1879 three columns totalling some six thousand British troops under Lord Chelmsford advanced over the frontier. Chelmsford took no intelligence officer on his staff, but attached to each column were a number of political officers. These were local men whose duties were very similar to the political officers of the Indian Frontier i.e. to act as interpreters, liase with the local population, employ guides and control spies. They included Captain George Shepstone, Mr Bernard Fynney, Mr. Llewellyn Lloyd,, Mr. John Dunn, and, with Chelmsford in the Central Column, the Honourable William Drummond, also known as the 'Staff Interpreter'. In the pre-invasion period Chelmsford had asked Fynney to write a report on the Zulu Army which Donald Morris in his excellent book 'The Washing of the Spears' has described.

> Fynney had his faults as a border agent but he had been collecting just such information for years as a hobby, and he soon produced a few packed pages that outlined in precise detail how the Zulu forces were raised, armed, drilled, officered, organised, fed and doctored. To this succinct compendium he added a complete list of the Zulu regiments, giving for each one the Zulu name and its translation, who had raised it, the name of the commanding Induna, the headquarters kraal, a complete description of its distinctive uniform, a close estimate of the number of warriors and their average age. Chelmsford, much impressed, threw in the best map that could be produced and published the whole in Pietermaritzburg in November. When Fynney sent him a list of over a hundred of the chief Zulu Indunas, giving each man's father, age, strength, character and political leanings, Chelmsford promptly published a second edition of his pamphlet, and when his forces entered Zululand every company commander had a copy in his kit. No expeditionary force has ever started a native war so well informed about its enemy.

On 20 January the Central Column camped under the hill of Isandlhwana and at dawn on 22 January Lord Chelmsford moved out with six companies of the South Wales Borderers then the 24th Foot, in search of a Zulu force reported in the area; he failed to contact them and after a frustrating morning returned to the camp. All was quiet and the tents were still standing, but as they rode into the perimeter they realised, to their horror, that everyone was dead. Five companies of the 1st Battalion South Wales Borderers and one of the 2nd Battalion had been annihilated. A total of 52 officers and 1,277 men had been killed. It was the largest loss of British life in a single engagement since the Crimean War. Captain George Shepstone, the Political officer, had been out on patrol with some mounted natives when, attracted by their shouting, he saw to his alarm an entire Zulu Impi of 15,000 men advancing at a run on the camp, it stretched over two miles, a great torrent of black skin and glittering steel pouring down over the hills onto the plain. The camp was not sited defensively, most of the men were having their dinner. Within twenty minutes all organised resistance had ceased and the scene was one of isolated groups of red-coated figures systematically being hacked to the ground. Lieutenant Colonel Pulleine commanding the 1st Battalion had, at the last moment, ridden over to the Guard Tent, taken out the cased Colours and given them to his Adjutant, Lieutenant Melville, ordering him to safety. By nightfall of the 950 Europeans who had reached Isandhlwana only 55 were still alive and, lying among the dead, were Shepstone and Melville. But the Zulu fury had not been spent and the Impi swept on to attack the 139 men, 110 of whom were South Wales Borderers, garrisoned in the two stone missionary buildings known as Rorke's Drift. The epic defence of these men is part of British Military History and eleven Victoria Crosses were awarded for the action.

On 4 February the body of Melville was found. Nearby, floating in a pool were the Queen's Colour and the Regimental Colour torn, tattered, but in one piece. They were carefully collected and taken back to the South Wales Borderers Company Headquarters at Rorke's Drift where they were returned to Major Glyn, who had had the honour of receiving them under very different circumstances thirteen years before at a regimental parade in Ireland. A little later the pole of the 2nd Battalion Colour was found but the Colour itself was never recovered. When the Regiment eventually returned to England Queen Victoria asked that the Colours be taken to Osborne where she placed a small wreath of silver immortelles about the crown. Tattered and torn as they were, the Colours then continued in service eventually crossing the Rhine with the Battalion in 1918. In 1933 they were finally laid up In the Regimental Chapel in Brecon Cathedral where they are to this day, together with the pole of the 2nd Battalion.

The two other columns also had little success. With no military intelligence officers appointed, the political officers, being mere civilians, were accorded scant recognition by the Army Commanders. On the right, Colonel Pearson stumbled into five regiments of Zulus and was surrounded at Eshowe; on the left Colonel Wood with Colonel Buller reached Kambula where, exhausted and immobilised, they remained. The whole Army had therefore been brought to a halt and was surrounded. There were no reserves in Natal, a second British expeditionary force would take at least two months to arrive and the long border with Zululand now lay undefended.

But fortunately Cetewayo did not seize his opportunity and attack. Chelmsford was able to return to Durban, gather reinforcements and on 29 March, march back across the frontier with scouts from the Natal Volunteer Guides in the lead. This time he took with him two intelligence officers designated as such, the Honourable William Drummond and Mr. John Dunn. Dunn could speak Zulu like a native and was an excellent shot. At the age of eighteen he had run off with a fifteen year old coloured girl and, after a series of adventures, had become a border agent and a man of wealth on the Zulu frontier. Although he had strong allegiances to the Zulus, he agreed to join Chelmsford and raised his own unit of 112 men called the John Dunn Scouts.

This time the advance was cautious and prepared. William Drummond organised his intelligence service by sending out the scouts, collecting their reports and matching them with other facts gleaned from spies and deserters. On 1 April when just short of the beleaguered Colonel Pearson, the scouts reported a Zulu Army massing at Umisi. Dunn rode forward alone and covered by a blinding rainstorm, stripped naked and carrying only his rifle swam across the river to have a look. He returned with the news that the Impi was indeed there and preparing to attack. Thus forewarned Chelmsford had the bugles sound and the camp stand to arm. This time as the Impi swept forward it was shattered by the infantry and naval brigade supported by rockets, gatling machine guns and field guns; for the loss of two officers and eleven men killed, over a thousand Zulus were slaughtered. John Dunn emerged unscathed, and when he died on 5 August 1895 he left 49 recorded wives, 117 children and a small 'empire' in the Lower Drift of the Tugela.

This battle marked the end of the second phase of the Zulu War Chelmsford regrouped his force then plunged direct for Ulundi, Cetewayo's Capital. William Drummond was redesignated 'Head of Intelligence'. He, like Mr. Calvert in the Crimean War, had graduated to the post, in default of any military officer doing the job. The son of Lord Strathallan, Drummond had been a Natal Civil Servant and had the two attributes also peculiar to Calvert, local language and local knowledge.

On 4 July the Force came to Ulundi. Chelmsford formed his regiments into a square and with bands playing and the colours of the Royal Scots Fusiliers uncased, prepared for the final battle. Buller and his Frontier Light Horse rode ahead and discovering 20,000 warriors in battle array, they halted, opened fire and stung the Impi into a charge. Once again the volley of lead that erupted from the waiting soldiers decimated the Zulus. They fell by the hundreds and as they began to retreat, the 17th Lancers galloped forward, spitting the remnants with

their lances. 'Who's to be first in Ulundi?' cried Buller and with a gallop
the cavalry spurred into the Capital. Amongst the leaders, pushing his
horse to the front, and leaping over the thorn barrier surrounding the
Royal Kraal was Drummond, anxious to capture the King. By mid-
afternoon the 1,500 huts had been set ablaze and the force began its
march back across the plain. The House of Shaka had been destroyed,
the Zulu empire was no more. Among the hundreds of dead lying
around the Kraal there were only ten Europeans, and to everyone's grief
they included William Drummond, the Head of Intelligence.

One man who received the news of the victory with very mixed
feelings was General Wolseley. Three months before, on returning from
a picnic trip in Cyprus he had received a cipher telegram ordering him
to return immediately to London. The casualty lists from Isandlhwana
were just arriving in the Capital and the Government, horrified by the
disaster, had decided to send out a further expeditionary force and, in
spite of Wolseley's comparatively junior rank, had selected him for
command. Wolseley was delighted, he collected the members of his
'Ring', Brackenbury as Military Secretary, Maurice as Intelligence
Officer, Lord Gifford as Aide-de-Camp and set sail. But on arrival at Port
Durnford the raging surf had prevented the party from landing, and to
their intense chagrin they had to waste six days going on down the coast
to Durban. By 28 June when they arrived, Wolseley was in an agony of
frustration, he knew the final battle of the war was imminent, yet here
he was in Durban, three hundred miles away. He immediately
dispatched the following restraining telegram to Chelmsford:

> Concentrate your force at once and keep it concentrated.
> Undertake no serious operations with detached bodies of troops.
> Acknowledge receipt of this message at once and flash back your
> latest moves. I am astonished at not hearing from you.' But
> Chelmsford was not to be deprived of the fruits of victory, he
> received the message only four miles from Ulundi, ignored it,
> continued his advance and won his battle. He then went home to
> a hero's welcome and left Wolseley the tiring task of catching
> Cetewayo.

Throughout July, and for three weeks in August, the hunt continued;
Wolseley set up a cordon of troops around the area then criss-crossed the
land with detached parties of mounted men. In one group under Major
Barrow 19th Hussars, Wolseley sent his Deputy Assistant Adjutant and
Quarter-master General (Intelligence) Captain Frederick Maurice. After
seventeen days of hard continual trekking in the heat, the English
cavalry horses became exhausted and Barrow decided to send on Lord

Gifford and Maurice in separate detachments to continue the chase. For Gifford it was a repeat of his Ashanti experience, completely cut off from ordinary supplies he lived off the land, plundered kraals and followed up every chance rumour. In one village he caught five Zulus, and a flogging having failed to get them to talk, he blindfolded the most aggressive, led him into the bush and fired his rifle in the air. Then he returned alone and began to blindfold the next man. This tactic proved successful and the terrified native agreed to lead Gifford to the King's latest hiding place. When they reached the kraal, however, Cetewayo was not there, only two boys were sitting in the hut. Using the same ruse, Gifford 'persuaded' the youngest to lead them to the village hidden in the valley, and there looking down Gifford recognised the portly figure of the man for whom they had searched so long. He sent a messenger back to Maurice telling of his discovery, but as there was no easy path down to the village decided to wait until dark before attempting his attack. The messenger, loping down the track with the intelligence report wedged securely in a cleft-stick, met a party of the 1st King's Dragoon Guards. The note was a little ambiguous so the Dragoons decided to act immediately and drawing their sabres cut their way down the hill to burst in and capture the unsuspecting Cetewayo. The campaign was over, but as a final effort Wolseley decided to subdue another native chief, Sekukuni, who had established a 'Bandit fastness' in a kopje in the hilly country some 150 miles north west of Pretoria. The attack was completely successful and the kopje was captured in a rush, but leading the assault and shot down at close range from the mouth of a cave, was the Intelligence Officer, Captain Frederick Maurice, wounded by a bullet which penetrated his right shoulder and lung.

The Ashanti and Zulu Campaigns are typical examples of the way intelligence operated in the field during this period. The appointment of a military officer to be intelligence officer was not mandatory and depended largely on the personality of the commander. If a civilian was made head of intelligence he was kept very much 'Under the eye' of the General and had little executive power. If a soldier was appointed, he tended to take part in personal reconnaissances and assume command of local scout units. In no case was a regular intelligence staff or regular intelligence unit in existence before a campaign began. In each case however, by the close of the campaign there had emerged a unit working specifically for an intelligence officer. These units were composed of men who had knowledge of the local language, the local area, or a flair for guessing correctly what the enemy was going to do.

Whilst these fighting campaigns were being undertaken overseas, another aspect of intelligence in the field, was gaining in importance.

Not so dramatic, but as times equally dangerous. In the last quarter of the nineteenth century the suggestion made originally by Colonel Jervis and then repeated in the 1870 Report, that officers from the Department should be allowed to visit foreign countries gradually came into effect. Armed with a multitude of pretences British officers visited Russia, Germany, Italy, Belgium, Denmark and Egypt, enjoying the social life, but scribbling away industriously on their observations each night. They discovered much useful information but, as an official report in 1877 explained:

> The information in their reports was based upon knowledge personally acquired, much of it obtained with great difficulty and without official facilities, the nature of the enquires precluding these being asked or granted.' It is not surprising that those officers, taken from a regimental background and sent on 'spying' tours, ran into a host of troubles. One while making up his notes in a hotel room heard someone knock fiercely on the door and without thinking pushed the papers into his pipe and lit the bowl, only to have the chambermaid discover him red faced and spluttering; another who was making a series of notes on some coast defences in France met two gendarmes, and so bad was this officer's conscience that he pulled out his notebook, tore out the pages and gallantly tried to swallow them. Astonished at this performance, the gendarmes, who had approached merely to ask for a light, solemnly decided that there must be something wrong with a man who liked eating paper, and arrested him.

The information acquired by the officers was at times also suspect; one officer when visiting the Paris Exhibition was highly impressed with a new naval gun being shown. It appeared to have that characteristic so long sought after by ship and subsequently tank designers, a stabilizing system, which would enable the gun to remain on target irrespective of the movement of its carriage. It was only later, when the report had been proudly dispatched, that the officer learnt that the gun had been made of papier-mâché. The 'tours' were eagerly sought by the Intelligence Branch Officers. Count Gleichen who was sent with a naval intelligence officer on a trip to the Tunisian and Algerian coasts managed to combine business and pleasure very well and for most of the time, 'to put the local authorities off the scent, shot snipe and wild boar'. Their biggest coup was in obtaining a 'secret naval code'; they had gone to check on a re port that a submarine station was being built near Bougie and in order to have a good look, they asked the keeper of the local semaphore station if they could see the view from his roof. Half way up the stairs they saw on the wall a table of flags. The Naval Intelligence officers whispered urgently that these were secret and Gleichen stopped to memorise them. After a few minute the keeper returned with 'face as black as thunder and threw them out' but Gleichen had already memorised the series. The count later recalled that these were delightful days and strongly recommended that 'sport of battery and fortress hunting to all who had a taste in that direction, especially as there was the zest of a ten thousand franc fine or five years inside the fortress if you were caught'. Several officers were in fact arrested, one had hidden incriminating documents under his mattress and was discovered, another was arrested on suspicion and questioned for several days, but as nothing incriminating could be proved, was just about to be released when he received a letter from England written on official notepaper – his alibi of being a tourist thus shattered, he was sentenced to several years imprisonment.

In the British Army today, if an officer wishes to travel to countries whose Governments are considered unfriendly to Great Britain, the officer must first apply for permission from the Ministry of Defence. Before this permission is given many intelligence factors might be considered e.g. would the arrest or disappearance of the officer result in grave embarrassment to the British Government; has the officer recently held an appointment which gives him access to vital secrets; it is likely that an attempt might be made to compromise or subvert the officer. At the end of the nineteenth century however there was no such cautionary control and any enterprising officer who wished to act as a temporary military sleuth could go abroad and travel where he wished.

One to do so was a young officer serving with the 13th Hussars in Colchester, Essex, Robert Baden-Powell (later the hero of Mafeking and founder of the Boy Scout Movement), Baden-Powell learnt from newspaper articles that the Germany Army was carrying out experiments with a revolutionary type of machine gun which did not have to be hand-cranked. They had developed a new type of smokeless propellant that enabled reloading to be done automatically. On his own initiative therefore, Baden-Powell decided to spend his leave on the Continent and attend the German Army manoeuvres as an 'Uninvited guest'. In Germany he found that the machine gun trials were being held in a camp near Spandau that was surrounded by a wooden fence and guarded by sentries. The inquisitive Hussar prowled round for some time and then lay in the grass pretending to be a asleep. There, by timing the shots against his watch he was able to calculate the rate of fire and by listening to the 'ping' of the bullets against iron targets, was able to gauge the accuracy. But 'Baden-Powell' was still not satisfied and wanted to have a look himself. He noticed a gap in the boarding and when the sentry had moved on, sauntered casually forward to take a peep. Unfortunately, the German sentry was well awake and seeing a stranger in the forbidden area came up 'Looking uncomfortably grim'. Baden-Powell, in line with his famous motto, was 'prepared' and pulling out a bottle of brandy took a gulp, spilling some over his clothes 'to give the right atmosphere'. He then insisted on sharing the remainder of the bottle with the sentry, whose attitude gradually changed from suspicion to sympathy, finally advising him gently to go away.

Later when Baden-Powell was appointed Intelligence Officer in Malta, in addition to his post of Aide to the General, he continued his espionage trips and made a worthwhile visit to Algeria to confirm that the French intended to establish a new naval depot at Bizerta. On these occasions, his gift for painting and sketching came in very useful and he cleverly drew picturesque scenes of harbours and coastlines, which included hidden dots and dashes to represent fortresses and defences. On a trip to Dalmatia, he posed as a butterfly collector and drew specimens caught in the area. His masterpiece was a coloured sketch of a local 'Lepidoptera' on which the delicately drawn veins were exact delineations of the lines of a fort and the spots on the wings denoted the number and calibre of the guns. The exploits of Baden-Powell typify a development of field intelligence during this period. Although Baden-Powell did receive forty pounds from the War Office 'To cover the expenses' of his trip to Algeria, there was no real control or co-ordination from a central headquarters. It was a very ad hoc and amateur state of affairs. Where success was achieved, it was not by a planned concentration onto specific intelligence targets, but rather the result of a haphazard gathering of information by individual officers with initiative and enthusiasm.

The motto of the Intelligence Corps 'Knowledge gives Strength to the Arm' – is a positive statement but it can, on occasion, be a dangerous statement; it reflects the constant and often misplaced, confidence of British Forces before the initial battles of any campaign. Perhaps a more pungent and arresting motto would be 'lack of knowledge makes the arm ineffective', and the 1,329 killed at Isandlhwana, compared to the ten killed at Ulundi must bear testimony to this.

CHAPTER THIRTEEN

The Sudan Wars

*B*y 1882 the concept of the Intelligence Branch in London had become accepted and its contribution to the War Office and Government recognised. But at this stage the big difference between the nineteenth and twentieth century Army was that officers either posted or attached to the Branch were still expected to carry out more 'legitimate' soldiering. The Staff and Staff College were very suspect and a staff tour was still regarded by the majority of officers as a sign of weakness as it directed an officer away from his 'true vocation' i.e. serving with his regiment. One young subaltern, who, on arrival in his regiment mentioned that he hoped to go eventually to Staff College was taken quietly outside by an embarrassed friend and warned not to let the other mess members know, as indications of ambition were considered rather unseemly. For the officer who was ambitious however, the Intelligence Branch did offer a vehicle for promotion. It had soon been realised that officers from the Branch stood a very good chance of securing an appointment on any active service campaign. Mr. Cardwell had but recently abolished the system of purchasing commissions and, as a result, promotion had become extremely rigid and slow. Only on active service could accelerated advancement be obtained, and it was this opportunity for promotion which drove the enterprising officer to extreme lengths in order to get a posting to the Intelligence Branch and thus to the scene of action.

In 1881 Major Tulloch, who was finishing a tour in Portsmouth as Movements Officer, decided that war with Egypt was a distinct possibility. He therefore, on his own initiative, resurrected the military report he had written on a holiday in 1875 and sent it to the Quarter-Master General. He also decided 'It would be a move in the right direction if I paid another visit to Egypt and made myself acquainted with its military resources, so that in the event of hostilities I might have a fair chance of being employed on active service.' He had two months leave due to him, so called at the Intelligence Branch headquarters in Adair House to let them know of his intended visit. General Alison was delighted with the news, for the Branch had wanted to send out two officers on a surreptitious reconnaissance mission, but this had been refused on political grounds. As Tulloch was 'Going out at his own expense – no one could interfere, nor need know where he had gone'.

Ever since the purchase of the Suez Canal shares in 1875, Britain's involvement in the affairs of Egypt had gradually increased. Although Egypt was still theoretically under the suzerainty of Turkey and in 1878 the Sultan of Turkey had displaced the ruler by putting the Khedive Tawfiq in his place, the finances and therefore the policies of Egypt were controlled by an International Commission the leading members of which were Britain and France. Not unnaturally this foreign control caused dissatisfaction among many Egyptians and in 1881 there had been a mutiny in the army led by a young Egyptian officer, Colonel Arabi. Colonel Arabi had surrounded the Khedive's palace and demanded the dismissal of all existing ministers; the establishment of a new constitution and an increase in the size of the army from 4,000 men to 18,000. In January 1882 whilst the International Commission debated what they should do, the Khedive capitulated to the rebel's demands and Colonel Arabi was appointed Minister of War. The European Powers again began a criss-cross series of negotiations.

It was against this background that Major Tulloch went on his excursion. He shot snipe, he toured ancient ruins and he compiled an excellent intelligence report. Using all manner of legitimate and illegitimate means he visited Egyptian barracks, examined forts, counted soldiers, surveyed routes and railways and formed contacts with many of the Bedouin. When at Port Said he walked over the beaches testing the mud-crust by pushing his stick into the ground to gauge its capacity for troop carrying. He was later highly amused to discover that the ubiquitous German officer who had stayed in the same Weston-Super-mare Hotel whilst carrying out his survey of the English coast, had also been seen assessing the mud-crust at Port Said.

His final report was very well received by the Government, was printed by the War Office and copies presented to Cabinet Ministers as well as the French and Indian Governments. Once again individual initiative had helped our intelligence operations. Major Tulloch received £100 to cover his expenses, and a commendation from His Royal Highness the Commander-in-Chief, a very satisfactory, but very unusual intelligence interlude for a Portsmouth based Deputy Assistant Quarter-Master General (Movements). Major Tulloch's luck continue to hold, for on 11 June 1882 when news reached England that Colonel Arabi's followers had rioted in Alexandria and had killed over fifty Europeans, Tulloch happened to be visiting the Admiralty in London explaining certain points in his Egyptian report. He used the opportunity therefore to mention, that if the Navy were to mount a punitive expedition and wished for a 'Spare fore-top man', he was only too eager for the post. To his great delight the offer was accepted and Tulloch was appointed 'Military Liaison Officer' to the naval force, which sailed almost immediately.

There was another officer also busily planning and scheming how he could get to Egypt, and the War. His father had been a long service soldier but had never seen active service or gained a medal. His son, Horatio Herbert Kitchener was determined to do both. Horatio had been posted to Cyprus in 1878, a slim handsome bachelor subaltern, to carry out a survey of the island and by 1882 had become as a well-known figure on the island. He had organised archaeological excavations, become the first Curator and Honorary Secretary of the Cyprus Museum, gained notoriety by being shot at by an escaped convict near Pissouri, a small village near the present Sovereign Base Area of Episkopi, and is traditionally held to have brought to the island the pack of hounds, whose descendants still roam the streets of Limassol in such large numbers. But for all his entreaties and telegrams he did not have enough influence to get himself to Egypt. Accordingly he set in action a plan of deception, which one feels he would have condemned heartily in others during later years. He applied for, and was granted, a week's sick leave, which the General Officer Commanding in Cyprus presumed, would be spent on the Island instead, Kitchener secretly took a ship from Limassol to Alexandria, where the invasion fleet had just arrived, and reported himself to the Liaison Officer, Major Tulloch, as 'Ready to do anything'.

After Kitchener had demonstrated his ability to speak Arabic, Major Tulloch decided to take him on a reconnaissance he planned to do that night. Tulloch had grown a beard and so, disguising themselves as shabby Levantine seamen, the two officers were rowed quietly ashore, bought train tickets for Zagazig and travelled for some way along the line taking notes and making sketches. Then, slipping off the train, they returned to an agreed rendezvous where they were picked up in a boat in the early hours of the morning and rowed back to the Admiral's Flagship. Colonel Arabi's followers heard about this trip by the British officers, and seven days later a fair complexioned Syrian was noticed on the train at Zyat. Under the mistaken impression that he was European working as a spy, they dragged the wretched man from his compartment and slit his throat on the platform.

After this taste of adventure Kitchener was more determined than ever to stay in Egypt and obtained a promise that if his own General would release him, he would be employed in the Expedition's Intelligence Department. Fairly confident that this application would be refused, 'by a calculated act of indiscipline' he concealed himself until the weekly mail ship to Cyprus had departed, and then returned to H.M.S.Invincible to express surprise at the adverse result of his application. Major Tulloch and Kitchener remained on Invincible for the bombardment of Alexandria and towards evening noticed that one of the forts seemed to be deserted. They therefore volunteered to lead ashore a party of twelve seamen to spike the guns. 'Kitchener, the tall engineer officer slipped quietly into the boat, but the naval officer in charge said he could not take a man in plain clothes, even on the plea of being an interpreter, so Kitchener had, much to his disgust to return on board.' The party had great success and with a hammer and bag of nails spiked the great smooth bore guns that were menacing the Fleet. The massacre of the Christians at Alexandria took place on 11 June, the destruction of the Forts on 11 July. On 12 July Tulloch landed with the Navy and in his role as 'Military Liaison Officer' helped draw up and implement legislation to restore law and order. Kitchener, however, received another abrupt 'Return immediately' signal from his General and on reaching Cyprus it is surprising to hear that he was genuinely 'hurt' by the coolness with which his chief greeted him; but it is not surprising to learn that he was extremely incensed that Wolseley refused to allow him the Egyptian Medal, even though he had been ashore on his intelligence reconnaissance.

Waiting to greet the Fleet Commander, Admiral Seymour as he came ashore at Alexandria was Major General Sir Frederick Goldsmid who, after service as an interpreter to the Turkish forces in Kertch during the Crimea War, had spent twenty-five years planning and superintending the gigantic accomplishment of laying telegraphic lines from Europe across Persia and Baluchistan to India. In 1880 he had been appointed Controller of Crown Lands in Egypt and was witness to the massacre and subsequent bombardment of Alexandria. As Admiral Seymour had no intelligence officer in the Fleet, and the General was familiar with the country, Seymour forthwith appointed him 'Head of Intelligence'. For the next few days Goldsmid, helped by Tulloch, recruited an intelligence organization based primarily on newspapermen, businessmen and officials in charge of the telegraph stations throughout Egypt. These men were all British who had lived for years in the country, knew all the principal Egyptians and had many native friends. As a result, a flow of intelligence soon began arriving on the Flagship including copies of Egyptian government telegrams both internal and between Cairo and Europe. Tulloch also used this telegraph system to 'feed in false information. He knew that the Egyptians were intercepting telegrams, so to help Wolseley's cover story that the main invasion fleet was to disembark at Aboukir and not at Alexandria, he sent a telegram to the British correspondent of a London newspaper explaining that the force had received orders not to land in the Suez Canal. The correspondent unwittingly forwarded the cable to his Editor and an Egyptian clerk sent it clandestinely to Colonel Arabi – both recipients being deceived and highly annoyed when they discovered the truth.

General Wolseley arrived with the main expeditionary force on 21 August and although he brought 16,400 soldiers he, like the Admiral, had brought no Head of Intelligence, he therefore asked Major Tulloch to take the appointment in place of the elderly Sir Frederick. Tulloch grasped the opportunity with avid enthusiasm and by expanding his spy network, soon began to build up a comprehensive picture of the Arab forces. The post also had other responsibilities as he has described:

> Examining prisoners, checking the reports of spies and such like, was only a portion of my work. I found I had to act as general agent and referee not only to the army and navy, but also to civilians, who used to come to me when they got into difficulties or misunderstandings with the 'Authorities'. As a result, my office was always crowded with Arabs wanting compensation, staff officers seeking interpreters, or transport officers wanting facts on local supply systems.

However by the beginning of September he proudly managed to present to the Commander, what proved to be an extremely accurate forecast of the enemy's strength, both in men and material. It therefore came as a bitter blow when he was suddenly informed that he had been superseded as Chief of Intelligence.

> On 5 September I was exceedingly disgusted by the arrival of Colonel Redvers Buller, who had come out from England to be head of the Intelligence Department. The commander in chief, Sir Garnet Wolseley, wrote hoping that I would continue to serve under that officer. My reply was that, for the good of the service, I was ready to serve under anyone, much less such a well-known soldier as Buller, but trusted I might be left in charge of the Field Section of the Department. Considering what I had done for months past, I could not help feeling that I was badly treated.

This habit of Wolseley of bringing his own officers with him was a perpetual source of friction in the Army. His selected group of officers went from campaign to campaign rather as General Montgomery took members of the staff of the 8th Army in Italy back to England, when appointed in command for the invasion of Europe.

Buller had been enjoying the tenth day of his honeymoon in Holland, but on receipt of a telegram from Wolseley had immediately abandoned his bride and sailed for Egypt. After serving with Wolseley in the Canadian Red River Campaign and as his Head of Intelligence in the Ashanti Wars, he was a 'Charter Member' of the Wolseley 'Ring'. He arrived at the front line on 5 September, and whether Tulloch remained in charge of the Field Section is not clear, but that very evening Buller, as Head of Intelligence, with a ten-man escort, went out to reconnoitre the enemy's position.

> We wandered about a little in the dark and among other incidents I almost rode on to the enemy's piquets; luckily for us we saw their fires before they saw us. Eventually by great luck, just at grey dawn I found myself exactly where I wanted to be, immediately in front of the centre of the enemy's position, and about a mile from it. I was able to have a good look at it by the light of the rising sun and then get back safely before the enemy had a chance to catch us.

Each subsequent night he did the same thing and again was nearly caught by a strong Arab patrol, as he fled back to his own lines his horse suddenly stumbled and bucked him over the top. Luckily he fell lightly and after changing horses was able to see the Arabs beaten back by British pickets. By 12 September the combined reports of Buller and Tulloch gave the Commander an almost exact picture of the enemy lines at Tel-el-Kebir. It was based on these facts that Wolseley decided to form up his army in fighting formation and make a surprise night attack. It was a hazardous undertaking, 11,000 infantry, 2,000 cavalry and 60 guns marched out at half past one in the morning guided by a Lieutenant, Royal Navy, steering by the stars. To the monotonous tramp of boots and the occasional muffled neigh of a horse the whole army moved in impressive, sombre lines until dawn revealed the enemy trenches three hundred yards in front of the Highland Brigade. The Egyptians leapt to the defence but the Highlanders, in spite of some unexpected fortifications could not be stopped and by 6 a.m. the victory was complete and the cavalry loosed in pursuit.

Buller was greatly relieved by the outcome of the battle. He had spent the preceding night briefing the separate column commanders on their routes and it was at his recommendation, that surprise could be better achieved by attacking during the sleep-provoking hour just before dawn, that Sir Garnet had put back the start of the march from half past midnight to half past one. This delay of an hour proved the ideal time and Buller's contribution was recognised. He spent the next two days with Tulloch, helping to clear the railway lines and organise the advance and they arrived triumphantly in Cairo on 15 September. It had been an exhausting three days for them both, Major Tulloch, although sick with dysentery, had remained at his post but on reaching Cairo collapsed unconscious and 'was only brought round by being forced to drink a large quantity of champagne'. Two days later he was evacuated to England. Buller remained for two more weeks then also returned home.

'Intelligence' was considered to have done a good job; it had found the enemy, correctly assessed his strength and deployment and had then led the army to the right place at the right time. For his twenty-eight days in Egypt Buller was awarded the K.C.M.G. No one saw any reason for proposing that in future 'Heads of Intelligence' in the field should be employed quietly collecting and assessing intelligence, rather than galloping round the enemy's rear at night on personal reconnaissances, acting as claims officer, or clearing railway lines. A typical account of an intelligence officer's role in battle at this time is given by Captain Grierson R. A., who was Deputy Assistant Quarter-Master General (Intelligence) with the Indian Division at Tel-el-Kebir.

> 'My part', wrote Grierson, 'was the following, Colonel Tulloch of the Intelligence Department and I were first out, away to the extreme right to watch for any sign of an attack from that flank, as we were afraid of an advance of troops from Salaheih. However, only a few Bedouins appeared, and soon the Cavalry Division came up, so the Colonel sent me back to say that there was not the slightest cause for anxiety on the right. The rest of the day I rode about with General Graham's staff and acted as galloper to him, also going about the field with an interpreter and gathering what information I could from the wounded and prisoners.'

Captain Grierson had been one of the first officers appointed to the Indian Intelligence Department. Following the acceptance of Captain Collen's Report in 1878 the Department had been expanded and improved, but the selection of officers does seem to have been a little haphazard. Grierson was an enthusiastic soldier and after being commissioned from the Royal Military Academy had written a series of papers on military matters. In 1881 he sent an article to an Indian newspaper advocating reforms in the army, the final paragraph of which reads as follows:

> Until the great body of British Officers becomes convinced that the days of playing at soldiers are over, and that work, and work in the fullest sense of the word, must now be the watchword, we

despair of any attempt at re-organization. By work we do not mean the daily duty, which is carried out with the greatest conscientiousness by British Officers – in no army with more – but study, hard study, which must be encouraged and fostered in every way by the authorities.

The Editor of the newspaper had been impressed by the article and suggested that Grierson was wasting his time with a Gunner Regiment living in isolation on the Central Plains, and offered to mention his name to a 'friend' – the Head of Intelligence. The 'mention' was successful and Grierson was delighted a few weeks later to 'Treat his friends to phiz in Mess' when his attachment to the Intelligence Department came through. His first task was to edit and produce a gazetteer on Egypt and when war broke out and it was decided to send an Indian Division to Egypt, was even more delighted to be appointed to the Division as an Intelligence Staff Officer. On his return from the Campaigns in 1882 Grierson had every reason to be pleased. During the latter stages of the battle at Tel-el-Kebir he had acted as aide to the General and at the critical point in the battle successfully found the reserve Indian Army Pathan Battalion and led them to the fight. Not only did he receive the coveted medal with clasp for Tel-el-Kebir, the Khedive's star and his appointment to the fifth class of the Medjidie, but also was mentioned by Sir Garnet in his despatches – 'Lieut. Grierson, R.A., DAQMG for Intelligence. A very intelligent and capable officer whose reports are both instructive and interesting'. Grierson was then selected for the Staff College and on the long sea voyage home, to pass the time, translated a Russian General's 'History of the Campaign in Turcomania 1881-2' for the Indian Intelligence Department.

The defeat of Colonel Arabi did not however bring peace to the Middle East. Although Britain had subdued Egypt, the Sudanese who hitherto had been treated by generations of Egyptian rulers as easy prey in a gigantic slave-raiding trade, began to take their revenge. Mohammed Ahmed, the Mahdi, one of the 'holy men' who periodically arise in Islam, formed an army and by 1883 had three times defeated Egyptian Government troops. This was an uncomfortable and highly annoying situation for Mr Gladstone the Prime Minister, because in the British Public's opinion, when assuming responsibility for Egypt, Britain had also assumed responsibility for the Egyptian possessions and thereby the safety of all the Egyptians in the Sudan.

On 12th February 1884 therefore he very reluctantly decided to send a British Expeditionary Force of 4,000 men commanded by Major General Graham V.C. with Brigadier General Redvers Buller as Chief of

Staff, to rectify the situation. Colonel Ardagh was appointed Chief of the Intelligence Branch and Captain Slade R.A who was acting as a Lieutenant Colonel on the Staff of the Egyptian Army, and Major Schoefer of the Egyptian Suppression of Slave Trade Department, formed his intelligence staff. Colonel Ardagh was a sapper, and as well as being Chief of Intelligence was also made Commander Royal Engineers (CRE). With the heavy engineer commitment of getting water and supplies to the Force his intelligence activities were, of necessity, fairly restricted and for the most part were confined to running a number of spies and in co-ordinating the efforts those officers given intelligence appointments on his Staff.

On 28 February General Graham decided to try and negotiate with the Arabs and sent forward Captain Harvey of his Intelligence Department with a white flag on a pole, attached to which was a letter calling upon the sheikhs to disperse and recommending them to send delegates to Khartoum to negotiate with General Gordon. Captain Harvey advanced about two miles under an ill-directed musketry fire, planted the staff and retired. Next morning there was no answer but the pole had been removed, so at 8 a.m. General Graham ordered his 'square' to move forward with the 1st Battalion Gordon Highlanders in front. On the eve of this first battle at El Teb, Colonel Ardagh and the five other officers attached to the Intelligence Department dined together. As the duties of the intelligence officer in battle were to reconnoitre forward it is not surprising that the casualties in this little party next day, were one killed, three wounded and another's horse shot. The Sudanese fought with a fanaticism similar to that of the Japanese in the Second World War. They spared no wounded or dismounted men and 'Seemed not to dream of asking for quarter themselves. When they found their retreat cut off they charged singly or in scattered groups, to hurl their spears in defiance, then fall dead riddled with bullets'. General Buller writing home that night explained:

> When we got close, the enemy rushed out upon us with a very heavy spear in one hand, and a sword or knife in the other. For about three minutes, it was a very pretty bit of hand to hand fighting and for a second or two it was a question whether they would not force through. I confess I did envy the people who were in the scrimmage, and would have given a good deal not to have been a General, and to have been able to go, but of course that would have been 'infra dig', and I had to look on.

But he need not have worried, for fourteen days later he received his full share of hand-to-hand fighting at the Battle of Tamai. Colonel

New Model Army
Scoutmaster, drawn
by H.B. Eaton, Int
Corps.

The Queen's Own Corps of Guides. A magnificent fighting regiment but a
disappointing Intelligence Unit.

The Natal Corps of Guides. Raised by the Hon T.K. Murray, and Major David
Henderson on the outbreak of the South African War.

Memorial in Westminster Abbey to Major John Andre who was hanged as a spy.

Memorial in Tarrytown, near New York, to the Militiamen who captured Major John Andrei.

Major Thomas Best Jervis, prematurely retired officer of the Bengal Engineers, who became Head of Intelligence by finding a map in a second hand book shop in Belgium.

Scout Unit on modified tandem cycles, using the railway line to cross the Veldt.

Basuto members of the Intelligence Corps, part of the Kimberley Intelligence Staff.

Colonel M.F. Rimington, who raised the Imperial Corps of Guides in 1889. This unit was known at the time as an Intelligence Corps, also Rimington Tigers, from the piece of wild cat fur they wore in their hats.

Lt Col F.H. Damant DSO, who took command of Rimington's Scouts on the departure of Colonel Rimington and changed the name to Damant's Scouts.

Four of the original ten Intelligence officers sent to South Africa before war broke out. Lt Col R.G. Kekewich seated left. Major Scott-Turner seated right, was killed leading a sortie out of the besieged town.

Major Henry Brackenbury RA, one of the Wolseley Ring whose succesful combination of active service and intelligence appointments led him to a seat on the Army Council.

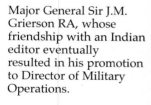

Major General Sir John Ardagh, who reminded Count Gleichen of a Maribu stork.

Major General Sir J.M. Grierson RA, whose friendship with an Indian editor eventually resulted in his promotion to Director of Military Operations.

Major Robert Baden-Powell, founder of the Boy Scout Movement who acted as a tourist and drew pictures of butterflies, where the veins were the lines of the fort and the dots were the guns.

Scout Balloon which, being perfectly spherical, made Count Gliechen feel sick.

Picture of Jan Smuts in 1900 in the FID Black List of Most Wanted Men. Jan Smuts later became a Field Marshal in the British Army.

French speaking Scotland Yard detectives who joined the Int Corps in 1914.

2Lt Arthur Bosworth, original
Int Corps Officer 1914.
Mentioned in Dispatches.
Rejoined Int Corps 1939.
Evacuated from Dunkirk.

2Lt F.E. Hotblack, the most decorated Int Corps
Officer in WWI. DSO and BAR and MC and BAR.

2Lt J.L.Baird, GCMG
DSO MP. Original Int
Corps Officer, later
Governor of Australia.

Major General David Henderson, who raised the Natal Corps of Guides in 1899, and can justifiably be called the Father of the Intelligence Corps.

General John Charteris, sacked for deceiving his Commander.

Front-line questioning for Immediate Tactical Information.

Brigade level interrogation.

Divisional level questioning.

Intelligence Police checking identification.

Capt Carrol Romer MC RE, an expert at reading aerial photographs, who identified locations where poison gas was to be released.

Line of exploding German gas shells, Carnoy 1916, WWI.

Remarkable aerial photograph showing British trenches and support trenches, Givenchy 1916, WWI.

Use of stereoscopes revolutionised the value of aerial photographs.

Pigeon who had avoided being in a pie is released from a tank.

Painting called *The Interrogation* held by the Imperial War Museum showing an attentive red tabbed staff officer, standing and listening to a green tabbed Intelligence Corps officer.

Captain Sigismund Payne-Best OBE, an original Int Corps officer wearing green tabs.

Unofficial badge devised by members of the Censorship Division, which subsequently was the basis of the Int Corps cap badge. The Greek motto means *In Secrecy We Work*.

Captain Sigismund Payne-Best OBE, taken after his release from Sachsenhausen Concentration Camp, 1945.

German snipers killed many front-line soldiers. A simple periscope gave some protection.

Corporal Vince Shirley, seen here on the left smoking a pipe, changed his name from Fritz Schurhoff in 1914 and won the Military Medal in March 1918 for operating his Interceptor Telephone Section until the very last moment and then taking up a rifle to help repel the German attack.

General Haig inspecting the Intelligence Police, 1918.

Field Security Police
in Occupied
Germany, 1923.

Ardagh, as intelligence officer, had ridden forward with the mounted infantry and located an enemy force about six miles ahead. General Graham therefore decided to divide his force into two brigade squares and give Buller command of the rear square.. The front line of the front square was shared by three companies of Black Watch and three companies of 1st Battalion York and Lancaster Regiment with the naval Gatling guns, as usual, in the corners. About 9 a.m. the enemy appeared at the edge of a ravine and, with a wild Highland yell the Black Watch surged forward. Unfortunately, at the same time a far larger number of Sudanese appeared against the York and Lancasters and charging fiercely they captured the guns of the Naval Brigade and burst into the square. All became bloody confusion. General Graham and Colonel Ardagh, reluctant to use their pistols in the tight throng, had to defend themselves energetically with their swords and one detachment of 6th Battery Royal Artillery particularly distinguished themselves by protecting their guns using wooden rammers and rounds of case ammunition. At this crucial moment, a volley from the rear square unfortunately struck their own leading brigade which 'Showed signs of unsteadiness'. But Buller, now in his element, spurred forward and bringing up a gun in line with the front rank, gradually eased the situation. He moved his Brigade forward and slowly pushed the Arabs back. This gave the Black Watch time to reform, which they did with considerable aplomb, putting out company markers, and then falling in at the double. By 11 a.m. the battle was over. The British had lost 109 killed and 115 wounded and the significantly high proportion of dead to wounded, as opposed to the normal ratio of one to four, reveals the savage nature of the fighting. It had become clear that the Sudanese, considering the weapons they used, were very formidable opponents and Rudyard Kipling has immortalised their bravery in his poem 'Fuzzy-Wuzzy.

> We've fought with many men across the seas,
> An' some of 'em was brave an' some was not:
> The Paythan an' the Zulu an' Burmese;
> But the Fuzzy was the finest o'the lot.
> We never got a ha'porth's change of 'im:
> 'E' squatted in the scrub an' 'ocked our 'orses,
> 'E' cut our sentries up at Suakim.
> So 'ere's to you, Fuzzy-Wuzzy, at your 'ome in the Soudan;
> You're a pore benighted 'eathen but a first class fightin' man

Colonel Ardagh continued to expand his spy network and wrote 'My spies have much improved and now bring very precise information.

They can recount names of the chiefs, the districts they come from their personal peculiarities and the number of their followers with as much system as the 'catalogue of the ships' in Homer'. Ardagh also advertised a thousand dollar reward for the capture of the enemy leader Osman Digna 'Dead or Alive' but this emotive phrase caused such a political uproar, that the advert was altered to 'Capture' - much to Ardagh's disgust, who felt that the delicacy of the British Public would make another war necessary.

The Government had decided to withdraw however, and on 3 April in spite of cries of 'betrayal' from the Opposition in the House of Commons, General Graham's Force was embarked for Suez, leaving Osman Digna subdued, but in no way defeated. Colonel Ardagh was made a military Companion of the Order of the Bath for his joint Engineer and Intelligence services, one of the few officers to obtain both the civil and military version of this award, and Brigadier General Buller was made a Major General. But even as the troops were sailing home, events in the Sudan were deteriorating. The Mahdi was going from strength to strength and was systematically, and successfully, annihilating all the Egyptians he could find. The fate of the remainder now became critical, and to help arrange their evacuation from Khartoum the British Government decided that, rather than send a military force, they would send one man, General Charles Gordon. It proved a classic example of military false economy. General Gordon, a Royal Engineer, 'With sword in one hand and bible in the other' had won universal fame for his ability to organise undisciplined armies, and this he was sent to do again in Khartoum. But it was a gross misappreciation of character by Gladstone to suppose that Gordon would ever leave the city, save his own skin and abandon the inhabitants to the Mahdi. By March 1884 Khartoum had been invested and a situation arisen where no British officer of the period, let alone a man of General Gordon's temperament, would have dreamt of 'Sneaking away' back to Cairo. The lack of any clear determined political aim thus created a military problem complicated and confused in the extreme, one very similar to other political fiascos – Suez 1956 and Afghanistan 2005.

Public opinion led by Queen Victoria, concerning Gordon's fate reached a crescendo and eventually grew too strong to be resisted. In August 1884, much against his will, Gladstone therefore decided he had to send out Lord Wolseley with a relief expedition. On 14 August Wolseley wrote to Colonel Charles Wilson in Dublin asking whether he would accept the position of Chief of the Intelligence Department with the rank of Deputy Adjutant General saying, 'You are the only man who can fill this office.' Wilson accepted and on 19 September he arrived in Cairo and set about creating his intelligence staff. As he wrote –

> All day I have been seeing people, engaging interpreters, servants, and picking up information. I have been much pleased at the way in which all who have worked with me have come forward. My interpreter is Mr. Van Dyck, son of a professor at the American College at Beirut, and an old friend – an unhoped-for piece of good luck. I have as my first assistant Major Slade, R.A, a first rate fellow, very plucky, with plenty of go and never failing spirits, he is doing caterer and has laid in a supply of delicacies. Bennet goes up the river with me as far as Assuan where I pick up McCulloch.

Two of Wolseley's previous intelligence officers were also recalled, but this time employed in administrative posts. Colonel Ardagh returned to Cairo and was nominated 'Commander of the Base Area' and Major Frederick Maurice now recovered from his Zulu War wound, was taken from the Intelligence Branch where he had been busy writing the History of the 1882 Campaign and made 'Commandant of Wadi Halfa'. Then, as now staff officers in the British Army often did one tour in an intelligence appointment and were then never again employed on intelligence work.

By November the situation in Khartoum was growing desperate. Gordon, in an attempt to save their lives, had sent out all the other Europeans under the care of his Second in Command, Colonel Stewart, and was then horrified to learn that the whole party had been captured and massacred. With no other white man to talk to, Gordon grew more and more bitter about the lack of information provided by the Intelligence Department. The only news that got through came from spies sent in by Kitchener, who was now an intelligence officer in the Egyptian Army. But as many of these messengers were caught the information that got through was disjointed and confusing. Gordon wrote in his journal:

> I reason thus respecting the slackness of the Intelligence Department in not sending me spies. On an average four or five Arabs came in daily therefore they do not keep so very strict a lookout. Also now there are vast gaps in their lines around the place, and one may say from here to Shandi is open. It is more difficult to go out than to come in, for in going out one may stumble on some new emplacement of the Arabs, while in coming in a man can ascertain such emplacements beforehand, it is evident that as all the information we have had has come from my returning spies, that no effort had been made by the Intelligence

Department. Had that Department initiated any such step, it is unlikely that all their men would have been stopped, my spies get caught, through so frequently passing the lines of Arabs.' The very last sentence in General Gordon's journal was this poignant message to the Intelligence Department 'You send me no information though you have lots of money.'

The most satisfying amount of news Gordon ever received, was in fact fortuitous. Kitchener had wrapped a bundle of letters up in some old newspapers and these revealed that Lord Wolseley had been seen off at Victoria Station for the relief of the Sudan Garrisons and expected to relieve Gordon 'Before many months had elapsed.' This news delighted Gordon and was a source of comfort to him for a long time.

But many months elapsed and eventually on 17 November Wolseley decided not to wait until the River Column had crept laboriously up the Nile but to save time and send a Desert Column overland across the bend in the Nile. The aim was not to relieve Khartoum as such, but merely to give Gordon moral support. On 30 December a force of 1,100 men under General Sir H. Stewart (as distinct from the murdered Colonel Stewart) left Korti and struck inland. With Stewart went the Chief of Intelligence Colonel Wilson, with no staff, no organization, and whose orders from Wolseley although extremely explicit and detailed, make little mention of intelligence. His main task was to give Gordon a letter, and General Stewart had been detailed to attach a small section of infantry, dressed in red coats to him so he could go ahead and reach Khartoum as quickly as possible. The Royal Sussex borrowed red coats from the Grenadier Guards for this operation.

> And upon arriving there you can, if you like, march these men through the City to show the people that the British are at hand, - you will only stay in Khartoum long enough to confer fully with General Gordon and then return. I do not want the British soldiers to sleep in the City. It is always possible that when the Mahdi fully realise that an English Army is approaching he will retreat.

It was a bluff and later became a matter of bitter controversy whether Wilson had been asked by Wolseley to persuade Gordon to leave and save his own life, but Wilson never admitted this and there is nothing in the written orders to say otherwise. On 16 January the force, having marched for sixteen tiring days across the desert, on a reduced ration of food and water, reached the area of the Abu Klea wells, here on 17 January they were attacked by a Dervish force of some 10,000 men. A desperate struggle ensued, the British bayonets bent, the Gardner gun jammed at the critical moment and with a triumphant yell the Dervishes broke into the square. But the Royal Sussex held, and after considerable loss the Arabs were finally driven out. One officer, fighting for his life in the Guards Camel Company was Captain Gleichen released from the Intelligence Branch to serve in Egypt. A bullet knocked Gleichen head over heels, tore away his watch chain, broke a pair of scissors in his breast pocket but amazingly did not pierce his skin. Another casualty, mortally wounded in the groin, was the Commander, General Stewart. The next in seniority was the Chief of Intelligence, Colonel Charles Wilson. When Wilson had left Korti it was intended he should act merely as an intelligence staff officer carrying a message to General Gordon. Now, suddenly, in the middle of the desert with no regimental background and no experience of war, he found himself foisted into command of a bloody and desperately weary force trapped in a very difficult situation.

On 19 November the Column under the command of Wilson reached the Nile, rested for four days, collected wood for the steamers and made armed reconnaissances into the desert. It is for the delay that the Government and General Wolseley later criticised Wilson for 'Lacking in drive'. Eventually on 24 January he set out, 'In two ancient river steamers with his twenty two men of the Royal Sussex, one hundred and ninety ill-disciplined Sudanese soldiers, no doctor and an interpreter who was suffering from a flesh wound in the side.' On 28 January, after sailing a hundred miles up the Nile through gorges and ravines all dominated by hostile, Mahdi supporters they finally reached Khartoum. Wilson himself has described the dramatic moments of their arrival.

> When about half way up Tuti, I thought for the moment that the island was still in Gordon's hands. A sort of dyke ran along the edge of the island, and behind this there was a long line of men firing away as hard as they could. I heard the bullets singing overhead, and saw them strike the sand amongst the enemy's sharpshooters on the opposite bank, and thought they were helping us. I then ordered the steamer to run in close to the bank, stop, cease firing and ask for news. This we did, getting within sixty or seventy yards. I felt so persuaded at first that they were Gordon's men that I got outside the turret, but the only reply to our questions was a sharper and better directed fire, which soon drove me inside again. It was clear that the enemy's riflemen were on Tuti, but Khartoum might still be holding out; so after a delay of about a quarter of an hour we went on. No sooner did we start upwards than we got into such a fire as I hope never to pass

through again in a penny steamer. Two or more guns opened on us from Omdurman Fort, and three or four from Khartoum or the upper end of Tuti island; the roll of musketry from each side was continuous; and high above that could be heard the grunting of a miltrailleuse, and the loud rushing noise of the Krupps shells, fired either from Khartoum or Tuti island. We kept on to the junction of the two Niles when it became plain to everyone that Khartoum had fallen into the Mahdi's hands; for not only were there hundreds of Dervishes ranged under their banners, standing on the sandpit close to the town, ready to resist our landing, but no flag was flying in Khartoum, and not a shot was fired in our assistance, though here, if not before, we should have met the two steamers I knew Gordon still had at Khartoum. I at once gave the order to turn and run down the river; it was hopeless to attempt a landing, or to communicate with the shore under such a fire. To me the blow was crushing. Khartoum fallen and Gordon dead; for I never for a moment believed he would allow himself to fall into the Mahdi's hands alive. Such was the ending of all our labours and of his perilous enterprise.

On the way back down the Nile both his ships were sunk and Wilson finally led out his party on foot. The skill of this accomplishment brought him great credit, but a scapegoat had to be found for Gordon's death, and Lord Wolseley felt it necessary to ask Wilson to explain, in writing, why he had not started for Khartoum before 24 January. The controversy raged and Wilson was blamed, but in retrospect one wonders if the arrival of a Staff Colonel and twenty two British soldiers dressed in borrowed red uniforms who had clear orders not to sleep in the City would have made any worth while contribution to Gordon's safety.

For distinguished services in the Sudan, Wilson was mentioned in despatches and was created a K.C.B. He then returned to Dublin and in November 1886 was appointed Director General of the Ordnance Survey and moved to Southampton. In 1895 he was promoted to Director General of Military Education as a Major General and subsequently died in Tunbridge Wells in 1905. His forty-two years in the Army had shown the value of clear thinking and forward looking personalities in the Intelligence Branch and the present Defence Intelligence Organization in London is to a large extent his legacy.

By a strange coincidence in the Sudan Campaign, another leading figure in the intelligence world also assumed command in the field on the death in action of his senior officer. Whilst Wilson was leading the Desert Column to Khartoum, General Earle with Colonel Brackenbury as his Second in Command were sailing and pulling their boats up the Nile to form the River Column. Brackenbury, after his long tour in the Intelligence Branch at Adair House, took a keen interest in Intelligence and had obtained Major Slade, from Wilson, to be his Deputy Assistant Adjutant General (Intelligence Department). Slade's duties were conventional for the nineteenth century; he carried out personal reconnaissances, interrogated prisoners, was responsible for liaison with local sheiks and organised the spies. He also had the traditional Quarter-Master General's tasks of finding camp sites and allocating guides to fighting patrols – not always successfully as Brackenbury writes 'Not liking the camp selected by Slade I rode out and chose another site about a mile further upstream.' On the second day of their journey up the Nile from Merawi, they came to a spot described in the Intelligence Department Gazette as the 'Gerendid Cataract', together with a picture to prove it. But the Cataract did not exist, nor had any native of the district even heard the name! As the Column advanced up the River the Arabs retreated before them until, suddenly, on 10 February 1885 they inexplicably decided to stand and fight on the low stony ridges at Kirbekan. It was a short, sharp, straightforward action. The British soldiers fixed their bayonets and advanced steadily up the slopes killing all the Arabs they could winkle out. This display of disciplined aggression broke the spirit of the Mahdi's followers and they fled in confusion. But, as in so many similar infantry engagement of this type, it was the officers who were called upon to pay the price that the privilege of their rank demands and among the twelve soldiers killed were the General Officer Commanding, General Earle, and the Colonels of the Staffordshire Regiment and Black Watch.

Later, Major Slade who had issued orders that all documents whatever their nature were to be handed to him for translation, was given a letter found in the saddle bag of a donkey. It proved to be from the Emir of Berber describing the capture of Khartoum and the death of Gordon. This explained the rise in morale of the Arabs and their decision to stand and fight. Command of the Column now fell upon Colonel Henry Brackenbury who, in this moment of crisis, maintained his reputation far more successfully than his former colleague in the Intelligence Branch, Charles Wilson. Fired by a desire to punish the murderers of Colonel Stewart and his companions, Brackenbury drove all resistance ruthlessly before him and eventually reached the site of the massacre.

Many relics of the murder were found there, including one of poor Stewart's visiting cards stained with blood and photographs of the Austrian Consul. All these were secured and carefully examined by the interpreters; and orders were issued for the troops to parade under officers from the Intelligence Department with axes, picks and shovels for the destruction of property. The troops set to with a will to destroy Suleiman Wad Gamr's house. It was a large one, standing on an eminence, with a colonnade supported by pillars, and several courtyards, each with several rooms. Roofs were pulled down, all wood available for firewood carried off, the walls shaken by charges of gun cotton, and then utterly destroyed by the pick and shovel. Beams and solid wooden doors, rare articles in this country, were destroyed by fire, and the house was razed to the ground. All his sakyehs were burnt, and his palm trees were cut down and destroyed with fire.

By this time a despondent Charles Wilson had returned to Korti following his abortive attempt to save Gordon and command of the Desert Column went to Sir Redvers Buller. Ten days after the Battle of Kirbekan Wolseley signalled Brackenbury that Buller was in difficulties near the battlefield of Abu Klea so, reluctantly, Brackenbury had to withdraw to help him. It took them nine days to descend the cataracts which had taken thirty-one days to ascend, but during this time Buller had successfully withdrawn from Abu Klea so Brackenburys help was not required,. Both the River Column and the Desert Column were then disbanded and the troops went home. The British press called long and indignantly for Gordon's revenge, but the Government decided against any further action – and thus only postponed the date.

The British Army had departed leaving their task uncompleted; it was now left to a handful of European officers, including Kitchener to rebuild the Egyptian Army and prepare for the next phase. In these first desert battles, of all the officers in the Intelligence Department it was perhaps Kitchener who had emerged as the most successful. After his return to Cyprus from the 'Illegal trip to Alexandria' he had used all his ingenuity in obtaining a posting back to Egypt. The plot which he had hatched was as follows, he persuaded the Commander in Egypt, Sir Evelyn Wood, to send a cable to Cyprus offering him a two year engagement in the Egyptian Army. Kitchener was confident that with at least a year's work remaining to do on the Cyprus Survey his own General would not let him go, so he immediately replied to the cable 'Very sorry – present work will not permit me to leave Cyprus for one year.' However, he had already reached a private understanding with Sir Evelyn to send a second telegram again asking for his services and had correctly calculated that his own General would be reluctant to stand in the way of an officer wishing to go on active service – especially as that officer had demonstrated his loyalty by refusing himself. Thus did Kitchener leave Cyprus.

The freedom of action Kitchener found in Egypt proved a turning point in his career. He had the two traditional qualities required for a good field intelligence officer, fluent local language and good local knowledge and these he combined with intense ambition and the ability to write clear reports. As a bonus, he was serving in the exciting environment of potential conflict where an intelligence officer is not merely a spare staff officer used for 'liaison duties' or 'odd jobs', but becomes someone on whose advice the commander depends. The years 1882-1885 provided just this scenario and Kitchener grasped the opportunity with both hands. By ruthless energy and planned determination he made himself an indispensable source of intelligence to his senior officers. He enlisted the services of a local holy man to administer a solemn blood oath of brotherhood to an escort of twenty tribesmen and, wearing Arab dress he made deep reconnaissances into the desert, arranging contacts and writing reports. On these trips he always carried a bottle of poison for use in case he was captured, as he had once been present at the execution of a spy and had been horrified by the tortures inflicted upon the wretched man. On one occasion he was arrested inadvertently by his own side and put in a tent with two genuine spies. These also mistook his identity and talked freely on their plans and intentions. Count Gleichen has described him during this period:

> It was at Kurot that we first came across Kitchener then a Major in the Intelligence Department. He had been sent ahead with some troops, mostly Bashibosuks, belonging to the Mudir of Dongola, and was busily collecting information about the enemy. I remember well my first sight of him – a tall spare man with a fair pointed bearded and wonderfully piercing grey eyes, dressed in a khaki jacket and trousers, which had shrunk very severely in the wash. He looked suspiciously at us, and did not seem at all glad to see us; but at luncheon he thawed a good deal, and though we never could get very much out of him, we became excellent friends, and he was made honorary member of our Mess. He lived with us until we reached Cakdul; but there, much to his disgust, he was sent back to headquarters at Korti in order to palaver with the tribes and collect camels and supplies.

In July 1882 Kitchener had been a 'Lanky unknown subaltern' trying to slip into Tulloch's boat at Alexandria, in July 1885 he sailed for England an imposing brevet Lieutenant Colonel with a reputation already established. 'Every war brings its heroes; and when the military operations in the Sudan are over the names and deeds of Kitchener will

be remembered' (Western Morning News). His last task in the
Intelligence Department was to help compile a report, which expressed
its unanimous conviction that the re-conquest of the Sudan would have
to be undertaken within the next ten years.

He was proved right. Seven years later in 1892 he became, to his great
satisfaction, Commander-in-Chief of the Egyptian Army, and
immediately began to plan a methodical advance back to Khartoum. In
order that the Government and public opinion in Britain would not take
fright and stop him, he had two guiding principles, minimum money
and minimum casualties. By taking his time, he was successful on both
counts. The senior intelligence officer in the Egyptian Army was Colonel
Reginald Wingate, who had used the intervening years to build a picture
of the enemy as complete as Kitchener would wish.

> 'Wingate's spies and agents' wrote Winston Churchill 'disguised
> as traders, as warriors, or as women – worked their stealthy way.
> Sometimes the road by the Nile was blocked, and the messengers
> must toil across the deserts to Darfur, and so by a tremendous
> journey creep into Omdurman. At others a trader might work his
> way from Suakin or from the Italian settlements. But by whatever
> route it came, information – whispered at Halfa, catalogued at
> Cairo – steadily accumulated, and the diaries of the Intelligence
> Department grew in weight and number, until at last every
> important Emir was watched and located, every garrison
> estimated, and even the endless intrigues and brawls in
> Omdurman were carefully recorded.'

The value of Wingate's intelligence service became apparent as victory
followed victory. From Firket in 1896 until the battles of Atbara and
Omdurman in 1898, Kitchener was constantly able to take the initiative
because of Wingate's accurate reporting. Even after Khartoum was re-
occupied and the Union Jack few again over General Gordon's
residence, Wingate, using his spy and informer network was able to
complete the subjugation of the Sudan by a successful pursuit of the
Khalifa. The Sudan/Egyptian Wars had lasted seven years and in that
time the intelligence organization had developed from one Major who
happened to be visiting the Admiralty and a retired General working in
Alexandria, to a staff-organised intelligence service acknowledged by
the world to be the finest. But at this stage there was a clear distinction
in the minds of British Army officers between the Intelligence
Department in the Sudan and the efforts of the Intelligence Branch in
London. Kitchener, who leant so heavily on his own Intelligence
Department, was always extremely jealous of his knowledge and

resentful of any 'outside interference'. When Gleichen was sent back to the Sudan by the Director of Military Intelligence in London, to be his official representative, he was treated with great suspicion. 'Although Kitchener was very civil to me' Gleichen has written 'he never gave me a hint of what he was doing, or going to do, whilst my inquiries in that direction were skilfully fenced with. Wingate, however, knowing both sides, told me as much as it was good for me to know, and in return I helped him to the best of my ability in drawing maps and collecting bits of information'.

This uncooperative and slightly contemptuous attitude by Kitchener towards the Intelligence Branch in London reveals how little he valued its contribution. The sad fact is that Kitchener was not alone in his attitude; it well represents the general body of Army opinion towards the British Military Intelligence Organization during the last decade of the nineteenth century. There was a growing awareness of the need for a centralised intelligence organization covering both staff and intelligence agencies when in the field, and this was to result in the creation of a Field Intelligence Department during the South African War. But towards London and the Intelligence Branch, the universal feeling was distrustful and disdainful.

CHAPTER FOURTEEN

Brackenbury and Ardagh and the Developing Years of the Intelligence Division in London

*A*t the end of the Zulu War Lieutenant Colonel East had returned from being Assistant Quarter-Master General to Wolseley, and reverted to his original position in the Intelligence Branch in London working for Major General Sir Archibald Alison. In the Branch a prodigious amount of work was being done, particularly in the Map Section, which was busily preparing many thousands of maps of the Nile cataracts and their surrounds. So great was the volume of work that on 19 December 1884, the Branch moved once more, from Adair House to a combined 16 and 18 Queen Anne's Gate. The new premises had a pleasant view over St. James Park and were more roomy than the old, but had the disadvantage of Victorian London houses in having two floors with fine large chambers and the remainder of the house containing numerous, but very small rooms. It was also an inconveniently long way from the War Office. Unfortunately the habit of posting officers away from the Intelligence Branch when operations began was still the accepted practice, and when fighting finally did break out in the Middle East, General Alison promptly left for Egypt and took four of the majors then serving in the Branch with him. At Alexandria, although he was still the Senior Intelligence Officer in the British Army, he was not employed as an intelligence officer, but was first given command of the City after its capture by the Navy, and then command of the Highland Brigade which landed at Ismailia and took the brunt of the fighting at Tel-el-Kebir. Thus for three years when the new Branch was dealing with its first large scale conflict and was committed to producing intelligence for the Cabinet and for the Commander in Chief, the 'Head of Intelligence' was living in a tent in Egypt and the responsibility of intelligence production in London fell to his Second in Command, first Colonel East, and then Colonel A.S. Cameron VC.

Colonel Cameron, although a gallant soldier with service in the Crimea and who, as a Seaforth subaltern had gained the Victoria Cross by slaying three Sepoy mutineers in successive personal combats after having his left hand lopped off, was not outstanding as an Assistant Quarter-Master General. His staff officers were constantly leaving for operational service and in the last Suakin Expedition in 1885, four out of his six Deputy Assistant Quarter-master Generals were sent out to form the Expedition's Intelligence Department. As a result the London Branch rapidly began to lose ground in its intelligence contribution and was beginning to slip from the position of influence and trust established by Macdougal and Wilson.

The withdrawal of troops from the Sudan however, marked a significant turning point in the history of British Intelligence as, for the first time, a number of officers were posted back to the Branch who had served there before. These men now returned after a tour on active service and in a more senior rank. Foremost amongst them was Major General Henry Brackenbury fresh from his success commanding the River Column. On 31 December 1885 Colonel Cameron left to become Commandant of the Royal Military College Sandhurst, and on 1 January 1886 General Brackenbury took up the lapsed post of Head of the Intelligence Branch and Deputy Quarter-Master General, the Assistant's position not being filled. Brackenbury, described by one of his staff as having a 'Pasty yellow black moustached face, with an almost uncanny power of using one word to get to the root of the most complicated matter' had been Professor of Military History at the Royal Military Academy in Woolwich and had successfully managed to combine staff appointments with active service. He had taken part in the Indian Mutiny Battle of Banda and had then participated in the Franco-Prussian war of 1870-1871 as a member of the British Hospital Unit, for which services he had received decorations from both sides, i.e., the Iron Cross and Legion d'Honneur. He had been Military Secretary for the Ashanti Campaign and Chief of Staff in the Zulu Wars. Henry Brackenbury like Charles Wilson proved the 'right man for the job'. In his five years as Head, the Intelligence Branch in London matured and developed to become, once more, an integral and important part of the War Office.

In the previous ten years there had been a series of committees and reports all amending and reorganising the Branch but these had had the effect of 'tinkering' with the organization rather than making any radical improvement. General Brackenbury's first step was to form a 'Ways and Mean's Committee of only two, the Permanent Under Secretary for War and himself. The conclusion of this 'Mini-Committee' was that the product of the intelligence staff must be linked with the operational requirement and that, as the greatest potential danger likely to face Great Britain would be from the quick concentration of an aggressive European army, intelligence and mobilization must be untied to prepare for this contingency. The report was accepted and a further committee set up to work out the establishment for a Home Defence Force, consisting of a field army plus garrisons and a force for service abroad of two army corps. But the task of determining an order of battle of two corps to go abroad on mobilization soon grew out of all proportion. It also attracted a great deal of emotional discussion when initial recommendation included such controversial measures as converting 'Redundant' Horse Artillery Regiments into Field Artillery Regiments. General Brackenbury therefore asked for additional staff and suggested that his old colleague Colonel Ardagh, be given the appointment.

Lord Wolseley approved and in November 1887 Colonel Ardagh moved into Queen Anne's Gate as Assistant Adjutant General with special responsibilities for mobilization and home defence. But it proved difficult, painstaking and detailed work, so much so that after three months General Brackenbury felt it was no longer a suitable commitment for the Intelligence Branch and in February 1888 a new Mobilization Sub-Division led by Colonel Ardagh, moved out of Queen Anne's Gate to the offices of the Adjutant General in the main War Office Buildings Pall Mall. Mobilization planning involves continual hard detailed work that, unless a war breaks out, is never used or recognised. The debt the country owes to Brackenbury and Ardagh therefore, only became apparent in 1899 when, within a matter of weeks, a cavalry division and eight complete infantry divisions were mobilised and embarked to serve in South Africa.

Freed from these other distractions the Intelligence Branch was now able to settle down and concentrate on its legitimate task of producing information and intelligence about foreign countries and armies. On 1 June 1887 the title of Deputy Quarter-Master General for Intelligence was changed and General Brackenbury became the first holder of a title which lasted until 1965 – Director of Military Intelligence (DMI). He was now graded as a Deputy Adjutant General and reported direct to the Commander in Chief. All the other staff officers then assumed the corresponding grading and when Major General Brackenbury was promoted Lieutenant General in 1888 the status of the Intelligence Branch was raised and it became the Intelligence Division organised as follows:

DMI	Lieutenant General H. Brackenbury, GB	
Section A	DAAG Staff Capt Mil Clerk	France, Belgium Italy, Spain, Portugal, Central and South America, Mexico
Section B	DAAG Staff Capt Mil Clerk	British Colonies and Protectorates, Cyprus Polynesia, South African Republic, Orange Free State and adjoining native territories
Section C	DAAG Staff Capt Mil Clerk	Germany, Netherlands, Scandinavia, Switzerland, USA.
Section D	DAAG Staff Capt Mil Clerk	Russia, India, Afghanistan, Burma, Siberia, China, Japan, Siam, Central Asia, Persia.
Section E	DAAG Staff Capt Mil Clerk	Austria, Hungary, Balkan States, Ottoman Empire, Egypt, Independent African States.
Section F	DAAG Staff Capt Mil Clerk	Compilation and preparation of maps.

It was a great achievement but Brackenbury had difficulty in getting the War Office to fill the vacancies. To solve this problem and get the officers he wanted, he used the stratagem of 'Attaching officers' to the Branch. This gave him great flexibility. The Staff Captain he chose for Section 'A', the Latin Section, was that experienced intelligence officer Captain Gleichen, Grenadier Guards. Gleichen had been on leave in Italy when he had received a letter from Brackenbury offering him the job as an 'Attached officer'. He had accepted immediately but being only attached, was still officially on the strength of his own battalion. The Grenadier Guards were in London at this time and Gleichen was therefore required to do his regimental duty either before, or after, office hours. This meant that for eighteen months before the Regiment moved to Ireland, he was on guard duty in the Bank of England every fourth night. One wonders how staff officers in the Ministry of Defence today, would react to doing regimental guard duties every fourth night. Gleichen has described his work:

> Among other tasks I had to compile handbooks on all sorts of subjects, including the Portuguese Army, the New Hebrides and Morocco, but the chief work was keeping information up to date concerning foreign armies and theatres of war, the sources being mainly official military books of the different countries, magazines, maps and periodicals of all sorts and the foreign daily press. How I used to hate the 'Temps' and the 'Journal des Debats', the 'Stampa', 'Diario de Governo' and all the rest of them. It meant a good deal of work looking carefully through half a dozen foreign daily newspapers a day, besides many other weekly and monthly ones, with very little result. Items of military interests were few and far between, but when one did run any important ones to ground, each had to be carefully indexed – some under four or five headings – and if from the daily press, cut out and stuck into a big cutting book.

This cutting out of pictures intrigued his fellow Grenadiers, who were convinced that Gleichen intelligence duties consisted of extracting interesting items from 'La Vie Parisienne'.

Another officer attached to the Division was Captain J.M. Grierson R.A. who, after passing out of Staff College, had been informed that as there was no job for him in India, he would not sail that trooping season but should report to Section D the Middle and Far East Section at Queen Anne's Gate. After a few weeks in London he was sent off to Russia as a language student where he combined passing the interpreter's examination with writing intelligence reports home. Brackenbury commented 'I have just received and read your most valuable and interesting letter and am sending it at once to the Secretary of State to see. You have given us exactly the information we require.'Grierson eventually sailed for India where he took part in the Black Mountain Expedition but three years later, again at the invitation of Brackenbury, he returned to the Intelligence Division as an attached officer. During these years at Queen Anne's Gate Grierson lived at Woolwich, first in rooms at 48,The Common, and afterwards in the East Wing of the Artillery Barracks. The main current of his life flowed in a well-defined channel. He had the habit each morning of rising early, dressing in Staff uniform and riding on the Common. He would then return, change into civilian clothes, breakfast and journey to London by 'that awful S.E.R.' In the train his day's work would begin and fellow passengers would see Grierson, the inevitable cigar in mouth, ensconced in a corner seat behind the 'Militar Wochenblatt' or the pages of a Russian newssheet. In due course 18 Queen Anne's Gate would engulf him and work on the 'Notes on the Army' would begin. He also produced such works as 'Twenty years of Russian Army Reform' and, based on a German Manual, the first edition of a book still used by all British officers as a guide to staff procedures, 'Staff Duties in the Field'.

This system of attaching officers to the Division, however although sometimes satisfactory could be very upsetting. On one occasion, just after Brackenbury's arrival, three Royal Artillery majors were ordered back to regimental duty on the same day. Brackenbury therefore began a long battle to reduce his dependence on attached officers, and eventually the War Office agreed to reduce the number of those attached and to increase his permanent strength by seven staff captains. Another of Brackenbury's successes was to wheedle £600 a year out of the Treasury to help pay the expenses of officers who wished to travel to countries for which they were responsible. Using this grant, Grierson, with his interest in Russia and Germany, took every opportunity to visit both of these countries. His fluent German gave him easy access to the German Staff and a senior German Officer once commented 'Grierson, that excellent comrade, is almost as well know in Berlin as in Woolwich and the whole German Staff of our Army values his knowledge of Germany.' Grierson made a point of being present for German divisional and corps manoeuvres and when in 1890 he was not selected to go in the official party to witness the Austrian exercises, went at his own expense, complaining in his diary – 'Just my luck to be out of it. They suck my brains dry when they want to know anything about the German Army, and then won't do a hand's turn for me when I want to go to the Austrian manoeuvres, it is all work and no glory; but H.M. will get more work out of me yet before I give up trying to get on. I suppose that other charlatans, who don't know an Uhlan from a pioneer will be sent and will boss it in British uniform while I play the civilian and write the report.' Perhaps because of his pique, Grierson did write a particularly good report which won high praise from his senior officers, for not only did it contain remarks and criticisms of the handling of infantry, cavalry and artillery, but also, for the first time in a manoeuvre report, had detailed notes on the logistic organization including transport and administration.

Grierson's dual responsibility for Russia and Germany proved particularly appropriate during the period of his tour. In 1885 war with Russia had seemed almost certain and for the next ten years both the German General Staff and the British Intelligence Division assessed that an attack by Russia into Europe was extremely likely. Grierson turned down the tantalizing appointment of Private Secretary to the Viceroy of India because he felt it would debar him from all chance of active service for five years 'And war must come within that time.' He thus found himself working with German Officers, against the 'common threat' of Russia and it was in this atmosphere of rapprochement, that he successfully managed to satisfy his intelligence gathering responsibilities towards both countries. Brackenbury was full of praise for his summary of the German armed strengths and sent it on to Lord Wolseley to see.

In 1891 Grierson managed to arrange a 'staff tour' and again visited Germany, Austria and Russia. He was most impressed with the amount of information the Germans had on Russia and felt this was due mainly to the fact that 'They were willing to spend a lot of roubles' but in Austria where he called upon the Head of Intelligence Division he felt the Government was far from well informed about Russian affairs and that 'Red tape predominated'. In Russia itself he visited the Quarter-master General, but managed to get very little military information. He felt the Russian people were very secretive and sensitive to spies. On his way by train to visit the Crimean battlefield, an English speaking civilian 'attached himself' to Grierson and after talking a great deal of obvious nonsense, announced that he had an English friend pronounced 'Fool', Grierson asked if he came from the well known family of 'Bloody Fool' to which the Russian gravely assented. The trip was worth while however and on 31 December 1891 Grierson was able to write in his diary 'Finished order of battle of the Army in the Caucasus, my topographical and military report, plan of operations, maps and order of battle are now ready for war, and so I end 1891 with a clean sheet in Section D'.

Throughout Europe it was a time of constant alarms and tension, it was commonly said 'There was always to be war next spring'. Once when Grierson was taking part in an exercise at Petersfield he was called suddenly to London as the 'Emperor of Germany is getting alarmed at the Russian concentration and you are wanted back badly'. It is in this type of disturbed situation that intelligence organizations flourish – provided they are staffed by the right quality of officer. Brackenbury and his selected officers were the right quality and although small in number, only sixteen officers and half a dozen clerks they established themselves more and more as advisers, not only to the Commander-in Chief, but also to the Foreign office. There were no typewriters in the Division, so all the reports had to be written in long hand; some tasks subsequently proved of little value (Gleichen was employed for many months compiling the Armed Strength of Portugal) but a prodigious amount of useful information was produced. In addition, the Intelligence Division had a new task, Brackenbury had secured a small grant to give to officers who did translation work. The rates offered were from 3d to 5d per 72 words for Russian works and from 1d to 2d for French and German, the price depending on the technicality of the work. Thus many books written by Continental and Asian Generals were being translated by officers in their spare time and then sent to the appropriate Intelligence Section for editing and distribution.

During this period, as well as numerous almanacs on various armies, the reports of British officers who had taken part in military expeditions while attached to foreign armies were also being collated and distributed, as were the Official Histories of British campaigns. One of these latter works aroused a whirlwind of controversy at the time. Frederick Maurice, who had been awarded a brevet Lieutenant Colonelcy for his services in the Nile Expedition, returned to the Intelligence Division to continue the 'History of the 1882 Campaign'. His aim, he stated, was 'To address his fellow-countrymen rather than his own brother officers, as no real progress was possible in the Army, unless it had behind it the driving power of public opinion. I happen in this instance to have something to say which I want to reach the ears of English men and women, not only of soldiers. I believe the facts of the next expedition which leaves the shores of England may be most seriously affected by my success or failure in bringing home to our people the experiences of the 1882 Campaign'. This policy of emphasising mistakes to act as lessons for future battles, not surprisingly upset the senior officers concerned, especially those still serving, and their vigorous objections delayed the publication of the History more than a year. However Maurice must have had influential friends for his next posting was 'Professor of History and Military Arts' at the Staff College, Camberley.

Another major task of the Division, perhaps the most important, was the continual effort that had to be given to the completion of a series of projects posed to it by the Commander-in-Chief:

a. A study of the defence problem of the North West Frontier of India, from an impartial and non-alarmist point of view.

b. An examination of the problem of an invasion of this country by France, from both the British and French stand points.

c. Preparation and printing of reports on the frontier defences of European Countries in view of any of them being at war with an adjoining country or countries.

Brackenbury had by now become a member of the Colonial Defence Committee and was helping organise a scheme of defence for the colonies on the same lines as the defensive plans for Great Britain. He had begun the practice, advocated by Charles Wilson, of circulating foreign military information to other War Office departments and had established a close liaison with the Director of Naval Intelligence. He was instrumental in getting intelligence officers established on the staffs of Generals commanding overseas garrisons and had increased the size and scope of the library. He had established an interchange of information with the Colonial and Indian Offices, the Foreign Office and even the Cabinet (it was still only a tentative interchange, as the Foreign Office viewed the military intelligence organization with the suspicion of the professional to the amateur) and had managed to obtain the significant concession that he could correspond semi-officially, provided he did not touch on matters of policy, direct with the Foreign Office and the Private Under Secretary for the Colonies, rather than through his own Secretary of State. Above all, he had established the principle that the Head of Military Intelligence should be consulted on military mattes concerning foreign countries.

It was all a great step forward but still, up to this stage, there was no War Office branch or department responsible for co-ordinating the assessments of the Intelligence Staffs with any possible overseas expedition. In fact there was no branch or department responsible for the pre-planning of any offensive action by the British Army. This situation was not merely lack of foresight on the part of senior offices but was a matter of general policy. Britain neither wanted, nor expected, to go to war. As late as 1888 a Committee under the Right Honourable Edward Stanhope, Minister for War, whilst accepting the need for a mobilization plan of two corps to go abroad in case of necessity commented: 'It will be distinctly understood that the probability of the employment of any corps in the field in any European war is sufficiently improbable, to make it the primary duty of the military authorities to organise only for the defence of this country'.

And so, apart from the fusion between intelligence and home mobilization, no pre-planning for possible operations throughout the Empire was carried out. Britain was the only European country, which had no General Staff system. Camberley-trained officers were sent almost exclusively to 'A' Branch (Personnel) appointments and officers of the Quarter-Master General's Branch whose duties, as laid down in the 1885 edition of Queens Regulations were still 'To conduct reconnaissances, to superintend the arrangements necessary for collecting information regarding the movements of the enemy and the local resources of the country' were mainly officers of the Army Service Corps who had not received any staff training.

The situation was blatantly unsatisfactory and in June 1888 a Royal Commission under Lord Hartington, which included the Director of Military Intelligence, was appointed to look into the War Office organization. The report was published on 11 May 1890 and recommended the creation of a new department under a Chief of Staff 'Which was to devote itself entirely to collecting information, to thinking out great military problems and to advising the Secretary of State for War on matters of general military policy'. The concept, however, ran into strong opposition. Apart from upsetting His Royal Highness the Duke of Cambridge, as it advocated the abolition of his post as Commander-In-Chief, one of the Committee members, Mr. Henry Campbell Bannerman felt that such a department would be 'Unnecessary' and that 'Although they existed in continental countries, those countries differed fundamentally from Great Britain in that they are concerned in watching the military condition of their neighbours and in planning possible wars against them, but in this country there is no room for a general military policy as we have no designs against our European neighbours'.

This idealistic concept of Britain's role in the world has always been a popular theme for British Politicians, and Campbell-Bannerman, although in the minority on the Committee, had his way and in 1892 became Secretary of State for War. But, willingly or unwillingly, Britain has continually found herself committed to using force when other countries have failed to agree with the British point of view. The desire not to plan and gain intelligence in time of peace has always produced its day of judgement in time of war. On this occasion the price of neglect was to be paid in South Africa – as the Report of the Commission which sat in 1904 to examine the initial catastrophes of the Boer War subsequently stated: 'If the recommendation of the majority of the Hartington Commission had not been ignored, the country would have been saved the loss of many thousands of lives and many millions of pounds.'

In 1891 General Brackenbury finished his five-year tour in charge of the Intelligence Division and left for India as Deputy Adjutant General and Director of the Indian Intelligence Department. He had proved himself to be a remarkably capable 'Intelligencer'. His successor was Major General E. F. Chapman, another Gunner. General Chapman's appointment was not a great success. He had spent all his service in India where after taking part in the Afghan War and the relief march from Kabul to Kandahar he had had long staff experience as Deputy Assistant, Assistant and finally Quarter-Master General in Bengal. Then, contracting a disease that had precluded further service in hot climates, he had been sent home and chosen to be Director of Military Intelligence. The motive behind his selection was the fear of a Russian invasion through India. In this event Chapman's experience would have proved useful but, as it happened, the next five years passed from crisis to crisis in Europe and Africa, not in India. General Chapman took over on 1 April 1891, and under his leadership the Division went for a while into the doldrums.

Not unnaturally perhaps, the officers who now came into the Division tended to have served in India – and tended to be Artillerymen. One such was Captain W. Waters who having become 'Heartily sick of India' had managed to exchange postings with another officer and came home to a regiment in Ipswich. Here he received a letter from General Chapman offering him a tour of two years in the Intelligence Division on a 'Purely temporary basis'. This would mean that his Battery Commander would be without a Second in Command for a long time, however the Battery Commander was on leave, so Waters took his application direct to the Colonel who was obliging enough to agree. The next day when the Battery Commander returned and objected vigorously, Water had already seized the initiative, left the Regiment and reported to the War Office.

Brackenbury's directive that all possible countries should have a brief prepared about them covering armies, routes and logistics was still being continued, and Waters was given the two year task of preparing 'Notes on Finland'. Many years later Waters met the British Representative in Helsinki who commented 'Some time ago the War Office sent me a military report on Finland, I forget who wrote it, but he must have been an ignorant ass, for I can't make head or tail of the names.'

The practice of sending officers 'on tour' was also continued, the most notable being a Major Wemys who persuaded his superiors of the desirability to visit Canada and prepare a plan for the defence of the 3,000 mile border against invasion from the united States of America. He was away for many months, and then returned to retire from the army. This visiting by officers from the Division was not always well received by our Diplomatic Staff in the countries concerned. The officers would return after a quick trip around, and in their report it could happen that only a rather general appreciation of the personaliites and problems of the country would emerge. The Ambassador in Russia once 'Picked a vulturesque crow' with General Chapman over an officer who arrived unannounced and then toured the country giving instruction to various consuls.

One officer to benefit from his touring was Count Gleichen. In 1893 he was returning by train from a day's shooting in Oxfordshire, when he read in the paper that a British Mission was visiting Morocco to 'Bolster British Prestige'. On the strength of having written 'Notes on Morocco' Gleichen jumped off the train at Reading, and sent a telegram offering his services to the Head of the Mission, whom 'He didn't know from Adam'. Such was the method of selecting intelligence officers that he was chosen to go, provided he could get four months leave from his battalion. This he did.

In 1892 Captain Waters was transferred from the 'Finnish Desk' to the section dealing with Spain and Egypt; the big event of the year was the purchase, by Spain, of a Krupps six-inch gun, which was mounted to dominate Gibraltar. It could outrange all our weapons and generated a great deal of paperwork in the War Office. Waters was also involved in a security matter, which at the time aroused little or no comment. The Cabinet had been considering the feasibility of a naval attack on the Dardanelles in case Turkey should refuse Britain passage in the event of an Anglo-Russian War. A committee came to the unanimous decision that it would be suicidal and impossible although in 1892 the Straits were not nearly so well defended as in 1915. But, because of its far-reaching implication only four copies of this important and sensitive report were distributed. A short time later Waters, to his surprise, was sent to collect and burn them. At the War Office he was very positively informed by the Principal Private Secretary that it was not Waters' business and anyway, as the Government was changing, the paper had been put away somewhere; the First Lord of the Admiralty said he couldn't lay his hands on his copy but would institute a search; Lord Salisbury thought it was at home in the pocket of an old gardening coat, and Mr. Balfour had no idea what had become of his. The four documents were never recovered.

Security was a matter that, although beginning to be recognised as a responsibility of the Intelligence Staff, was not taken very seriously. When Waters was a Military Attaché in Berlin a visiting British Cabinet Minister left a top-secret document in his hotel, and it was not missed until two weeks later when a Prussian Intelligence Officer handed it back. There was always a good market for War Office documents and French agents are believed to have obtained a complete set of drawings of the Dover and Channel defences, from a writing table in the Secretary of State For War's locked offices in Pall Mall. To guard against this type of danger one Admiral rigged an attachment to his drawer that rang a bell in his secretary's office if the drawer was opened. One lunchtime, on the departure of the Admiral, the bell rang and the secretary came into discover an Admiralty messenger with his fingers in the desk. He proved to be working for a Foreign Embassy and was dismissed. The printing of classified material was also a problem and to reduce the danger of compromise, the various 'Notes on Foreign Armies' were divided into small sections and sent to a number of different compositors.

In November 1895, after a decade of rather unpleasant internecine politics His Royal Highness the Duke of Cambridge at last retired, and his place as Commander in Chief was taken by Lord Wolseley. But in reaction to the Duke's detailed and autocratic domination over all military matters, Wolseley did not inherit the powers of his predecessor, he became merely an 'Adviser to the Secretary of State, with only a general command of the forces'. The Adjutant General, the Quarter-Master General, the Inspector General of Fortifications and the Inspector General of Ordnance were now required to by-pass the Commander in Chief and report direct to the Secretary of State but strangely, the Director of Military Intelligence, the Director of Mobilization and the Military Secretary remained on the staff of Lord Wolseley. It was a complicated organization, pregnant with potential troubles, one more factor that contributed to the forthcoming disasters of the South African War.

On 27 March 1896 General Chapman left to command Scottish District and in his place Colonel Sir John Ardagh was notified that 'Her Majesty the Queen had been graciously pleased to approve of his being appointed Director of Military Intelligence with the temporary rank of Major General'. In the second half of the nineteenth century four men share the credit for creating a British Intelligence organization, Jervis, Wilson, Brackenbury and now Ardagh. For twenty years Ardagh, like Brackenbury, had managed to intersperse his career with intelligence appointments, active service and diplomatic assignments. After leaving the Mobilization Department he had spent six years as Private Secretary to the Marquis of Lansdowne, then Viceroy of India and on his return a year as Commandant of the School of Military Engineering, Chatham. He now returned to the Intelligence Division with the reputation of being the foremost politico-military officer, an authority of international law and an outstanding staff officer. He also had that priceless advantage of being a personal friend of the Commander in Chief, most of the senior officers, and many of the leading statesmen, e.g. the Adjutant General Sir Redvers Buller, the Quarter-Master General Sir Evelyn Wood, the Director General of Ordnance Sir Henry Brackenbury and his former master in India Lord Lansdowne, now the Secretary of State for War. The 'Ring' had now reached the top of the tree.

The next three years proved to be the most difficult in the history of the Intelligence Division. Following General Ardagh's appointment there erupted almost immediately an era of colonial expansion in North, East and West Africa. Vast, unsurveyed and only partially explored regions were divided up by various European politicians, sitting at home, often using nothing more than small-scale sketch maps. Treaties were drawn up and new countries established on completely erroneous facts, watersheds of mountain ranges were unknown locally, rivers proved to have several main channels and degrees of longitude when verified by actual astronomical observations cut towns in two, or separated tribes from their pasture lands. These errors eventually brought European soldiers face to face in desolate spots, each convinced of their own legal position.

The outcome of these military confrontations were settled however, not by shooting, but at the conference table. The 'winner' proved to be the side that could produce sound arguments supported by precise knowledge. In this environment the Foreign Office turned to Sir John Ardagh and his Intelligence Staff. It proved easy, not only because they knew him from his days in India, but also because his office was almost next-door. Happily this flow of information was not completely one-sided. Into the Foreign Office each day poured a stream of reports and assessments from ambassadors, consuls and agents stationed all over the world. These constituted gold mines of information to the military intelligence officer, but were of course, written in the strictest confidence to their own departments. It was General Ardagh's great achievement that he had so won the confidence of civil servants and diplomats that they were prepared to send them to Queen Anne's Gate for perusal and collation. General Ardagh's intellectual ability plus his extreme tact had managed to win the trust of the most cautious of statesmen. Gleichen has written –

> Ardagh, silent, monocled, skinny-necked, he always reminded me of a marabu stork I fear, the writer of beautifully expressed far-seeing memoranda on the most abstruse questions, was always something of a mystery to us. He never spoke, and when he sent for us to give him information on certain subjects, there was dead silence on his part whilst we talked. I once gave him a full account of Morocco matters during the space of something like half an hour. He leant back in his chair, never interrupted once nor took a note, and at the end he slowly screwed in his eyeglass and said in a hollow, faded voice, 'Thank you'. Yet he had absorbed painlessly all that I had told him, and the issue was a masterpiece of writing. Over this head was a placard in large letters, which the interviewer could not possibly fail to see:

When you come to see a man on
Confine yourself to stating your
Be lucid and brief about your
And leave him to his
BUSINESS

Seldom can Britain have been so involved with events around the world, during General Ardagh's first three years of office British Troops undertook no less than thirty small wars or expeditions. From China through to British Guiana and Nigeria, Whitehall was controlling men's destinies. A typical incident in 1898 was the Uganda Mutiny. At 5.30 one afternoon the Foreign Office notified the Intelligence Staff of trouble and requested an immediate verbal opinion of the action to be taken. General Ardagh made his appreciation took it to the Commander in Chief and by 7 p.m. orders had been dispatched to Simla for a force to be sent from India to 'Suppress the mutiny'.

More and more work now came to the Colonial Section of the Intelligence Division. This Section had not only forty distinct and dependent governments to look after, but also a number of areas some of which came under the jurisdiction of the Sovereign and some of which were controlled by independent British Companies, such as Somaliland and British East Africa. The Intelligence Division, for some strange reason, was responsible for the training, equipment, administration, organization and employment of all the local forces in these areas, and, as the forces were mostly only just establishing themselves, the need for guidance was continual. Complicated questions concerning the armament of overseas garrison and the establishment of coaling stations were sandwiched between intelligence reports describing General Kitcheners methodical avenging of General Gordon in the Sudan, and the disturbing indications from South Africa of impending bloodshed.

Another factor that prevented the Intelligence Division from concentrating on the problems of potential enemies was, paradoxically, the ' general acceptability' of Sir John Ardagh himself. As well as being constantly required to attend conferences on frontier disputes, he had been appointed member of a Cable Landing Rights Committee formed to advise the Board of Trade as to the many complicated questions connected with the granting of crown licences for telegraphic cables. The strategic implications of controlling the new submarine cables, which linked the Empire, had just been realised, and the degree to which the Government should impose its will on the privately owned cable companies was proving a difficult and controversial problem. As

Director of Military Intelligence Ardagh was also, ex officio, a member of the Military Committee on Defence and the Colonial Defence Committee.

Additionally, in 1899, in spite of all his other commitments, General Ardagh was sent to The Hague as military adviser to a peace conference. In August 1898 the Russian Government had proposed an international conference 'To investigate the best means of securing a durable peace and for limiting the progressive development of military armaments'. In 1899 the conference met and the agenda, which bears a remarkable similarity to those currently debated in the United Nations, was under eight headings:

1. The limitation of the effective strength of naval and military forces.
2. The prohibition of new types of firearms and new explosives.
3. The restriction of the use of existing explosives and in particular the prohibition of throwing of projectiles or explosives from balloons.
4. The prohibition in naval warfare of submarine torpedo boats and of vessels armed with a ram.
5. The application of the Geneva Convention of 1864 to naval warfare.
6. The neutralization of boats and ships employed after an engagement in saving men overboard.
7. The revision of the laws and customs of war, drawn up at the Brussels Conference of 1874, but still unratified.
8. The acceptance of the principle of arbitration, and the organization of machinery for giving effect to that principle.

Sir John Ardagh took a major part in these debates and, as Senior Military Representative, suddenly found himself the centre of an international controversy for using 'Dum Dum' bullets. In 1895 during the Chitral Campaign it had been shown that the new small-bore Lee Metford rifle, which had a lead bullet, covered by a hard casing, when passing through the body made an extremely small hole and if it met a bone drilled neatly through it. This had proved inadequate to stop a charging tribesman and so, after a series of tests, the Government had approved the manufacture of a bullet known as the 'Mark IV' which had a slightly cylindrical cavity at its head, again covered by a hard envelope. This gave it the equivalent stopping power of a much greater calibre weapon and caused a very nasty wound. Sir John found himself assailed from every quarter and found it necessary to make the following defence:

> I explained to the Sub-Commission that in our savage warfare it had been found that men who had been penetrated through and

through several times by the latest model of small calibre projectile which made a small clean hole and which the savage regarded as a scratch, meant a more effective means of disabling him was necessary. Your civilised soldier when he has had a bullet through him knows that he is considered as wounded; he recognises the fact, lies down on his stretcher, and is taken off to his ambulance to have attention from his doctor or his Red Cross Society according to the rules of the game. But your barbarian, when he received wounds of a like nature which are insufficient to stop or disable him, continues to rush on, spear or sword in hand and before you have had time to explain to him that he is not playing according to the rules of the game, and that his conduct is in flagrant violation of the rules of the Peace Conference, he may have succeeded in killing you.

But the argument proved inadequate and Britain was condemned by a majority of eighteen votes. Other resolutions prohibited the dropping of explosives from balloons and the employment of projectiles whose sole object was to spread asphyxiating gas. More important, but equally ineffective, were the long debates which tried to 'Secure a durable peace.' These debates kept General Ardagh heavily committed defending British interests and each night trying to keep in touch with Downing Street and Queen Anne's Gate by letter. On 27 July when the Conference ended he returned to England and collapsed with fever and exhaustion. He was away from work for three months. War with South Africa was declared in October and thus for five months before the biggest conflict since the Crimea, the Head of Intelligence was away from his desk.

His Second in Command, Colonel Everett, had also shown a remarkable flair for tact and diplomacy and, like Ardagh, had also been employed unravelling the complicated tangle of frontier questions. In 1898 he had been created a K.C.M.G. for his services in connection with the treaty delimiting the frontiers of Nigeria and the Northern Gold Coast and was travelling to Paris and Berlin much of the time in 1899. The Head of the Colonial Section, which dealt with South Africa, was Major E.A. Altham, but a month before in September, he had been posted to Natal as Intelligence Office to General White's force concentrating there in case of trouble. Thus when war did break out a staff captain was in charge of this all important section, Captain W.R. Robertson, the first man from the ranks to go to Staff College, the first man to enter the army as a private and reach field marshal's rank.

On the outbreak of the war Robertson took charge of the Section and another officer filled his Staff Captain's chair. This officer was posted to

Africa two weeks later and by Christmas Day no fewer than five different officers had passed through the appointment of Staff Captain, this at a time when the volume of work descending on the Section was growing more formidable each day. All reports and suggestions as to how the war should be waged, and won, from people who had private or commercial interests in South Africa were channelled to the Colonial Section and as these often came from 'Very Important People' they had to be considered and answered in detail. When a particularly difficult question was posed, Robertson would go to General Ardagh's bedside, otherwise he coped himself.

> Another task which took much of my time' wrote Robertson 'was the preparation of a summary of events for the Queen, the Cabinet, and various departmental heads, showing the dispositions of the troops and the reinforcements in course of transit. Information as to these dispositions was difficult to obtain, as it always is when the military situation is unfavourable, for often the local authorities themselves may not have it, and such as they have may be doubtful or unpalatable, and therefore they sometimes hesitate to forward it until it has been confirmed. Again, when information reached the War Office it had to pass through rigidly prescribed channels, and was often hours and sometimes days before it arrived at my table in Queen Anne's Gate. The Intelligence Branch was treated as a separate, and not very important, part of the War Office organization. The consequence was that I had to rely for my data largely upon the reports of war correspondents which would often appear in the Press before the same information reached me officially, As my Summary was the only document of its kind produced, the demand for it soon rose from half a dozen copies to five times that number.' Small wonder Robertson subsequently wrote 'I could but try, with the help of my ever changing assistant to deal with the more important matters, so far as an average sixteen hour day would permit, and leave the remainder to look after themselves.'

In December, Robertson's former tutor at the Staff College Colonel G.F.R. Henderson, who had just been appointed Lord Robert's Director of Intelligence asked for him to go to South Africa and when this was approved Robertson himself, on 30 December 1899, sailed gladly away. He was the fifteenth officer to leave the Division since the fighting had begun in October.

'The 'pigeons had now come home to roost' complained the Secretary of State 'The Government had as little expectation of war with the

Orange Free State, as they had of war with Switzerland. 'We find the enemy who declared war against us is much more powerful than we expected' added the Commander in Chief. Both used a phraseology, which bears an amazing resemblance to that uttered by their respective predecessors forty-five years earlier at the beginning of the Crimean War. From persons less highly placed the statements were more vitriolic though less specific: 'The armament and strength of the Boers greatly exceeded anything anticipated; the theatre of war was a 'terra incognita' to the troops; the provision of maps, essential to the conduct of successful operations had been totally neglected'.

Three years later the Intelligence Division was put on public trial before the War Commission charged formally:

1. That it had failed to correctly assess the numerical strength of the Boers.
2. That it was ignorant of their armament, especially their artillery.
3. That it had failed to fathom the Boers' offensive designs on Natal.
4. That in any case, no warning as to the above had been given to the Government and
5. That our troops were left unfurnished with maps, and were without topographical information.

The Commission marked the climax of three years bitter criticism against the Intelligence Division and the pre-war intelligence Staffs. The Army and the Public positively and aggressively believed, that in spite of all the past experience, in spite of all the money they had spent, the Military Intelligence Organization had failed – failed most wretchedly.

CHAPTER FIFTEEN

The War in South Africa

*O*n July 1899 General Redvers Buller, then commanding at Aldershot, was recalled from leave and told, under great conditions of secrecy, that in the 'Unlikely event of a war in South Africa' he would become Commander in Chief of an Expeditionary Force totalling 10,000 men. But, he was emphatically warned that this plan must be kept a close secret, as any suggestion that such a move was being prepared might give the Boers and their allies the excuse to declare a defensive war. Throughout the summer therefore, Buller was in the invidious position of knowing he was to command the biggest British battle force to go overseas since the Crimea War but not being able to make any preparations for it. Even his suggestion that an exercise should be held on Salisbury Plain, so the battalions and staffs could get to know each other was refused, on the ground that this might 'Antagonise the Boers'. More depressing still is the fact that he was not allowed to discuss the future operation with the Director of Military Intelligence and when asked about this after the War by the Elgin Commission replied, 'The Secretary of State had told him not to do so, as the appointment was strictly confidential.'

In September a number of reinforcements were sent to South Africa and included amongst these was a new commander, General Sir George White. White knew that Buller was to be Commander in Chief in the event of war and knew that war was extremely likely, but he did not have any talks with Sir Redvers because as Buller's biographer has explained, 'The two were not intimate'. Like Buller, General White also did not discuss the situation with Sir John Ardagh, as the Elgin Commission discovered. Elgin Commission: 'Did you see the Director of Military Intelligence before you sailed?' General White: 'I really forget. There was no interview of mine with the Director of Military Intelligence of sufficient importance to impress itself deeply on my memory' and a few minutes later the General admitted that he had not spoken to Sir John at all.

General White arrived in Africa on 7 October and on 12 October an excited Boer Army crossed the Natal frontier. They met no opposition, no sentries had been posted, no roads had been mined, no bridges had been blown and the railway line remained intact. The first police posts surrendered in astonishment when told that war had been declared and the Boers, using the railway, swept South and East. About which The Times History, perhaps a little unjustly considering how long Sir George had been in Africa, subsequently commented: 'The least damaging explanation is that Sir George White never fully realised the Boers were civilised opponents who could make use of a railway for military purposes'.

For the next three months the British Army suffered reverse upon reverse. During the preceding forty-four years the British soldier had been outstandingly successful in a series of short campaigns. Comparatively small numbers of soldiers, supported by native troops and often led by the same select band of officers, had fought large numbers of Afghans, Zulus and Sudanese who, in the critical battles, had charged to self destruction in massed attacks against infantry 'Squares'. In 1899 Britain faced with an enemy using modern weapons, modern communications and the ability and capability to adopt a strategy of dispersal and concentration. When the Boers attacked, there were 20,000 British troops in South Africa who had the advantage of army discipline, a superiority in artillery and a long tradition of success in battle, facing some 45,000 Boers who had the advantage of combat experience in the veldt, strategic and tactical mobility and the confident comfort that God was on their side. After the initial battles of the war at Talana Hill and Elandslaagte a stunned British Army found itself forced to retreat and then, to its amazement, besieged in the three towns of Ladysmith, Kimberley and Mafeking. Isolated and impotent in Ladysmith, together with General White, was the Head of Intelligence, Major E. A. Altham.

On 9th October 1899 General Buller, still in London, was officially appointed. Commander in Chief in South Africa, and on this day was allowed for the first time to see Intelligence Division's documents concerning Boer strengths and likely plans. Five days later he left to command the Army Corps now converging on Capetown. On his arrival he divided his Corps into three main battle groups and quickly thrust north to relieve the beleaguered garrisons. General Gatacre commanded the centre column and with 3,000 men moved forward to attack the Boer position at Stormberg. The Column, which had no intelligence officer appointed, moved without advanced or flank guards, had no maps, and although the British had previously held the ground, no field sketches. Dawn broke to reveal the British flank strung out in line beneath the Boer-held heights. In the resulting disaster seven hundred men were lost and Gatacre was compelled to withdraw.

On the left. Lord Methuen advanced on Kimberley and also launched a night attack, at Magersfontein. Daybreak came to expose his force concentrated and held up by a line of wire. Cut down by fire from trenches at ground level, and pinned down by fire from above, the wretched infantry lay throughout the day under a burning sun, and then retreated with a thousand causalities. One of the casualties, shot through the neck as he was taking a compass bearing, was Count Gleichen, posted from the Intelligence Division to be a company commander in the Grenadier Guards. The previous day a colonial scout and a native informant had reported the presence of the Boers, but as this did not coincide with Methuen's previous deductions he chose to ignore the reports and there was no intelligence officer appointed to his staff to advise him.

On the right, the Commander in Chief, General Buller moved towards Ladysmith. Stormberg and Magersfontein had shocked and grieved England, but Buller's 'Inevitable' victory would make up for this. On 15 December near the little tin-roofed village of Colenso, Buller confidently launched his main attack. It failed. 'It was' says The Times History 'A frontal attack directed on three points of an insufficiently reconnoitred position, held in unknown strength by an entrenched enemy – a worse plan could not have been devised.' On a front two miles wide and a mile deep, line upon line of khaki clad men had moved forward in silence, the whole force led by one terrified kaffir guide. With no map or sketch of the area, inadequate reconnaissance and no intelligence staff, Buller became confused by the bends in the river and slowly, to the astonishment and joy of the Afrikaners, the leading brigade moved into a re-entrant covered on three sides by Boer rifles. In spite of piece-meal attacks made with traditional gallantry the advance collapsed and Buller withdrew, suffering 1,100 casualties and, to his shame, losing ten of his twelve Royal Artillery guns. Small wonder England in horrified stupefaction called it ' Black Week'.

How was it the best British Generals, the best British cavalry and line regiments had been beaten in battle by a horde of 'uneducated ill-disciplined Boer farmers?' Public opinion turned to the obvious solution, 'Our soldiers had no idea of what to expect, how could they hope to fight under such conditions, and against such odds – they should have been informed, - then they could have been prepared.' General Ardagh and his Intelligence Staff suddenly found themselves the target and scapegoat for all the humiliation and anger of Victorian England 'It was obvious to everyone that war with South Africa had been imminent for months; why hadn't the Intelligence Division given adequate warnings?' In Parliament, and out, Ardagh was personally accused of a neglect which to many people seemed almost treasonable, but Ardagh remained silent and only 1903, four years later, did the report of the Elgin Commission reveal what in fact the Intelligence Division had done.

The first discovery made by this Commission was that, in spite of all the accepted beliefs, the Intelligence Division had in fact issued a succession of documents all emphasising that war in South Africa was extremely likely and, that it would be both costly and sanguinary. As early as October 1896 Sir John had submitted to the Commander in Chief a paper entitled 'The Transvaal Boers from a Military Point of View'. This showed that the South African Republic was spending £2,350,000 a year on military preparations and that 'This large expenditure can have no other explanation than an anticipation of war, or an intention of aggression against this country.' The paper had concluded, 'That action now would ensure success, give confidence, attain the object quickly and in the end save men and money.' On 5 April 1897 Mr. Chamberlain had expressed his acknowledgement for 'The most valuable reports submitted by the Director of Military Intelligence as to the importations of vast quantities of munitions of war into the Transvaal' but in spite of these warnings Chamberlain and his Cabinet remained unwilling to accept the likelihood of war.

In a subsequent memorandum, drawn up by the Intelligence Division on 21 September 1898 on 'The present state of preparation for frontier defence in South Africa in a war against the Dutch Republics', it was pointed out that:

> The Transvaal has, during the last two years, made military preparations on a scale which can only be intended to meet the contingency of a contest with Great Britain. These preparations still continue, and the condition of affairs in South Africa has practically become that of armed neutrality, which may last for years, or may culminate in war at very short notice. At the outbreak of such a war we should, at first, be in a decided numerical inferiority; moreover, we should have to face the problem of protecting a very long frontier, and should be handicapped with a certain amount of disloyalty (passive, if not active) within our own borders. At least a month or six weeks must elapse before any appreciable reinforcements could arrive from England or India. The problem would, therefore, be a difficult one, and its difficulty will be enhanced by the fact that any mistakes or lack of finances at the outset would seriously affect subsequent operations.

This memorandum gave the latest information as to the armed strength of the Republic and, after pointing out that 'There are reasons to believe that, in a war against the Transvaal, we should certainly find the sister Republic ranged against us', estimated that 'After deducting all local garrisons and non-effectives, the Republics could organise for offensive operations beyond their frontiers a force of not less than 27,000 men.' It was further pointed out that 'The Transvaal had laid in reserves of over 30,000 rifles surplus to their own requirements, and that these reserves were avowedly intended to arm loyalists in the Colonies in the event of war.' It also explained that projects for offensive operations had been drawn up in Pretoria, although at that time, September 1898, it was held by the Intelligence Division that these attacks would be limited to an attempt on Kimberley, the occupation of the northern apex of Natal, and raids of 2,000 to 3,000 men in other directions.

In another memorandum prepared in the Intelligence Division and submitted on 7 June 1899 to the Commander in Chief, stress was laid on the probability of the active co-operation of the Free State with the Transvaal in the case of war, and after making deductions for detached Boer forces watching Rhodesia, Mafeking, the Basutoland border and for men left at home on their farms, it was estimated that the Republic would be able to place in the field at the outset of the war a main army of 34,000. Finally, a memorandum was written, dated 8 August 1899 on 'The Political and Military Relations existing between the Transvaal and the Free State', which stated: 'The conclusions seem clear, that our plan of campaign, as well as our preliminary defensive preparations for the first phase of the war, should be based on the definite hypothesis of a hostile Free State.'

In addition to these warning memoranda, in April 1898 a handbook about South Africa was printed and issued, first as a secret publication and then de-classified, revised and brought up to date in June 1899. In 1903 a critical and hostile committee aided by the priceless gift of hindsight dissected this book sentence-by-sentence, item-by-item. Such an examination must constitute the ultimate test for an intelligence staff. The results are remarkable.

Item	Number Reported in Military Notes	Number actually in Possession September 1899
Field Guns in Transvaal	83*	71
Field Guns in Orange Free State	24	28
Machine Guns (total)	34	27
Rifles (total)	64,950	70,091
Rifle Ammunition (total)	23 million rounds + 10 million ordered	33,050,000
Men who could take up arms	47,600	45,000

Note: The over estimate of guns rose from the fact that whereas it was known that sixteen 'Long Toms' had been ordered, only four had arrived when the war started.

The Elgin Commission had thus shown that the Intelligence Division had warned the nation and had, with great accuracy, estimated the enemy strength. It now considered the more significant problem of what action had resulted from the warnings. Poor intelligence can lose battles, but good intelligence cannot, by itself, win battles. As the Commission continued its investigations the trail, for many reasons, became a little blurred; however it was proved that a number of documents issued by the Director of Military Intelligence had not been shown to members of the Cabinet also, that so strong had been the desire to avoid talk of war, that other memoranda had been deliberately altered before circulation. Abruptly, over night, attacks on the Intelligence Division ceased. General Ardagh and his staff were now bathed in a warm flood of sympathy and forgiveness. In the public press it became fashionable to praise 'The quiet backroom boys who had worked so diligently and successfully to predict the outbreak of the war'.

But in retrospect the Division had fallen short in its service, and one reason for this was lack of money. During the two years before the war the Boers had spent £170,000 annually on their 'Secret Service'. Sir John asked for £10,000. He was given, as a great concession, £100. As the Editor of The Times explained to the Elgin Commission: 'We did not spend nearly enough money, or send enough officers. The eight or ten who went out did very good work, but they were fewer than the men I employed myself as Times correspondents, and I should have been ashamed to have sent correspondents anywhere, or even a commercial traveller with the sums of money they were given.' And *The Times History* also pointed out that 'Whereas the German General Staff employed over three hundred officers spending £270,000 the Intelligence and Mobilization Divisions of the British Army only employed seventeen officers at a cost of £11,000.'

But lack of money was not the main cause of failure. *The Times History* pinpointed a more damaging factor:

> Far worse than the starved condition of the Intelligence Division was its lack of authority. It was a mere information bureau with absolutely no control over military policy. Its investigations were not directed with the sense of responsibility that belongs to those who inquire in order to act upon their own information, nor had it the power to insist upon the taking of those measures of the necessity of which its special knowledge convinced it.

This was the tragedy of the Intelligence Division. They had yielded to a temptation which all intelligence officers must be aware of, and resist, that of continually calling 'Wolf'. It is the duty of the intelligence officer to alert his commander of impending danger, but the warning must be presented in such a responsible way that there is a clear, sharp distinction between general worry over a deteriorating situation and the crucial moment when positive action is required. During the years 1896-1899 the Intelligence Division although, they had produced numerous warnings, had not done this with a conviction that had persuaded their seniors that defensive measures were required. The blame can in part be put on the structure of the War Office but General Ardagh and his staff cannot be completely exonerated.

CHAPTER SIXTEEN

The Field Intelligence Department

𝒪𝓃 spite of all the published fears of the Intelligence Division, in the spring of 1889 there were only two intelligence officers stationed in South Africa. These two men both had other staff appointments and both subsequently admitted in evidence that 'As war became more and more likely, so their other staff duties became increasingly onerous and thus the time they could give to their intelligence responsibilities became less and less.' In July 1899 the War Office did send ten officers to South Africa on 'Special service' and included in their brief was the requirement to ascertain 'What persons would be available to act as agents, runners, interpreters etc'. One of the ten, Colonel Baden-Powell, went to Mafeking, three others, Scott-Turner, MacInnes and O'Meara went to Kimberley and two, Major A. E. Altham, still holding the appointment of Deputy Assistant Adjutant General (Intelligence) in Queen Anne's Gate and Major David Henderson, Argyll and Sutherland Highlanders went to Natal. Their intelligence gathering activities were, however, rigorously restricted by the authorities in South Africa. These local officials, supported by the British Government, were anxious in the extreme that nothing should be done which the Boers could publicise as provocative. The final decision to carry out intelligence work against another country in peace time, is correctly a political decision, but the events leading to the South African War provide a good example of a situation where unwillingness to take the risk of political embarrassment has subsequently resulted in military defeat.

The 'Special service' officers were not allowed to develop their own sources of information and had to content themselves with cycling along the frontier pretending to be tourists, and surreptitiously making sketches. But this was only done for a short time, as hardly had they settled in and began to learn about the country when war broke out. Immediately, all the restrictions were swept away and the officers set about contacting men who could help form an intelligence organization.

With this in view Major David Henderson approached a well-known South African personality, the Honourable T. K. Murray. Murray had been born in Natal and at the age of seventeen was one of the original 'peggers' in the Colesberg diamond fields. He had acted as a scout in the Langalibalele Rebellion and Zulu Wars and had then settled down to be a farmer and politician. He was a member of the Natal Legislative Assembly and was Minister of Lands. As a result of Murray's efforts forty five white men and fifty natives were enrolled 'Selected from Natal, the Orange Free State and Transvaal for their special acquaintance with the different districts, knowledge of the Dutch and Kaffir languages and experience of the veldt life including riding and shooting.' The men were all volunteers, had to find their own horses, saddlery and rifles, serve without pay and were to provide local language and local knowledge. Henderson thought briefly about what to call them and then chose that traditional, and most appropriate of titles – 'The Corps of Guides'.

In Cape Colony another of the ten 'Special' officers, Major Mike Rimington, Inniskilling Dragoon Guards, was raising a similar Corps. Rimington, who enlisted only those who spoke Dutch, established a high standard by ruthlessly discharging anyone who failed to be absolutely efficient. The unit was initially known as the Imperial Corps of Guides but following the contemporary habit of calling newly raised units after their commander, it soon became Rimington's Guides* and then 'Rimington's Tigers' from the piece of wild cat fur they fastened to their hats. On 24 February, 1900 Corporal Clements of Rimington's Guides won the Victoria Cross, 'When dangerously wounded through the lungs and called on to surrender, Clements threw himself into the midst of a party of five Boers, shooting three of them with his revolver and thereby causing the whole part to surrender.' In Kimberley, Scott-Turner, subsequently killed leading a sortie out of the Town, raised the Kimberley Light Horse and the Diamonds Field Horse, but these two units were used more as mounted infantry rather than scouts or guides.

General Buller arrived in Capetown in November 1899 and brought with him a full Army Corps with all its supporting staff and services. He brought with him not one single intelligence officer. By this time, of the ten 'special service' officers holding intelligence appointments, Altham and Henderson were trapped in Ladysmith, Baden-Powell was besieged in Mafeking and O'Meara was caught in Kimberley. There were thus no intelligence staffs waiting for him. The only one of the ten still available was the most junior. Second Lieutenant A. N. Campbell, RA. Campbell therefore became Buller's 'Intelligence Staff' but there remained the problem of selecting a Head of Intelligence. This was to be a man capable of creating and co-ordinating a military intelligence system for a Corps of 20,000 regular soldiers. Buller chose the Natal farmer, T. K. Murray:

> 'The formation of the Intelligence Department', wrote Buller, 'was undertaken by the Honourable T. K. Murray who placed his thorough knowledge of the country and his unbounded energy at our service. He obtained for us a Corps of Guides whose services were invaluable, but all this work had to be begun from the beginning. The threads of the Intelligence Department that had been prepared being all in Ladysmith and inaccessible'.

Thus it was that Murray, a civil servant, who had had no military training but who had the attributes of local language and local knowledge, followed exactly the precedent set by Calvert in the Crimea and Drummond in Zululand and became Head of Military Intelligence. There was no intelligence officer available for General Gatacre to help him avoid defeat at Stormberg, nor for General Methuen to avert disaster at Magersfontein and although Murray's Corps of Guides received information that the main body of Botha's force was concentrating along the line of the Tugela, it was not sufficiently specific to enable Buller's reconnaissance patrols to find the enemy on the ground and thus save the shame of Colenso. Many factors contributed to the events of 'Black Week', but the complete lack of a military intelligence system of any kind, played its significant part.

Two days after the news of the defeats reached England the Government decided that a new commander and staff have to go to South Africa. Without consulting Lord Wolseley, their own Commander in Chief, the Cabinet selected Lord Roberts. Roberts was offered the post, and told of the death of his only son, killed trying to save the guns at Colenso, on the same day. But he accepted, and before sailing on 23 December gathered a small staff to take with him. Amongst these were General Kitchener called from the Sudan to be his Chief of Staff, and Colonel G. F. R. Henderson called from Camberley to be the Head of Intelligence. Henderson had commanded a company at Tel el Kebir and had later been posted as an instructor to the Staff College, Camberley. Here, his ability to teach and develop new ideas had become celebrated throughout the Army and the publication, after eight years effort, of his history of 'Stonewall Jackson', together with other military books and articles made him an understandable choice for Lord Robert's team. It was Henderson who successfully asked Lord Roberts that his ex-pupil Captain W. Robertson should leave his desk in Queen Anne's Gate to accompany them as an intelligence officer.

On the boat trip to Africa, Roberts, Kitchener and Henderson planned their war. It was to be based on two major factors, first the army must become mounted and so diminish its reliance on railways, and second that the defeat of the Boer armies, rather than capture of ground, should be the main aim. The final plan, agreed after their arrival in Africa, was that 30,000 men including a strong cavalry force under General French, would leave the railway some fifty miles south of Cronje's strong position at Magersfontein, march East into the veldt then swing North and cross the Modder River. If successful, this would help relieve the pressure on Buller in Natal, open a route to Kimberley and cut Cronje's lines of communication with the Boer capital in Bloemfontein. All depended on secrecy, and until the last minute only Roberts, Kitchener and Henderson knew the details. Henderson was charged with creating a deception plan and was so successful that even Majors Hume, Davies, Milne and W. Robertson, the four Deputy Assistant Adjutant Generals (Intelligence) living in the same tent, did not know the proposed route. Fictitious telegrams were sent out ordering a move in clear then, on a pretext, cancelled in cipher. False orders were circulated to imply a concentration of troops at Colesberg and to aid the deceit a newspaper man was given 'Confidential tips' about this concentration together with the strictest injunction to keep it to himself. When, as Henderson hoped, it duly appeared in the London Press the War Office, which was also deceived, telegraphed Roberts pointing out a 'Serious indiscretion on the part of someone on his staff'. Later when the real line of advance became clear the newspaperman complained formally to Roberts about his 'unfair and dishonest treatment'.

The deception was successful. Cronje had no idea of the plan and, as General French left his tents standing when the cavalry moved out, news of the march did not reach him for twenty-four hours. The plan was good, the surprise complete. It now all depended on the fighting ability of troops pouring up from the coast, tired, confused and lacking in organization, a mixture of cavalry, mounted infantry, regular and yeomanry regiments, Australians, Canadians and New Zealanders. The man who turned this chaos into a degree of order, who by his own personality got an incredible scene of disorder pointed in the right direction, was Kitchener, who became loathed, hated and cursed by everyone for his ruthless personal intervention. As units arrived at the railhead they were formed into brigades and staffs allotted. One story, perhaps apocryphal, concerns an officer returning from convalescent leave who was waiting at the station when Kitchener and a Colonel stopped close by. Kitchener had evidently just appointed the Colonel to command a Brigade.

Kitchener: 'All right; I will soon find you a staff. Let me see; you have a Brigade Major?

Colonel: Yes but he is at Hanover Road.

Kitchener: That's all right; you will collect him in good time. You will want a chief for your staff now. Here, you' and he beckoned a Colonel in palpably just-out-from England kit, who was standing by. What are you doing here? You will be Chief of Staff to the New Cavalry Brigade'

New Colonel: But sir …'

Kitchener: That's all right. Now you want transport and supply officers. See that depot over there; go and collect them from there – quote me as your authority. There, you are fitted up, you can round up part of your brigade tonight and be off at daybreak tomorrow. Wait, you will want an intelligence officer. Here he swung round and ran his eye over the miscellaneous gathering of all ranks assembled on the platform. He singled out a bedraggled officer from among the group who had arrived the preceding night.

Kitchener: What are you doing here?

Officer: Trying to rejoin, Sir.

Kitchener: Where have you come from?

Officer: Dreifontein – convalescent, Sir.

Kitchener: You'll do. You are Intelligence Officer to the New Cavalry Brigade. Here's your Brigadier; you will take orders from him'. Turning again to the Colonel and holding out his hands, 'There you are fitted out. Mind you move out of Richmond Road tomorrow morning without fail. Goodbye!'

February is the hottest month in the month in the South African summer, water was extremely scarce and the sand plain offered no fodder for the horses, Roberts had to march round the flank of a mobile enemy knowing every inch of the way, while he knew little or nothing of the ground. It is perhaps understandable that Cronje did not believe it possible. But the plan worked. Led by Rimington, British troops crossed the River Modder and General French in an exhilarating cavalry charge broke through to relieve Kimberley. The problem now was to determine what Cronje would do next and Major Robertson prepared an assessment:

I knew that Cronje had three courses open to him; it was as yet impossible to say which of the three he would choose. He might retreat either by the west or the east side of Kimberley and unite with the force just driven back by French, or he might try to escape to the eastward and make for Bloemfontein. Strategically, either of the two first would have been the safest, but, as so often happens in war, the least likely route – the third – was selected. At midday on the 16th all our doubts were dispelled by the arrival at Headquarters of one of the men whom we had previously introduced into the commandos at Magersfontein. His account of Cronje's movements was evidently reliable, and being corroborated by the information we had received from other sources, it became possible to form a definite opinion upon which the Commander in Chief could safely determine his future action.

As a result of this information, one of Rimington's Scouts found Cronje in the riverbed at Paardeberg and in the ensuing battle 4,000 Boers surrendered. It was Britain's first major success of the war and enabled Roberts to carry out the third phase of his plan, the capture of the Capital at Bloemfontein. Unfortunately on reaching the City, Colonel Henderson fell sick and had to be evacuated from Africa and. Lieutenant Colonel C. V. Hume, RA, took his place as Director of Intelligence On 3 May 1900 General Roberts began his march to the Boer centres of Johannesburg and Pretoria. The plan was to advance on a front extending from Ladysmith to Kimberley with Buller on the right, Hunter and Methuen on the left, and the columns in the centre directed by Roberts himself. The troops marched three hundred miles, crushing all resistance in their path. By the first week in June, Johannesburg and Pretoria had been occupied and by August the Boer army under Prinsloo had been defeated on the Basuto border. On 1 September the Transvaal was annexed once again to the British Dominions and a victorious Lord Roberts then handed over command to Kitchener and went home. With him went Major Robertson, back to resume his appointment in the Intelligence Division.

The war had been won and the Intelligence Staffs now reviewed the developments in Field Intelligence. In making this review it became clear that a subtle but highly significant re-organization had taken place. At the beginning of the War, intelligence staff officers, following the traditions of the past hundred years, had galloped around with their commanders, made personal reconnaissances, drew topographical sketches, selected camp sites and interrogated prisoners. As a result they found themselves harried, hot and continually under pressure. But the great size of the country, containing as it did numerous enemy columns which could communicate quickly between themselves, brought the need for a pivotal point where all intelligence could be collated centrally, analysed and then presented to the commander. The need had arisen therefore for two sorts of intelligence officer, one to sit back quietly and collate and the other to accompany commanders in the field.

One weakness, quickly exposed by the early defeats, was the penalty incurred from the absence of men trained in the skills of intelligence gathering. Early intelligence officers had had to develop their own sources and agents from the people whom they chanced to discover in their area. Although these local men might produce admirable information, unless they had a degree of training or experience which enabled them to realise what subjects were of particular significance and, more important, how to report their information in a form understood by the military commander, the result was often a waste of effort and lives. To solve these problems and achieve a measure of continuity, certain colonial units who had shown themselves to be adept at this sort of work, were eventually officially designated 'Adjuncts to the Intelligence Department' and thereafter were continually employed under the direction of Intelligence Staffs. Foremost amongst these were Rimington's Tigers and the successors of Murray's Corps of Guides. Initially, Major Altham called all these men and units connected with intelligence the 'Local Intelligence Organization' but by July 1900 this rather ad hoc grouping had developed into a recognised part of the Army and was called the Field Intelligence Department (F.I.D.). The man primarily responsible for this new concept was Colonel G.F.R. Henderson.

In 1897 Colonel Henderson in his definitive book on Stonewall Jackson had highlighted the exploits and capabilities of locally formed scout units:

> On outpost and on patrol, in seeking information and in counteracting the uses of the enemy, the keen intelligence of the educated Volunteers was of the utmost value. History has hitherto overlooked the achievements of the 'scouts' whose names so seldom occur in the official records, but whose doing was unsurpassed and whose services were of vast importance. In the Army of Northern Virginia every commanding general had his own party of scouts whose business it was to hear everything, to visit the base of operations, to inspect the lines of communication and to note the condition and the temper of the hostile troops. Attracted by a pure love of adventure their private soldiers did exactly the same work as did the English Intelligence Officers in the Peninsula – more admirable material for the service of intelligence could not possibly have been found, they were acquainted with every country lane and woodland track. They had friends in every village and they knew the names of every farmer. The night was no hindrance to them, they knew the depth and direction of every ford and could predict the effect of weather on stream and track.

Having thus studied and described the characteristics of scout units only three years before, it is not surprising that Colonel Henderson took a great interest in the development of similar units in South Africa. It was this interest, plus the fact that he had been appointed Head of Intelligence direct from the post of instructor at the Staff College and so was fully conversant with staff procedures, helped in the formation and rapid expansion of the Field Intelligence Department. The Field Intelligence Department was to become the first blending into one army organization, of a headquarters intelligence staff, field intelligence officers, and units whose primary role was to gain intelligence.

In July 1900 Colonel Hume, now called Director of Military Intelligence (South Africa) continued George Henderson's good work and wrote a paper describing the progress of a new Field Intelligence Department; he also made recommendations for its future. He explained that at the beginning of the war no formation below division was established to include an Intelligence Officer and even divisions were often without a man in post. He now recommended that all columns regardless of their size should have one – 'It is most essential that in campaigns such as this, every unit which may have to move independently should possess a staff officer for intelligence duties. This is recognised in India, where an Intelligence Officer is allowed for each mixed brigade.' An equally momentous point made in his paper was that these Intelligence Officers should be allocated various grades of assistants to help them, i.e. Interpreters, First and Second Class Scouts, Guides and Native Scouts. The Interpreters were to be selected from 'Well educated men' and given honorary ranks. First Class Scouts were to be recruited to accompany different headquarters but were to act on the orders of the Director of Military Intelligence, whilst Second Class Scouts could be used by unit commanders and were to be 'Intelligence men, good riders, with an eye for the country.' Colonel Hume also urged that pre-planning was essential to ensure the early provision of interpreters:

> Such men cannot be obtained on the spur of the moment, the names and addresses of any willing to serve with a British force should therefore be registered in peace time. The terms of engagement must be a private arrangement with each man, and should be of a liberal value. These men would be used for penetrating the enemy's lines, destroying railways etc.' Colonel Hume also covered another important aspect of intelligence when he explained that there existed the requirement for a military counter-intelligence unit. 'Detective work in connection with rebels although essentially for the Civil Authorities, is for obvious

reasons, necessary to be concluded by the Military Authorities and therefore by the Field Intelligence Department.' He concluded, 'Press censorship and the reading of private mail should be affiliated with the Field Intelligence Department as should the Topographical Department.

This document marks a watershed in the story of British Military Intelligence. It set out formally, for the first time, the requirement for an establishment of Intelligence Officers deployed at all levels who were to be co-ordinated and controlled from a central headquarters. It asked that Intelligence Officers should be allotted specialised staffs to help them and above all it gave these officers executive control over intelligence gathering units. It recognised the advantages of having operational intelligence and counter-intelligence duties organised by the same unit and pointed out that the preparation and training of those concerned with intelligence should be started in peacetime.

Revolutionary proposals indeed, written in the light of sad experience, but as likely to be filed away and forgotten as were the majority of other reports which came from a rapidly reducing army in South Africa. But suddenly, a new factor emerged. The Boer army obstinately refused to accept that they had lost the war. Inspired by their elusive leader Christian de Wet, they had discovered a new and far more rewarding way to continue their fight against the British – commando raids.

A new phase of the war developed in which the Boers achieved great success by launching a myriad of attacks against extended British supply lines. Stores dumps, depots, ration convoys and railway stations, all were quietly pounced upon and destroyed, but only when the commandos had a superiority in numbers and the clear advantage of surprise. Their units were widely dispersed, moved swiftly and continually changed in size. British casualties began to rise and several Generals lost their reputations by being caught unawares and routed. It soon became clear that the only way to beat these pestilent commandos was by combining good intelligence with swift retaliatory action. It was in this atmosphere of defeat, humiliation and exasperation that the proposals made by Colonel Hume to improve the intelligence organization were extracted by those in authority, examined and then implemented.

CHAPTER SEVENTEEN

The Intelligence Corps

*B*y the end of 1901 the British Army had more intelligence officers than ever before in its history. Their number had increased from 10 in July 1899 to an eventual total of 132 officers, of whom 74 were gazetted staff officers, 2,321 white soldiers and a host of native scouts. The Director of Military Intelligence (South Africa) had established his Headquarters in Pretoria and had divided the country into four districts, Transvaal, Orange Free State, Cape Colony and Kimberley. Each district had a Deputy Assistant Adjutant General (Intelligence) and was divided into sub-districts each having a Staff Intelligence Officer. Every column, regardless of size, also had an intelligence officer, and when a column came near a Sub-District Headquarters these intelligence officers would meet and exchange information.

But it proved an easier task to decide on the necessary intelligence organization than to provide sufficient men of the right calibre to fill the posts. There were no officers trained in intelligence procedures and so regimental officers who showed a flair for languages, scouting, or who just happened to be 'spare' at the appropriate moment were arbitrarily selected. One of these young regimental officers, plucked abruptly from his routine life to become an Intelligence Officer, was Captain J.F.C. Fuller, later General Fuller the celebrated Royal Tank Corps Historian. He reported to headquarters and received short sharp orders – 'Find the enemy, report his whereabouts and keep him under observation.' 'What is my area?' Fuller had asked 'Oh roughly between the railway and the Vet River' (some 4,000 square miles) he was told, and then given a 'Staff of two European agents and seventy Kaffir scouts to get on with it.' Another man who found himself in an intelligence post was the naval officer who had accompanied Count Gleichen on his snipe shooting/spying tour of Algeria. He was appointed Deputy Assistant Adjutant General (Intelligence) in Bloemfontein and was also confused as to his duties:

I found that the intelligence officer was looked upon as a sort of handy man, expected to undertake odd jobs of every description. In Kitchener's small army, which had conquered the Sudan, Staff

Officers had exchanged duties constantly, and Kitchener did much of his own staff work. The precedent was followed, and intelligence officers did so much of other people's work that they had little time for their own. I soon found myself employed as a sort of mayor of an occupied town, where I had to arrange for all police duties, for the baking of bread and for pacifying old Boer women who complained that they were running short of matches. I was a requisitioner of sheep and responsible for the custody of hundreds of prisoners, their arms, horses and saddlery, this all in addition to the responsible work of locating the enemy, providing maps, guides and interpreters and all the usual matters which come within the scope of the intelligence officer. I had no office equipment whatever, and no staff.

About this time Army Headquarters published an order to all column commanders explaining that 'Column Intelligence Officers should be concerned with the enemy, and that the herding of cattle was not an intelligence duty.' One new Brigade Intelligence Officer did receive a short course of instruction from his Brigadier:

Brigadier: 'Do you know anything about Staff work?'

New Intelligence Officer: Nothing, Sir.

Brigadier: So much the better; you will have a mind ripe for tuition. Now I will give you a lesson. You have two pockets in your tunic. The right pocket will be the receptacle for 'business' telegrams, the left one for 'bunkum'.

In the next forty-eight hours, of the one hundred and four telegrams given to the new Intelligence Officer, ninety-seven went to the 'bunkum' pocket and only seven were classed as worthy of action. The officer wrote later 'It is superfluous to mention that the whole of the messages sent by the local Intelligence Departments were dismissed as 'bunkum', often without perusal. As the Brigadier remarked; 'I suppose that the poor fellows have to justify their existence as members of the great brain system of the army. The only means by which they come into prominence is by squandering public money and they only hurt those who take their information seriously.' The Brigadier had concluded his 'Course of instruction' by turning to his new aide and stating 'Look here, Mr. Intelligence, you have got to form an Intelligence Department tonight. You had better set about it, at once.' The young man had then walked sadly into the Veldt:

It was too dark to see his face; but there was that something in his attitude that betrayed the feeling of utter hopelessness which possessed him. It is in just such an attitude that the schoolmaster detects young Smith's failure to prepare his homework before that youth has hazarded a single word. The Intelligence Officer had been ordered to raise an Intelligence Department for the Brigade and, trained in the stern school of army discipline, he had no choice but to obey. With this end in view he left the precincts of the station. Then, the absolute impossibility of the situation dawned upon him. Not a soul was in sight, and even if there had been, though the powers in the press-gang officer were invested in him, he did not know a word of the Kaffir tongues. He stood upon the fringe of the gaunt Karoo. On either hand stretched a waste of lone prairie – a solitude of gathering night.'

The sad experience of this young man, as described by the officer himself, illustrates the predicament of many other officers who suddenly found themselves designated Intelligence Officers. They represent the product of three hundred years lack of preparation and failure to provide intelligence training in peacetime. Small wonder that given this haphazard method of selection and such complete lack of experience, commanders tended to have little faith in the official intelligence assessments. Although the intelligence service received more money in the first two years of the twentieth century than at any time since Mr. Thurloe's regime, senior officers remained extremely critical of the service provided.

In contrast to this and perhaps as a result of it, when someone was discovered who did manage to provide accurate and reliable information he was treated with an almost exaggerated respect and often won an international reputation. One such was the American scout, Frederick Russell Burnham. Burnham was born in a frontier hamlet on the edge of the Indian Reserve of Minnesota. As a child he had been saved by his mother from New Ulm when the town had been burnt and the residents massacred by Red Cloud and his braves. By the age of thirteen he had begun a life of scouting in which he fought Apaches, Mexican bandits, horse thieves and rustlers. In 1893 he had gone to South Africa to look for gold and had become involved in the Matabele War. He had been scout to a party of thirty-five when they had been surrounded by a large force of natives and was ordered by the commander to escape and fetch reinforcements. After an epic ride he had reached the main force, only to discover that they too had been surrounded. Six weeks later when they managed to get back to the site, the bodies of the patrol were found lying in a circle, each shot many times. A son of the Matabele King who had witnessed their massacre told how the last five men having run out of ammunition, had stood up singing 'God save the Queen'. For his part in this campaign Burnham received a gold watch and, at the suggestion of Cecil Rhodes, a tract of land of three hundred acres.

In 1896 the Matabele had risen again and inspired by a new leader gathered secretly to destroy Bulawayo. At that time Lieutenant Colonel Baden-Powell was Chief of Staff to General Carrington when late in the evening on 5 June, two excited horsemen had galloped furiously up, dismounted and rushed into his office. One of these was Frederick Burnham who had been out on patrol and had discovered a large Impi encampment only three miles away. Baden-Powell hastily gathered two hundred mounted men and in the early hours formed them into cavalry line and led a charge straight into the Matabele camp. Two hundred natives were killed. Baden-Powell was surprised at the blood-thirsty rage with which some of his men wielded their weapons but he had not seen, as they had done, the mutilated bodies of European men, women and children left behind after a merciless Matabele attack on some isolated farm.

One evening in January 1900, as Lord Roberts was in the Bay of Biscay sailing to command in South Africa, talk on the future campaign turned on the need for scouts, and Sir Frederick Carrington who had commanded Burnham gave instances of his marvellous powers as a 'tracker'. 'He is the best scout we have ever had in South Africa.' Carrington declared. 'Then why don't we get him back?', asked Roberts. Burnham was at this time searching for gold in the Klondyke so, at the next port a cable was sent to Alaska. The telegram was delivered to Skagway by steamer, where Burnham, when asking for his mail, received it. The boat was scheduled to leave again in two and a half hours and within this time Burnham had packed his belongings and was on his way to Capetown. After his arrival he joined the Field Intelligence Department and was pleased to discover that its members were often called upon to take part in expeditions deep behind enemy lines either to gain information or disrupt communications. Burnham enjoyed doing this and during the advance north spent most of his time inside the Boer areas. Twice he was captured, but twice he escaped. The first time he had to live for two days in an anthill surrounded by a Boer laager, the next time while reconnoitring alone in the morning mist he came upon a Boer ambush lying in wait for an approaching British convoy. As the Boers were all around him, he had to choose between abandoning the column to its fate or, exposing himself to capture. He decided to stand up and wave his red handkerchief in warning, but the column, which had no advance guard, did not see him. The Boers did, and he was caught. In the ensuing fight, Burnham pretended to be wounded, bound his leg with a swaddle of bandages and groaning dreadfully, got himself placed in the car with the wounded. Later that night, when the cart driver jumped out to belabour a span of oxen, he rolled out and escaped. After four days on the veldt, with only one biscuit to eat he regained British Lines.

On 2 June 1901, while trying to blow up the line between Pretoria and Delagoa, Burnham was surprised by a Boer party and throwing himself Indian fashion across his horse galloped away. But a bullet hit the animal that, without faltering in its stride, crashed dead to the ground crushing Burnham beneath it. He lay unconscious and alone for twenty-four hours, then dragged himself painfully to the railway and successfully placed his charge. The explosion brought the Boers to the scene and he was forced to crawl on his hands and knees for two days and nights before being picked up by a British patrol. His injuries were such that he was evacuated to England, where he was made a Major in the British Army. He later dined with Queen Victoria and after her death, was presented with the Distinguished Service Order by King Edward, a rare distinction for an American.

Another well known Intelligence Officer and scout, was Aubrey Woolls-Sampson. Brought up in South Africa, Sampson had, by 1899, thirty years of experience in fighting. He had been a scout for Lord Wolseley in Zululand where he had been sent as an emissary of peace, together with another famous scout, G. C. Dennison to King Sekukuni. But King Sekukuni had been rather unsympathetic to peace talks and before releasing them had them bound to stakes and allowed his native women with 'Sharp thorns and thin pointed sticks to have their way with them.' In the Boer War Dennison raised his own unit called Dennison's Scouts, was promoted major and was also awarded the Distinguished Service Order.

Early in 1899 Woolls-Sampson, by then a prosperous farmer and growing anxious at the belligerency of the Boers, had approached the senior British General in South Africa, Sir William Butler, with the suggestion that a militia regiment of Imperial Light Horse be formed in case of war. The General, following a very clear directive from London had refused point blank. 'England is not preparing for war, even if the Transvaal is', was his exact reply. So it was left to Sampson himself, using his own initiative and private means, to organise a volunteer group of young South Africans who could ride.In the first battle at Elandslaagte, Woolls-Sampson led a squadron of the Imperial Light Horse into action and had fallen in the final charge with an explosive bullet in his thigh. He had been carried back to Ladysmith and on its relief returned to the regiment as Commanding Officer. But Sampson, although recognised by Roberts, Kitchener and others as an 'Exceptional intelligence officer', was not so successful as a commander. Having found the Boers, his handling of troops in battle was a little too impetuous and after several actions, which resulted in heavy casualties for the Imperial Light Horse, he left the regiment to form his own small scout unit. General Blood had described his activities at this time:

> I first met him at Machadadorp Station, in March 1901, when I was having my first look at the District. Woolls-Sampson was somehow at a loose end and joined me to help in the Intelligence Branch of the Staff, which I found to be in a very elementary state. He had a sort of 'following' of six or seven natives, who made themselves very useful on many occasions – especially as guides. He himself was of the greatest assistance to me in many ways, as of course he knew the country thoroughly, while I knew very little about it.

Later Woolls-Sampson was recruited into the Field Intelligence Department and joined the column commanded by Bruce Hamilton. The two men respected and trusted each other and achieved extremely good results.

> 'I first met Woolls-Sampson', Hamilton has written, 'when I took over Benson's command after Bakenlaagte and soon realised that I had got an exceptional Intelligence Officer. He had a collection of specially chosen native scouts, mounted on chosen ponies and had great knowledge and experience of the native character. I don't think anyone else could have got them to work so reliably as he did. As we moved about the country, with the help of those boys he found native agents in all the villages, had long talks with them, explaining what he wanted to know, gaining their confidence, and promising them rewards and safety. When we halted at a camp he would send off his boys at sundown, each with two horses and each told to go to the agent in a certain village, not too far away for them to be able to visit it and return after daylight. Thus next day he would have heard of any Boer commandos within a radius of about twenty-five miles from our camp. He would spend hours talking to his boys on their return, encouraging them, cross-questioning them, and checking what they told him. It was dangerous work for the boys, as the Boers killed any they caught and we found their bodies left as a warning on the veldt. It was due to Woolls-Sampson's unceasing efforts to take care of his boys and gain confidence, and to his great attention to detail that this information was so wonderfully

accurate. He had an extraordinary sense of what the Boers were likely to do, and over and over again, after marching all night, we would find them at dawn almost exactly where he expected.

But apart from these well-known names, the main body of the field intelligence officers, scouts and guides came from locally raised colonial units. In December 1899 when Murray had joined Buller, the demand for scout units had increased so rapidly that it was decided to disband the Corps of Guides and use the men to form the nucleus of other units. Major Menne took one squadron and formed Menne's Scouts, another followed Major Bethune and became Bethune's Mounted Infantry. Six went off under the Squadron Sergeant Major, F. Von Steinaecker, on a daring raid through Zululand and Swaziland to the Transvaal. Steinaecker's unit which eventually totalled 450 men served the whole war in the unhealthy regions along the eastern frontiers and as well as many casualties caused by enemy action, lost a dozen men eaten by lions and crocodiles. In the official report of the F.I.D. at the end of the war Colonel Henderson speaks highly of the 'Native Police belonging to the Intelligence Department' who were attached to Steinaecker's Horse.

As the war progressed still more scout units were required and eventually certain men who had distinguished themselves in battle or shown a flair for this type of work were asked to raise additional units. One such was the dark handsome Irishman, Captain D.P. Driscoll. Driscoll had been in business in Burma when the war started and held a commission in the Upper Burman Volunteer Rifles. When he heard of the initial British defeats, he had abandoned his private interests and 'Overcoming a yard of red tape' arrived in Capetown where he became an orderly to General Gatacre. He had then moved to the Border Mounted Rifles and in the attack on Labuschagne's Nek, achieved fame by being the first man to reach the Boer position. After this he was commissioned and asked to raise a unit of fifty scouts. By the end of the war Driscoll was a Major, had been awarded the Distinguished Service Order and commanded nearly three hundred men of his own Driscoll's Horse.

Other men who raised scout units in their own names included Damant, who took over Rimington's Tigers when Rimington went back to command his own regiment, Captain Beddy, Captain Warwick and the gallant Captain The Honourable R. de Montmorency who had been Adjutant of the 21st Lancers in the Sudan when he had won the Victoria Cross. Montmorency himself was killed in 1900 – witnesses reporting that 'He fired eleven shots after receiving his mortal wound'.

But although a few regular British Officers did succeed in this type of command it is interesting that the majority of the men who commanded successful scout units came from younger countries. Canadians, Australians and New Zealanders particularly showing an ability to match the Boer in stalking and 'slimness', Captain Doyle of the New South Wales Bushmen and Major Arthur Gat-Howard, an American commanding the celebrated Canadian Scouts being two who were quite outstanding in this respect. The Canadian Scouts, which was one of the many units raised in the Empire to go to South Africa, was composed mainly of 'ex-Mounties' (North West Mounted Policemen) and prairie cowboys. They were the successors to a long line of scout units raised in Canada throughout the nineteenth century. The last time being only fifteen years before, when the French Canadian, Louis Riel, had returned from exile in the United States and caused such unrest, particularly amongst the Indians, that the Minister of Militia and Defence had ordered the Canadian Army to mobilise and restore law and order. At that time the wild rugged regions of Western Canada were being surveyed by a hardy group of men known as the Dominion Land Surveyors. These men on hearing of the impending fight had volunteered to serve 'en block' and because of their local knowledge were known under various titles including the 'Intelligence Corps (Militia Order)', the 'Intelligence Mounted Corps' and the 'Land Surveyor Scouts'. They had remained embodied until the final battle at Lake Loon, when the rebellious Chief Big Bear was defeated, and had then been disbanded.

The need to raises specialist intelligence gathering units was not however confined to the Allied side. It took only one defeat for the Boers to appreciate that they also required such men. On 24 February 1900 Cronje was besieged in the Paardeberg Drift, for the first time the British Army had trapped a large force of Boers into a confined space and Kitchener, fired with the savage combination of revenge and personal ambition, was pressing home his attacks with a steadfast disregard for his own casualties. De Wet who commanded the nearest relief force was most anxious to let Cronje know that if he could break out at night, then his retreat would be covered by a diversionary attack. But the rain poured down and the Boer's signal heliograph could not be seen, so a young commando called Daniel Johnnos Stephanus Theron volunteered to carry the message. Before the war Daniel Theron had been an enthusiastic member of the Radical Young Afrikander Party and had achieved a degree of notoriety by thrashing a correspondent of The Times with a horsewhip because he had disagreed with his reporting. Now, covered by a thunderstorm, Theron crawled through the British Lines, swam the dangerously swollen river and reached Cronje. But the encircled Boers were in no mood to continue the fight and so Theron, once more alone, braved the night and slipped back through the pickets to reach de Wet. Here he sent the following report to President Kruger:

> Your Honour, the night before last I took a report to General Cronje, and got back safely again last night, thanks to God's guidance. The English piquets are stationed around the laager about ten paces apart, and consequently it took a long time and was difficult to creep through them. My knees are bleeding. The state of affairs in the laager is indescribably miserable and dreadful. I went to propose to General Cronje a plan to break through – how, where and when. He agrees with it, but most of his officers and men are unwilling. The General, I, and a few others went about among the men and did everything to encourage them and to make them willing, but half of them are so disheartened and depressed that they really no longer mind falling into the enemy's hands. Very many of them say straight out that they are not going to leave the trenches, but are going to surrender to the English as soon as General Cronje makes a dash out. President, I do not send you this telegram to depress you, but to let you know exactly how things are there, so that you may not have a false impression about the peril of our position.

Cronje did surrender three days later and Daniel Theron, bitter at the lack of information available to the commando leaders submitted a proposal to a member of the Executive Committee, Mr. A. D. W. Wolmarans, recommending the establishment of an Intelligence Corps 'Composed of high calibre scouts with authority to go where and how they wished in order to gain intelligence.' The Boer Government were already worried by lack of intelligence and Mr. Woolmarans was an influential man, so it was, on 3 March 1900 that President Kruger authorised the raising of 'Theron's Verkenners Korps' (Theron's Intelligence Corps). At the same time Theron was made a field cornet and became a members of the Council of War. Unlike most other Boer units, the Afrikaans Intelligence Corps was based strictly on a military system. Theron was commanding officer and he alone could appoint or discharge officers. He personally submitted every member of the Corps to a severe test of courage and initiative before accepting them, and wisely did not restrict his selection to Boers. The Corps consisted of Dutchmen, Germans, Frenchmen, Russians plus a Greek, a Bulgar, a Levantine, a Turk and an Algerian Arab.

The activities of Daniel Theron and his cosmopolitan Intelligence Corps soon became renowned on both sides and in British Intelligence summaries he earned the title 'Ubiquitous'. During the retreat to

Pretoria, Botha often gave him the responsibility of being the 'Rear-rearguard' and, as the Burghers withdrew, some of Theron's men remained in Bloemfontein, Johannesburg and Pretoria to act as agents. At one stage Theron is alleged to have worn the uniform of a British Major and accompanied by a suitably dressed orderly 'Visited' British forward positions. In July 1900 when de Wet and Prinsloo were 'pinned' against the Basutoland border, Prinsloo surrendered but de Wet successfully broke out taking with him some 2,600 of his best fighters. Included in this number were the two hundred strong Intelligence Corps now using all their skills to keep de Wet out of the clutches of the pursuing columns. Eventually however, de Wet was forced to disperse his commando and he sent Theron and his Corps to the Kleritsdory area to create diversions and attack lines of communication. On 1 October Theron derailed a train carrying the 2nd Battalion Coldstream Guards, but on 5 October, when, leading three of his Intelligence Scouts (called as such in the Official History of the South African War) he was endeavouring to discover the position of Commandant Liebenburg at Gatsrand, they were surrounded and the party all killed. The Boer leader Deneys Reitz who met him just before his death has described him as a 'Light wiry man of about twenty six, dark complexioned and short tempered, and although I never once saw him really affable, his men swore by him for his courage and gift of leadership.' British contemporary accounts, biased as they were, also spoke highly of the 'Redoubtable and intrepid Theron, a man of great dash and cunning.'

After his funeral at which the lamentation of Saul was read (11 Samuel 1:19-27), a cousin of Theron was chosen to command the Intelligence Corps. But he did not possess the same qualities as Daniel and within a short time the members were scattered amongst other commandos. By December 1900 the Boer Intelligence Corps had ceased to exist. It had had a brief, but highly successful existence and its title was now known throughout South Africa. For a hundred years the British Army had been calling the specialist units who gathered field intelligence, intelligence corps, now following the precedent established by the Canadians and Boers the British also, at last, began to think in terms of an Intelligence Corps.

CHAPTER EIGHTEEN

The Growth of Professionalism

hroughout 1900 and 1901 the Field Intelligence Department in South Africa settled down as an organization embracing all aspects of intelligence acquisition, analysis and dissemination.. Included in this organization were those units and individuals employed exclusively on the gathering of military intelligence and who, although not designated officially as such, were often referred to by commanders and staff, as the 'Intelligence Corps'. One to do so was Major Gleichen who had recovered from the wound received at Magersfontein and had been posted as a staff officer to Graspan. The situation he found there appeared a little precarious:

> The cavalry were on the move to relieve Kimberley, and as Graspan was now denuded of everybody except myself and about twenty five men, and as we might quite well be attacked by a roving commando, I drew up a defence scheme for my tiny command and awaited the arrival of the Intelligence Corps that I had been promised. I knew there were going to be Basutos – excellent scouts by nature – and had pictured to myself a number of swarthy brown men dressed in blankets and riding small ponies. All thirsting for a fight with Brother Boer. What was my surprise then, to receive a small band of extremely polite natives, attired in smart straw hats and tweed knickerbockers suits, the leader of whom took off his hat, introduced himself as Mr. Appollo and addressed me in excellent English. I liked the looks of them very much, and distributed them to patrol and lie out at night; but I was rather sorry for them. For, by mutual consent between ourselves and the Boers, no coloured man was allowed to carry arms, though there was a tacit but unexpressed understanding that there would be no objection to using them as scouts or spies.

This use of natives in the Field Intelligence Department gradually increased as the war progressed and as an inducement they eventually received higher pay than a major in the British Army. It was found that an 'Educated' Kaffir could go through Boer lines carrying dispatches, mix with Boers in their camps, hear the gossip then return to the British lines. But 'Many raw natives paid the penalty of their simplicity by being made more raw at the wagon wheel'. The Kaffir would know the country better than his more sophisticated countrymen and could crawl through the long grass to the edge of a Boer camp and back again, but when it came to standing erect and walking boldly among the burghers, they failed. The abrupt question, 'Who are ye? Where d'ye come from?' were enough to shatter their confidence and reveal their guilt.

In spite of Gleichen's statement and an assurance by the Secretary of State for War in the House of Commons that 'Not one armed Kaffir was employed in the country' as the war progressed, natives in the Field Intelligence Department were given arms. The nature of the guerrilla fighting, the large open spaces and the limited numbers of British troops available, forced a greater dependence on the use of these men. At first, the unarmed scouts if captured, were whipped, or maltreated by being dragged along behind a galloping horse, but then the powerful emotions of the Boer farmers towards any native he distrusts, became more violent. One Boer leader wrote the following compassionate letter to the 'Commander in Chief of the British Forces in Morresburh':

> Sir,
>
> We have captured several of your so called coloured scouts, who can be very easily shot by our men, but we have never in memory, shot men innocent of the present state of affairs. We beg your Worship kindly not to use the above-mentioned coloured scouts, but send men armed and ready for resistance. We consider it a disgrace that Her Majesty's Officers use unarmed men who are quite innocent of what they are doing. In future we will be obliged to shoot the so-called scouts, of which fact I trust you will make them aware. This time the scouts will be released unmolested, but this is the last warning.

The use of natives continued however, and when they were indeed shot by the Boers, it was decided to arm them in self-defence. But the wisdom of this decision is still debatable, although it raised the morale of the Field Intelligence Department and native scouts did obtain information, the policy resulted in an almost unconscious strengthening of resolve among the Boer forces. If many burghers felt lukewarm about the nationalistic cause of Kruger, they all felt very strongly about the threat of arming the 'coloureds'. A quick death was the kindest treatment any armed native caught by the Boers could hope for. Many of the atrocity stories that circulated in Britain at the time, stem from incidents involving the capture of armed scouts.

But the Boers could be equally as ruthless to any of their own white compatriots suspected of aiding the British. One alleged collaborator was caught and tied to his wagon wheel, as described by an eyewitness:

> Six burghers looked to the magazines of their Mausers, stepped off twenty paced, took deliberate aim and fired slowly one after the other. Andries shrieked at every shot, not because they hit him, but from surprise and fear. The bullets all struck the ground within a few inches of his feet. The Commandant shouted and waved his sjambok threateningly at the firing party. Shoot straight at his treacherous heart', he yelled. Again the firing began. The first bullet sent up a little clouds of red dust at Andries feet, the second struck his left foot. He did not shriek, but stooped his head and looked at the boot with stupid surprise. Then came a cry: 'My leg! My leg.' Eight shots followed in slow succession, each announced by a howl of remonstrance rather than of pain, blood was oozing from the trouser legs, a bullet had been placed accurately in each instep, and three in each shin bone, finishing with the knee-cap. When the shooting began Andries was a well set-up vigorous man of forty-five. A week later he crawled into Klerksdorp an old man of seventy and a cripple for life.

On the British side rough justice could also be meted out, as the Commanding Officer of a colonial unit has written:

> Double agents were also a problem. Did I ever tell you about the Boer spies? Well, in the early days of recruiting in Natal several Dutch agents were enlisted. They were paid by the Transvaal to enlist in British corps. When we got to Mooi River one of these men was discovered and a corporal came to me and volunteered some advice. 'You prove him a spy Colonel, and then turn him over to us: You won't have any more spies after that.' I had the suspect up. There was not a shadow of doubt about his identity, so I just said to the sergeant major 'this man is your property, the fair name of the Corps is in your keeping and there's a convenient donga over there!' I never saw the man again, nor did I ask what happened to him, but this I do know, that on the self-same evening five men came to me and asked to be allowed to resign. They came with faces as white as the coat of a mare. 'Yes', I said as I looked at them 'you may go. You leave for the good of all concerned, yourselves included.' And since that day I was never troubled by the enlisting of Dutch Agents.

But in the 'occupied areas' spies and informers abounded. One such agent was caught in January 1902 after the following letter was received from a Captain in the Field Intelligence Department. 'Yesterday about midday I met a man in full British uniform wearing six medal ribbons, who I knew before as Count von Danckberg. In 1894 I prosecuted Danckberg at Fauresmith, for the crime of diamond theft and he was imprisoned with hard labour for two years and paid a fine of £500. This morning I saw the same man in the uniform of a Lieutenant in the Imperial Yeomanry and I believe he is at present staying in No. 16 room, Grand Hotel, Capetown.' Danckberg was arrested but not executed. As the war became more savage and the concentration camps came into operation, the Field Intelligence Department not only had to deal with genuine agents, like Theron's men but virtually every Boer had to be regarded as suspect. Both in Johannesburg and Pretoria plots were discovered to kill British commanders and raise revolt. In Johannesburg Mr. Broeksma, an ex-public prosecutor in Kruger's Government was arrested for breaking his oath of neutrality and committing high treason. Letters found in his house contained anti-British propaganda together with lists of Boers serving with the British who Broeksma recommended should be 'buried alive'. Other conspirators planned to capture the garrison's officers when they were attending a race meeting and hand them over to a nearby commando.

In Pretoria a surrendered German, Hans Cordua, who had taken the oath of allegiance to the Crown, plotted to set fire to a number of houses in the west of the town and then, when attention was diverted, kidnap Lord Roberts. He had arranged that two hundred and fifty other 'Ex rebels' who had also been issued with British passes, were then to attack the police barracks and seize the 7,000 rifles stored there. All these plots were discovered in time and both Broeksma and Cordua were executed by firing squads, but the realization of what could have happened if the headquarters' staffs had been suddenly assassinated or kidnapped, provided a great stimulus to the counter intelligence aspect of the Field Intelligence Department. Members of the Department were encouraged to recruit their own agents and, as a letter from the Intelligence Officer with Colonel Haig to the Director of Military Intelligence reveals, at least one had achieved the greatest prize of all, a covert reliable source well placed in the enemies' headquarters.

> When in Calvinia a few days ago I had a long talk to Lieutenant Vice of Rimington's Guides and it is clear that he has one source which is particularly well posted in General Smut's plans and intentions. In order that those receiving Lieutenant Vice's telegrams may know when any news from this particular source is being sent I arranged with him to preface such intelligence reports with the words 'Mallett reports that…'

Lieutenant Vice was naturally extremely sensitive about his 'source' and when sending the next 'Mallet Report' emphasised that 'As this information is known only to Smuts and his Commandants, please do not give it as a report from Calvinia District. Agent is already suspect and should this be known he will be immediately shot.' Another agent in the Portuguese Colony of Mozambique managed to send a continual stream of messages to the Field Intelligence Department, but these became renowned for their alarming nature rather then their accuracy – 'A reliable source reports that Lord Roberts' life is threatened and no sum of money will be considered too high a price for his assassination; the source says powerful electric mines have been laid in the Johannesburg gold mines and that you should beware of cyanide in the dams along the Rand.'

The standard of intelligence reporting was however rising. In 1899 Major Altham in Ladysmith submitted a report each evening to General White. Initially it was a collection of facts gathered from various sources, without any comment, as this typical extract shows:

NEWS WHENCE RECEIVED	INTELLIGENCE
Intelligence Agent	3,000 Boers at Horgate.
	Buffel River has risen six inches.
Press telegram intercepted at Maritzburg	Mafeking is cut off by 3,000 Boers who have seized railway.
Intelligence Officer at Maritzburg	80 Boers with packs crossed Caffens Drift, our column fell back.
Officer Commanding 5 Lancers	All quiet.
Press Censor	Charter Capetown have arranged steam tug to carry mail to Boers.
Zulu Scouts	Commandos at Nelthorpe.
Balloon on Waggon Hill	Enemy cooking fires observed at Bulwhana
'JOE' Native Deserter	Kruger at Onderbrook
Major Murray	Reconnoitred Rifle Ridge with 10
Deputy Assistant Adjutant General, Field Intelligence Department	men from Corps of Guides.

Some of the reports were smuggled out to General Buller who in turn passed them back to Army Headquarters – 'General Buller directs me to send you the following message received from Ladysmith which he considers interesting as Ladysmith news is generally reliable. Begins

Ladysmith 29 January: Native reports four Field Cornets killed in fighting last week. Also your artillery broke seven guns and caused 1,000 Boer casualties.' Army Headquarters were however not particularly impressed with this particular intelligence 'tit-bit' and replied, 'More care should be taken, because people are becoming uneasy and beginning to doubt the accuracy of official reports.

The collating and analysis of intelligence reports was however gradually improving. The keeping of well-designed records is the most tedious, and often most unrewarding of all intelligence tasks and yet, it is unquestionably the most important. Just as an efficient police force can trace a criminal by reference to his habits and idiosyncrasies, so the intelligence officer can hazard a guess at his enemy's future intentions by an accurate knowledge of his habits and past actions. Without well-kept records an intelligence officer is no better than any other officer with similar experience; with records he has the potential to give his commander a unique service.

To help gain additional intelligence reports a multitude of other measures were also introduced. After Ladysmith, where captive balloons had been used successfully to gain better observation, they were issued to the intelligence officers of the various columns. Colonel Rawlinson, who went up in one to do a panorama, was hit 'in the bag' by a six-inch shell, but luckily sank only slowly to the ground and escaped with a severe shaking. Count Gleichen, when posted as intelligence officer to the 9th Division also received one, but was not over enthusiastic:

> Wishing to get some idea of the enemy's position, I went up in a balloon in the early morning of the day previous to the attack, but was not much the wiser for it. For the Boers had ensconced themselves under the high banks of the river and dug themselves in a narrow bottle-sectioned trenches among the trees and scrub so that there was remarkably little to see. Added to this was the disadvantage that the balloon was never still enough for one to get a compass-bearing for, being of a perfectly spherical shape it spun round on its cable, first one way and then the other till it almost made me feel sick. A few bullets in my direction added interest to the view, but they only pierced the balloon and did no practical damage.

Boer newspapers were now translated, and orders that all captured documents should be sent to the intelligence officers resulted in the establishment of translating cells in the Field Intelligence Department. Another unprecedented step forward, was the institution of a series of courses specially designed for intelligence officers. Here they were taught sketching, report writing and how to interrogate a prisoner to ensure that he was not 'over-interrogated' by the time he reached the Divisional Intelligence Staff. 1900 also saw the birth of a development in intelligence that was to produce such dramatic results in both the First and Second World Wars – signal intelligence. In 1900 small parties of signallers were sent out into the veldt to intercept Boer heliograph messages.

At the War Office in London, a Section 'H' was added to the Intelligence Division which took over responsibility for cable censorship and, in conjunction with Scotland Yard, the surveillance of suspected persons. The cable censoring proved most successful. In May 1901 the Afrikander Commander, General Botha, asked Kitchener for permission to hold a joint meeting with Smuts, de Wet and the Dutch Consul in Pretoria to discuss current peace proposals. This was agreed and after the meeting the Boers sent a long cipher message to President Kruger who was in Holland, explaining the terms. The message went via Aden where the British cable censor, who guessed that the cipher might come from a book, opened his dictionary – and broke the code. It showed that the Boer leaders in South Africa regarded their cause as hopeless and wanted peace. Kruger's reply was then intercepted, and revealed that he wanted the war to continue, 'As Europe felt the Boers were doing very well.' The Censor Section passed this, and other pieces of valuable intelligence secretly to Kitchener.

Like all field intelligence organizations the Field Intelligence Department had the problem of getting their information back to headquarters as quickly as possible, and to help solve this, on 1 September 1901, Lieutenant E. Abadie, 9th Lancers, was appointed to the Field Intelligence Department as Staff Officer (Pigeons). By February 1902, forty-two homing stations had been set up, and over 1,000 birds distributed to columns, individual scouts, and in some cases to local farmers living in occupied territory. This latter was a dangerous practice, as the birds were difficult to conceal and natives often reported their presence to the commandos. The staff of the Pigeon Service had their casualties; Lieutenant Wilson, formerly of the Cape Town Homing Society, was killed carrying birds in 1901, and Scout Grimes was killed carrying birds in 1902, two other scouts of the Cape Cycle Corps were captured taking pigeons to Colonel Doran's column and were stripped of their bicycles, birds, and boots and then released. A native scout sent out with three pigeons to learn the feeling of the Boers towards the current peace proposals, was also captured and released, but was first soundly sjamboked and his messengers eaten.

Difficulty was experienced in carrying the birds. Moving on horseback was found to upset them and the best way proved to be using baskets carried by the Cycle Corps. Scout Callister achieved great fame by 'cycling 120 miles gaining a point of vantage, lying 'perdu' for several days, and then releasing birds whenever he saw Boer activity.'Many birds were lost, both from hawks or being shot on the wing by Boers, but as several successful contacts had been made as a result of 'pigeon carried information' it was decided to expand the service. Homing societies in South Africa and Australia co-operated nobly, but when Lieutenant Abadie returned to England to obtain a fresh supply, he received a very mixed reception. The Prince of Wales donated his flock, but the publication 'Racing Pigeon' was 'Distinctly antagonistic' as their leading article on 23 April 1902 made clear:

> We publish a letter from Lieutenant Abadie, Superintendent of the Pigeon Intelligence of General French. This letter refers to the service that pigeons have rendered in the Transvaal, which is a matter for congratulation and we are pleased to note that the Admiralty is supplying 300 additional birds. With regard to the appeal to fanciers to contribute birds we have little or no patience. The country is not on the brink of ruin, more money is being continually voted to carry on the war, and if birds are really necessary and wanted, as Lieutenant Abadie states, the most reasonable course that suggests itself, is that they should be bought at fair valuation from fanciers, who, we think, would treat any agent appointed by the Government fairly and honestly, without any risk of pigeon scandals similar to the remount scandals. Does it not stand to reason that for such serious purposes as those for which these pigeons are required, only the very best birds are needed? With corn rising in price, with the Income Tax another penny in the pound and bread and other necessaries of life becoming dearer each day the war continues, combined with slackness of work, English fanciers will have difficulty enough in finding sufficient to pay the upkeep of their birds during the forthcoming season. Without wishing to be unpatriotic in any way, we must confess that we have little or no sympathy with Mr Abadie's appeal.

In spite of this 'righteous anger' from the Editor of the Racing Pigeon', more birds were donated, and at the end of the war Lieutenant Abadie received a Distinguished Service Order and Colonel David Henderson in his final report regretted the system had not been started earlier. He wrote: 'The excellent pigeon post arrangements reflected great credit on the Field Intelligence of Cape Colony.' The cost of the organization was later subjected to keen analysis and it was discovered that fifty birds cost £20. 12. 0d per loft per month, and that by the end of the war, as 1,600 messages had been carried, it came to two pounds ten shillings per flight.

David Henderson took command of the expanding Field Intelligence Department in February 1901. In this story of men who have influenced the development of British Military Intelligence David Henderson of the Argyll and Sutherland Highlanders stands out as a major figure. He had emerged from the siege of Ladysmith, not only with his reputation established as a sound intelligence officer, but also of being a brave and pugnacious fighter. During the siege, the Boers had brought up a 5-inch 'Long Tom' gun and a 4.7-inch howitzer, to shell and terrorise the town. They were placed 150 yards apart and protected by a mountain of sandbags, some thirty-one feet thick. As this made them impossible to destroy by shellfire, on the night 7 December a force of 650 men under General Hunter sallied out to destroy them. Henderson was selected to lead the attack, and together with eighteen men of the Natal Corps of Guides steered the party over two miles of rough scrub country, through the blackest of nights to reach the base of 'Gun Hill'. As they scaled the heights the Boer piquet had suddenly realised their presence and shouted – 'Shoot! Shoot! The Rooineks (Rednecks) are upon us!'. Fix bayonets – charge!' had come the answering cry, and with a rush the British force had swept over the position with Henderson still in the front, though wounded and bleeding heavily. The guns were destroyed, and the party had then returned exultantly to the encircled town.

After the relief of Ladysmith Henderson had been appointed Director of Military Intelligence (South Africa) and his great contribution to the Field Intelligence Department was to consolidate the framework of the existing centralised intelligence system. He, like Murray in the Peninsula, laid down the precise requirements of the intelligence staff, issued intelligence officers with a specimen report to ensure uniformity and ordered fixed times when these reports were to reach senior headquarters. Above all, he began to disseminate intelligence 'downwards' that is back to subordinate units. The reports included Boer order of battle charts, their weapon states, the condition of their morale, short and long term assessments of their probable courses of action plus personality lists of wanted men. These personality lists were divided into three categories, a black list describing known rebels, a grey list – those known to the disloyal and a light grey list – those whose loyalty was suspect. If possible a photograph was attached to each man's description. Press and letter censorship was also undertaken by the Field

Intelligence Department and a great deal of information obtained by reading the mail of Germans and other foreigners working for the Boers. The Boers also tried to extract intelligence from British mail. But once when de Wet set himself the task of reading sacks of captured letters he gave up in frustration commenting, 'I never realised how many love-sick women there were in Britain!'

Throughout the history of British Military Intelligence the sensitive problem of press censorship has always aroused very strong, but mixed feelings. By 1900 it had been accepted that there should be censorship and in each district one of the Deputy Assistant Adjutant Generals (Intelligence) was appointed 'Official Censor'. But what constituted an infringement of the law then, as now, was often the subject of most bitter debate. During the siege of Kimberley when Major O'Meara in his capacity of 'Intelligence Officer and Military Censor' classed two editorials of the Diamond Fields Advertiser as 'Extremely injurious to the interests of the Army and the defence of this town', the editor, in high dudgeon stopped printing completely.

In 1900 the censor's task was also made more difficult, as for the first time, the British lines were flooded with journalists from all over the world. Little restriction was placed on where these journalists went, but every effort was made to stop the flow of damaging information they produced. Unsuccessfully it would appear, as President Kruger subsequently admitted that he maintained his 'British Order of Battle' from the international press.

One of the most able at evading censorship was the 'Ex-cavalry officer' Winston Spencer Churchill. Of his visit to Rimington's Guides an officer wrote in his diary:

> Winston Churchill turned up to enliven us. There are several colonels and senior officers squatting about, and Churchill takes the opportunity of giving them a bit of his mind. He is much annoyed with the day's proceedings. He has been a good deal shot at so has the Duke, and so has the General. They have had to use their Mauser pistols. This sort of thing should not happen. Then where was French? Checked indeed! A pretty fine thing! And the Guards? Kindly tell him why the Guards were somewhere else? And Churchill, who has a face like a good-natured child, and looks about fourteen, eyes the old colonels, who fidget nervously round the fire like disturbed hens. He talks and argues incessantly, but very cleverly. Before he goes he dashes off a sketch of South Africa's future with a few words about farming and gold mining. He gives us a cup of hot cocoa all round, which he produces from nowhere, like a conjuring trick,

re-arranges our fire, tells us when the war will be over and strolls off, daring the old colonels with his eye to so much as look at him, to give the General his final instructions about tomorrow's action.'

A new use of the press was the sending to London, by the Boer Secret Service, of journalists to present the Boer case. One, Mr Statham, an Englishman who had lived for some years in the Transvaal was paid an 'Honorarium' and given a free hand to promote Boer interests. But Statham eventually revealed his purpose and newspaper editors learnt to recognise his style and stopped publishing his work. Dr. Leyda, the Boer Secretary of State and Head of Boer Intelligence then clandestinely 'Bought silence or even mild approval' from certain European journals, although after the war when asked about this he replied 'The papers I should have liked to buy I couldn't and those I could, were not worth it.'

When the war ended the standard of British Military Intelligence had reached an 'All-time' high. But it cannot be said that this had been achieved easily or naturally. The intelligence organization had been built up piece-meal to face various threats as they arose and to exploit different sources as they emerged. The overall impression is one of reluctant acceptance. The Intelligencers of the period did not grasp the opportunities for reform offered by the Commando Phase of the war with any great enthusiasm, it was rather that a continual lack of success forced improvements upon them.

The birth of the twentieth century British Army on the South African Veldt was a messy and premature affair and, although as General Fuller has written, it proved an 'Act of Providence' which gave Britain the time and stimulus to prepare for the First World War.

How did the intelligence lessons learnt so painfully in the Boer War help the British Army in August of 1914?

CHAPTER NINETEEN

The Planning Years

*W*hen we contemplate the perturbed state of the political world brought about, by the Anglo-Saxon race. When we note that the War in South Africa reveals, as a sudden flash of lightening illuminates a dark night, the hatred of Great Britain by all but the Anglo-Saxon people, then England as a world power supported solely by its fleet stands out in its proper perspective.' These were the words of Field Marshall Ritzenhofen at a lecture to six hundred officers of the Imperial Austro-Hungarian Army in November 1900.

On Major William Robertson's return to his post of Staff Captain in the Colonial Section, after a year in South Africa, the greatest worry in the War Office was not the Boer War conflict, still festering quietly, but the realization that it had absorbed the whole of the Regular Army and most of the Volunteer Army as well. 'When we speak of the critical military condition of England, we do not refer to that of the army engaged in South Africa,' Ritzenhofen had continued, 'But to the fact that, by this employment, England is all but denuded of troops.'

Ritzehofen suddenly made everyone aware that in the face of an intensely hostile, aggressive and well-armed Europe the entire British Army was deployed some 6,000 steamship miles away. A shiver of apprehension ran through Whitehall and a series of organization changes aimed at solving the problems of rapid mobilization began. In June 1901 Major General Sir John Ardagh finished his tempestuous tour as Director of Military Intelligence and was succeeded by Lieutenant General Sir William Nicholson. At the same time the Mobilization Division, which had been separated from the Intelligence Division in 1888, was brought back and Nicholson became Director General of Mobilization and Military Intelligence (DGMI). This raised the standing of the Division to that of a Department and gave Nicholson a seat on the Army Board equal with the Adjutant General, Quarter Master General and the Director General of Ordnance. He was also made a member of the Committee of Imperial Defence and was now required to report direct to the Commander in Chief. The remainder of the War Office must have regarded the new Department with some suspicion, for in the 1901 War Office List there is a delightfully pointed afternote 'The DGMI is authorised to correspond semi-officially with other Departments of the State on all subjects connected with his duties, in such correspondence however, he will not give information or express opinions which may be interpreted as pledging any other section of the War Office without the specific concurrence of the section concerned.

After two months in office General Nicholson decided what he had to do, and overnight abolished all the existing sections. He replaced them with only three. Colonel Altham was put in charge of one, Colonel Trotter another and as head of the third he chose a staff captain, William Robertson. Thus in one bound, to the chagrin of his more senior colleagues, and his own amazement, he moved from being the junior officer in a section of two, to chief of a section of nine. But Robertson was not over impressed by what he found:

> On taking over the new duties I found that, chiefly owing to an inadequate staff, imperfect organization and lack of clear direction there was not a single up-to-date statement giving a comprehensive and considered estimate of the military resources of any foreign country.

Since 1899 the Intelligence Division had been run by reserve officers and it was to this quiet organization that 'Wullie' Robertson burst like a pike in a tench pond. A close friend has written that in 1901 when he obtained his promotion he adopted his well-known 'Gruff manner in order to show people who was boss.' Certainly this period in the Intelligence Department proved the turning point in Robertson's career and when he left six years later he had won such a reputation that thereafter only key appointments were considered good enough for him – Brigadier General at Aldershot, Commandant of the Staff College, Quarter-Master General of the British Expeditionary Force to France and eventually Chief of the Imperial General Staff.

During his tour in the Intelligence Department, handbooks on foreign armies were produced, studies were written on 'The principal foreign powers and their resources for waging war', greater attention was paid to the selection of military attaches, language training was re-introduced including for the first time Japanese, the translation fund was increased and the grant to enable intelligence officers to visit other countries was made more generous. But these projects bulldozed through by Robertson are no different to those proposed by Colonel Jervis in the Crimean War, Robertson's exceptional achievement was that he had the ability, charisma and determination to make things happen. He also had that great advantage, so necessary for the success of any intelligence officer - a troubled environment. War with France, war with Russia, war with Germany all seemed imminent at some stage in his tour and it was against this worrying background that Robertson, supported by Nicholson, was given the opportunity and impetus to demonstrate his capabilities.

An Order in Council in 1901 had condemned the inadequacy of the Intelligence Division and Nicholson now emphasised that without more money and staff the inadequacy would continue. In August the Secretary of State therefore appointed a committee under the Earl of Hardwicke to review the 'Permanent Establishment of the Mobilization and Intelligence Department. The Committee sat until March 1903, and as well as reaching agreement on the more professional use of military attaches and closer links between Army and Naval Intelligence, spent a great deal of time discussing the problem of training intelligence staff officers. Following so closely on the sad lessons at 1899 it is strange that there was still doubt as to whether those charged with the responsibility of converting information into intelligence should receive specialised training. General French told the Committee that he had had only one trained intelligence officer in his Division and that this officer was 'Excellent and had an advantage over the rest in knowing from the beginning how to set to work.' General Sir T. Kelly-Kenny however, stated that he had had only two good intelligence officers and as neither of these had been intelligence trained he felt 'In the peculiar circumstances of South Africa it was not necessary for field intelligence officers to have any special training.' General Ian Hamilton had concluded the argument by asserting that he had had a large number of intelligence officers, that none had had previous intelligence training and that in fact the best was Colonel Woolls-Sampson who had received no military training of any kind.

The proposition that officers posted to the Intelligence Department should be graded in accordance with other staff appointments, have equal chances of promotion and tours of active service was accepted, but a statement by a Times correspondent that British Generals obviously did not attach sufficient importance to intelligence because they had not sacrificed enough scouts was not. This newspaperman had informed the Committee that 'A General ought to see that a certain number of his scouts get shot every day, as this shows they are in proper touch with the enemy.' But the point that aroused the greatest controversy was the degree of authority that should be given to the Head of Military Intelligence. To review the establishment properly, the Earl of

Hardwicke stated 'The Committee was bound to secure every possible means of finding whether the staff had adequately performed its proper functions.' This of course widened the terms of reference of the Committee quite considerably and they not only interviewed Colonel Altham, Colonel Trotter and Major Robertson, but also the Commander in Chief, Lord Roberts; the Adjutant General, Sir T. Kelly-Kenny and the Director General of Ordnance, General Brackenbury. The former group of officers were still smarting under the criticism that they had failed to warn the country of the dangers of war when in fact, so they protested, these warnings had been given and ignored. They therefore asked for more executive power to implement their own recommendations. The latter and more senior group, while recognising the need for the Head of Military Intelligence to have greater weight in Committee, felt that Intelligence should be an advisory service only, not an executive service. And that when the Director General of Military Intelligence was stated to be responsible for the strategical distribution of troops, it really meant 'Planning' the strategical disposition of troops, and that it was the Commander in Chief who approved the plans, the Adjutant General who selected and trained the necessary units and it was the Quarter-Master General who got the units to the required area and then maintained them. It is a strange fact that the fundamental responsibilities of the three General Staff Branches of the British Army today, 'G' (Operations) 'A' (Personnel) and 'Q' (Logistics) were first clearly defined, and accepted, in a series of sharp memoranda attached to a routine establishment proposal to increase the strength of the Intelligence Department.

This extension to the terms of reference caused great fury in the Intelligence Department itself, and General Nicholson who had by now been Head for three years took great exception to some of the remarks made by the senior officers. After reading the draft report he insisted on adding a further note:

> The enquiry, so far as I understand the matter, was whether the increase of establishment, which I had recommended, was needed for the efficient performance of the duties assigned to the Mobilization and Intelligence Department by the Order in Council dated 4 November, 1901. The enquiry was not intended to include a consideration of the propriety of such assignment of functions, or of the manner in which I carried out my duties as head of the department. I am responsible for my work to the Commander in Chief and, through him, to the Secretary of State; but I am not responsible to my colleagues, such as the Adjutant General and the Director General of Ordnance, who hold appointments at the

War Office equal, but not superior, to mine. I submit, therefore, that it was outside the province of the Committee to ask questions of Sir T. Kelly-Kenny and Sir H. Brackenbury, evoking an expression of their opinion on the above subjects.

Lord Hardwicke was not overawed by this display of pique however, and added a further note justifying the steps the Committee had taken and coming out strongly in favour of Intelligence being only an 'Advisory Department'. This ruling is still extant today and although Intelligence is a part of 'G' Branch which has executive control over troop deployments and battle decisions, the members of G (Intelligence) still have to convince their colleagues in G (Operations) of the reliability of their advice before action is taken on any intelligence produced.

Hardly had Lord Hardwicke's Report been published than a further three-man Committee began its investigations. Lord Esher, Lord Sydenham and Admiral Sir John Fisher made what was to be an extremely exhaustive and very critical examination of all the good and bad points arising from the War. After a comparatively short period of examination and research they came to two main conclusions, both of which were immediately accepted. First the necessity to abolish, after nearly two and a half centuries, the office of Commander in Chief, and second that there was a need to create a General Staff. It had taken many years of frustrating internecine warfare before the decision was taken to remove the Duke of Cambridge as Commander in Chief from his office. Perhaps as a reaction to this, no ceremony at all marked the abolition of his post. It happened quite abruptly. It is said that when Lord Wolseley went down to see him next morning, he found not only his appointment gone, but also his chair.

The new General Staff was to have only three Directorates, Military Operations, Military Training and Staff Duties. The Intelligence and Mobilization Department was to end its brief life and divide - Intelligence to become part of Military Operations, and Mobilization part of Military Training. General Nicholson who had actively helped to create the new General Staff and who had hoped to become its first Chief was passed over and selected, quite unexpectedly, to be the Director of Military Operations was Colonel J Grierson, the Gunner who had treated his friends to 'phizz' in 1881, when he had been posted to the Intelligence Department.

The careers of many British Officers at the turn of the century are truly Homeric in flavour but in the face of so much competition, it was necessary to show ability both in action abroad and at home on the staff in order to gain promotion. It is not surprising therefore; that in spite of the low opinion held by the Army as a whole towards Intelligence, so many officers who had held intelligence appointments did reach the heights of the profession. Grierson was one:

> I was offered head of the Operations Section with £1500 a year and rank of Major General. I said I would do as I was ordered and would come if I was wanted. There is to be a clean sweep at the War Office. I think it will be almost a record to have gone from Captain to Major General in eight years three months.

This 'Clean sweep' of 1904 marked the last major spasm of change engendered by the Boer War although in the Military Operations Directorate itself, a continual reorganization of sections took place. Initially there were four:

MO 1 – Strategical Section – Imperial defence, and Strategical distribution of the Army.
MO 2 – Foreign Intelligence.
MO 3 – Administration and Special Duties.
MO 4 – Topographical Section.

In 1907 two new sections were formed, MO 5 took over the functions of 'special duties', i.e. the controlling of spies and agents and MO 6 was created to deal with medical intelligence, which meant gathering of medical data about foreign countries.

During the South African War some members of the Field Intelligence Department had worked as spies among the Boer forces. When the war ended these activities virtually ceased although for some years a number of officers were employed in Africa as secret agents. One such young spy, who lived for two years in German South West Africa posing as an oxen-driver, later became a British Field Marshall and Chief of the Imperial General Staff – Captain Edmund Ironside, Royal Field Artillery. Throughout the Boer War the Germans had given both practical and moral support to the Afrikaners and in 1908 the War Office decided it would be a sensible precaution to have a good knowledge of what was happening along their South African borders. Captain Ironside who had taken an Army interpretership in German and had learnt both Cape Dutch and Afrikaans was therefore tasked to assume the identity of a German-loving Boer and get himself enrolled in the German Army. This he did and thereafter suffered all the mental agonies of a spy. On one occasion he nearly revealed himself when a German officer struck him in the face because his oxen were misbehaving – a severe test for the six foots four inch Highlander. After two years of espionage work Ironside told the Germans that he wished to return to his family and so impressed had they been with his services that they presented him with the German Military Service Medal. Another souvenir he brought back was a silver thaler, worth a few shillings, which had been given by another officer as a tip to the 'Humble German Soldier'. Ironside wore it for years on a chain round his neck.

Richard Meinertzhagen, at this time a young officer in the Royal Fusiliers was tasked to go to the Crimea clandestinely and discover the details of a new fort being built by the Russians. At one point on the tour he had left the road to get a good view of his target when he was spotted and two soldiers came running forward to arrest him. Meinertzhagen however, had planned for this crisis:

> Luckily I knew what to do. I rapidly unloosed my trousers and had the satisfaction of squatting down for at least three minutes in full view of the fort, whilst the soldiers, appearing to understand my embarrassment, and I suppose appreciating the fact that I was an ignorant foreigner, watched from a respectful distance.

In the First World War Meinertzhagen became head of General Allenby's Intelligence Section and was responsible for the celebrated ruse before the Third Battle of Gaza, when he rode out alone into no-mans land, contrived to be chased by Turkish cavalry, pretended to be wounded and let fall a haversack stained with blood containing papers which had been skilfully prepared to deceive the Turkish Intelligence Staff.

Another officer who carried on the tradition, actively encouraged in India and continued before the South African War of officers taking 'tourist' expeditions, which were intelligence related, was Second Lieutenant Bertrand Stewart, West Kent Imperial Yeomanry who in 1906 had published an 'Active Service Pocket Book' dealing with the art of reconnaissance. In 1911 Bertrand Stewart was arrested by the German police for carrying out espionage activities at the naval facilities of Bremen and Wilhelmshaven. The damming evidence against him was that he had tried to recruit an agent by paying him money for information about German naval mobilization plans. In spite of his vociferous and vitriolic protestations of innocence Stewart was convicted of being a spy and sentenced to three years in prison.

Bertrand Stewart's Father was an influential lawyer who began a lively public campaign to obtain release of his son and wrote from his home in Eaton Square to the Times - 'My sons actions which I venture to say have been grievously misunderstood and misrepresented to the court, are no proof of anti German feeling among the people of England. They merely show that 'young men will be young men' and that the guidance of international affairs must be entrusted to men with steady hands, discreet tongues and genuinely pacific intentions.'

In 1913 King George V was to visit his cousin the Kaiser and, as part of the visit, it was planned that the King would request that Bertram Stewart be pardoned. Preliminary enquiries failed to achieve this aim, Admiral Von Tirpitz objected on the grounds that 'The authorities were justly incensed by the violent criticism which the prisoner had passed concerning the sentence and the proceeding of the court.' The Admiral felt that 'The pardon would decidedly be declined so long as the culprit does not acknowledge the justice of his judges.' However, in May 1913 the German Ambassador in London wrote in confidence to Bertram Stewarts Father explaining that 'On the occasion of the Kings visit to Berlin your son will be released by the Emperor' and he was.

In 1913 the deterioration in Britain's relations with Berlin and the discovery that Germany was establishing a spy network in England, caused the Government to set up a sub-committee of the Committee of Imperial Defence to consider what improvements could be made in the counter-intelligence system of the United Kingdom. The Committee soon discovered that the laws dealing with espionage were inadequate and that a co-ordinated system to deal with foreign espionage was non-existent. They did not however, confine themselves solely to questions of counter-intelligence, but also looked into Britain's own secret service activities. Colonel J. E. Edmonds who was head of MO 5 (later the Official Historian of the First World War) explained that 'He was in charge of the section of the General Staff employed on Secret Service' and it was this direct link between the War Office and espionage activities that was strongly deplored by General Ewart. Ewart explained the system adopted by other countries, and pointed out that correspondence between Military Attaches and Secret Service Agents was not carried on direct, but through an intermediary. The General Staff were thus protected against being detected in any dealings with spies.

'We have no machinery of this kind' General Ewart continued, 'But it could no doubt be organised. We require information regarding espionage in this country so that we may keep suspicious aliens under observation, and be able to lay our hands on them in time of need. We also want to be in touch with foreigners with a view to ascertaining if there are any stores of foreign arms or explosives in this country.'

As a result of their deliberations the Sub-Committee concluded:

That the best method both of acquiring information of what is being done by foreign agents in this country and of procuring information from abroad, would be obtained by means of a Secret Service Bureau which should be separate from any of the Departments, but should at the same time be in close touch with the Admiralty, War Office and Home Office. This Bureau would deal both with counter-espionage, and serve as an intermediary between the Admiralty and the War Office on the one hand, and agents that we employ in foreign countries on the other ... the sub-committee consider that the organising of this Bureau should be entrusted to the Director of Military Operations in co-operation with the Admiralty and the Commissioner of Police, and that it should be undertaken without delay.

The Committee of Imperial Defence approved the recommendations and at the next meeting of the sub-committee it was decided, after some discussion, that the most junior man in the room should form the new Bureau. It was to be called the Special Intelligence Bureau, would be part of MO 5 and be responsible to the Director of Operations. Captain Vernon Kell, South Staffordshire Regiment was the 'Most junior officer' present and on 23 August 1909 he took possession of a tiny office on the first floor of the War Office and began work. For a year he was alone, with no records, no clerk and hardly any furniture. The story of his success is, however, the story of the present Security Service – MI5. In 1914 Kell was able to round up every single German Spy in Britain less one, and thirty years later when he retired as Director of MI5, he had seen the organization grow from one office with limited access to the Director of Military Operations, to the principal Service concerned with maintaining British security, an autonomous civilian department directly answerable to the Prime Minister. This is the system still in place today.

But the sub-committee of 1909 did not feel that there was any pressing need to create a bureau to control their own British spies. And it was not until 1912 that the Special Intelligence Section (later MI 6) was formed to co-ordinate the activities of British agents overseas. Commander Mansfield Smith Cumming R.N who was a member of the Directorate of Military Operations was given the task of raising this section.

This combination of all aspects of intelligence and all military planning into one department meant that the Director became a very influential person in Whitehall – a fact that was soon realised by General Henry Wilson who succeeded General Ewart in 1910. General Wilson foresaw that war with Germany was inevitable and also that Britain and France would be Allies. He kept two large-scale roller maps on the wall opposite his desk, one showed the lines of communication on the

Franco-Belgian-German frontier, the other the German-Austro-Hungarian-Russian Frontier, he made a personal reconnaissance of the Franco-Belgium area allotted to the British Expeditionary Force and insisted that the Handbook on the German Army was continually reviewed and kept up to date. German Field Service Regulations were translated and given a wide issue, as were handbooks on roads and billeting facilities in Northern France and Belgium.

At one stage in 1911 Wilson asked his two intelligence assistants Count Gleichen (ADMO 2) and Colonel Money (ADMO 3) to work out, without consulting each other, when and where the first collision would occur if Germany went to war with France. Using the known capacity of the German railways and roads and an 'acquired' German mobilization plan the two Branches decided quite independently that the first big clash would probably occur on the fourteenth day after mobilization near Montmedy. 'Very odd' mused Henry Wilson 'the French General Staff have also calculated that the first big battle will be on the fourteenth day of mobilization about Montmedy.' 'This was a wonderful coincidence' Count Gleichen has written – 'But we were all three wrong, a surprise Corps enabled the Germans to make that huge turning movement north of the Meuse which, had it not been for the little B.E.F. in the way would have rolled up the French left and maybe altered the history of the World.'

The title of the 'Planning Years' well describes this period. It had to be planning, as the Government would allow no actual expansion. What a frustrating period it must have been for Service Commanders:

> Wherever I look, to China, India, Egypt, South Africa, Morocco and to Europe, everything is restless and unsettled and everyone except ourselves is getting ready for war,' wrote General Wilson in his diary on 25 November 1913. 'This frightens me. Our territorials are falling down – witness the Deputations of County Associations who are going to Asquith tomorrow; our regulars are falling down – witness our recruiting returns; our Special Reserve is a thing 'pour rire'. And we are doing nothing.

Yet in spite of the efforts of those idealistic members of Government who imposed the cold dead hand of pacifism on service reforms, the Army and Navy did manage to prepare for the coming war. The success of the Japanese against the Russians, the Balkan Wars, the Dreyfus espionage scandal in France and above all the growing militancy of Germany, all provided a strong stimulus for thoughtful policy-makers. Winston Churchill as First Lord of the Admiralty and Admiral Fisher as the Senior Royal Naval Officer saw to it that the Navy was ready. The

Royal Navy came to the zenith of its power and with the creation of a Naval Staff, naval intelligence prepared itself successfully for 1914. Admiral Sir Henry Oliver established the concept of Room 40 and engineered an organization of radio interception, which was to produce the dramatic decoding of the Zimmerman telegram in 1917. This was a telegram sent to the German Ambassador in Washington from the German Foreign Secretary Herr Zimmerman. It explained that Germany intended to allow her 'U' boats to sink on sight neutral ships as well as those of the Allies, and instructing the Ambassador to conclude a Treaty with Mexico promising the return to Mexico of her lost territories of Texas, Arizona and New Mexico. This clandestine decoding precipitated the United States entry into the War.

Army Intelligence was also making plans. The 1914 edition of the War Office War Book lists the duties of the Intelligence Branches in three phases; peace, precautionary stage and war. Each phase is described in great detail showing the increased establishments required and the additional responsibilities to be undertaken, as this small extract from the plans for MO 5 reveals:

DUTIES IN PEACE

Traffic in Arms.
Secret Service at Home and Abroad.
Submarine cables and wireless telegraphy.
Censorship ciphers.

DUTIES IN A PRECAUTIONARY STAGE

Communicate to the Home office and Post Office the names of:
Individuals suspected to be agents of a probable enemy.
Firms likely to have business transactions in connection with the
  impending war.
Correspondents of foreign newspapers and request the Home Office to
  prepare for signature of the Home Secretary and, if and when signed,
  to forward to the Post Office warrants to open and detain
  correspondence of above.
Consult with Foreign Office, Admiralty and Post Office as to the
  imposition of partial or complete censorship of postal matter received
  from or destined for specified countries.
Present to Home Secretary for signature any warrants required for the
  scrutiny of Inland telegrams.

Matters affecting cable censorship.

Matters affecting Press correspondents.

Purchase for the Intelligence Section of GHQ of the Expeditionary Force copies of the best extant works on International Law.

Compile the daily summary and diary of operations overseas.

Purchase more Foreign Newspapers.

Close military telegraph stations.

Arrange with MT 1 for the issue of fresh keywords as and when required.

Before the precautionary stage is instituted MO 5 will ascertain from the Foreign Office if notices to Chief Constables regarding the treatment of suspects are to be issued.

If the scheme for secret service is put into force, two additional officers will be required.

DUTIES IN WAR STAGE

Arrange with the Chief Commissioner, Metropolitan Police, to obtain the services of men for the Intelligence Police to accompany GHQ Expeditionary Force.

In 1903 the Esher Committee had emphasised quite clearly that there was a requirement for two types of intelligence officer 'Both having certain qualities specially developed'. First, the staff intelligence officer 'Trained as to what information is wanted, the best way of getting it, the best way of collating it, and how to put it shortly and clearly before the General' and second, 'The field officers and scouts whose responsibility it is to obtain the information'. The report had emphasised that the two services were fundamentally different: 'The Intelligence Department officer must be accepted on general grounds, and his training should be done in peace time: The field intelligence staffs are a more difficult problem as their ability depends to a large part on local language and local knowledge, but even so, there exists the need for a department, organized so that, in the case of war it can be expanded rapidly.'

It was based on this conclusion that the first official announcement was made that the British Army was to have an Intelligence Corps. This was promulgated in 'Regulations for Intelligence Duties in the Field' published in 1904 which confirmed the requirement for an Intelligence Corps but stated that it should only be formed after hostilities had started.

Whenever possible, the interpreters, permanent guides, scouts and other employees of the Field Intelligence should be formed into a Corps. In civilised warfare they should be temporarily commissioned or enlisted and should wear uniform. Members of the Intelligence Corps will be paid from intelligence funds. Special scouts and Intelligence Police will form part of the Intelligence Corps.

This is an important document in the development of British Military Intelligence even if it includes the strange requirments that an Intelligence Corps is only necessary in the case of 'Civilized Warfare'.

Given the reluctance of senior army officers to consider forming an Intelligence Corps great credit must be given to David Henderson in maintaining his conviction for the need of such a Corps. In 1907 at a debate organised by the Aldershot Military Society he restated his conviction.

All persons, except staff officers and secret service agents, permanently engaged on intelligence duties in a campaign, should be formed into an Intelligence Corps. The advantages of such an organization are many; subordinates are more directly under control and know to whom they are responsible; their accounts, and the care of their horses and equipment, can be more easily dealt with; and there is the probability of the growth of an esprit-de-corps which may be invaluable.

It was an Army decision that an Intelligence Corps should only be formed after hostilities had started. It was left to Henderson, fortunately now Director of Military Training, to urge upon the War Office that at least they should compile a register of men capable of being used to gain intelligence in war. Prodded and jolted by these continual recommendations, in 1913 Major Macdonogh, who was head of Section MO 5 began drawing up a list of such men.

CHAPTER TWENTY

1914

*I*n comparison with the organization and preparedness of the British Army in 1899, the situation had significantly improved by 1914. Stimulated by experiences of the disasters at the beginning of the South African War and mortified by the sharp criticisms of post war reviews, the Operations Department of the War Office was well prepared. In a remarkable achievement, units were brought back from all over the Empire and in a complicated land and sea logistical exercise between the 12th and 17th August four infantry divisions and one cavalry division were dispatched to France.

In August 1914 there was no Directorate of Intelligence in the War Office as this Department had been amalgamated with the Military Operations Directorate in 1904 but, under this banner of Operations rather than Intelligence a number of very good staff officers had joined the Intelligence Department, including Captain A.P. Wavell, (later Field Marshal Lord Wavell.) These War Office intelligence officers, like their operational colleagues did well. For ten years there had been a firm conviction that war with Germany was inevitable and the Intelligence Department had developed a good understanding of German military capabilities and strengths. The Department had also produced a stream of intelligence reports that accurately suggested possible German axis of advance, timings and objectives. Unlike after the Boer War there were no subsequent allegations that the Intelligence Department had failed.

M.O.5 the section responsible for Counter Espionage also did well. They had been formed in 1909 tasked with investigating foreign espionage cases in the United Kingdom, and indexing all information on known spies, they influenced the drafting of the 'Official Secrets Act of 1911' and armed with this legislation and good intelligence in August 1914 they arrested all but one of the German agents in the country.

Analysis of information by the Army in London was good, but the Army's ability to gain information overseas was still very restricted. Senior officers felt very uncomfortable about using serving officers to reconnoitre foreign countries, feeling it was a form of espionage not suitable for gentlemen. The Foreign Office was also against using officers to reconnoitre potential enemy dispositions, fearing that their own finely balanced diplomatic manoeuvrings could be prejudiced by clumsy actions on the ground. This feeling was reinforced by the embarrassing case of Bertram Stewart and culminated in Section M.I. 6, like M.I.5 gradual moving away from army control to a predominantly civilian organization that is still the case today.

The Intelligence Department was small but had done well because it was manned by competent officers. These officers however were all very ambitious and it was this quality of ambition which was to prove counter productive - no way was any ambitious regular officer going to sit at a desk in London when there was a chance of taking part in a war especially as the war might be 'Over by Christmas'. In August 1914 therefore as soon as war was declared, the Intelligence Department, less one officer, moved across to France. The head of the Department, Lt Colonel G.M.W. Macdonogh was promoted and became Colonel GS (Intelligence) in the B.E.F. and a very disconsolate Captain A.P. Wavell was left to fill the intelligence vacuum in London.

In France the intelligence staffs had a very difficult task, the headquarters were constantly on the move and the tactical situation was a turmoil of advance and retreat. The intelligence staffs using prisoner interrogation and rudimentary aerial photography achieved some success and had a major coup when they identified three fresh German Corps on the flank of the British Army. This success however was based on astute reading of fragmentary information and not from planned acquisition and quiet analysis.

In the War Office the recommendations for improvement following the South African War had to a large degree been implemented. The London based intelligence staffs had done well both in the analysis of information and dissemination of intelligence before the war started, and then in coping in France with the heat of intense battle. Attention now focussed on the decision to form an Intelligence Corps after hostilities had broken out.

In 1913 in line with this recommendation and as part of the Mobilization Plan, Macdonogh had drawn up a register of potential members for an Intelligence Corps, as a result on the 5th August, eight hours after Britain's ultimatum to Germany had expired, university professors, journalists, business men, artists, musicians and professional adventurers received, to their surprise, a telegram asking them to join a new unit in Southampton called the Intelligence Corps. All had been previously earmarked and all had one thing in common, they were either linguists or experts in some aspect of European life. Also called up were twelve French speaking policemen from Scotland Yard to fulfil the requirement for an Intelligence Police Element.

These men had received no training, they had no idea of their duties and neither they nor their commanders had any idea of their role. On arrival in Southampton they had to find accommodation, buy a uniform from a local military tailor, put on General Service buttons wear a General Service cap badge and persuade someone to give them rations. Training began and was simple. Members of the Corps were required for liaison duties and so had to be mobile. If they could ride they were given a horse requisitioned from the Grafton Hunt, if they could not, they had to learn how to ride a motorcycle.

On the 5th August 1914 the Intelligence Corps had come into being, but there remained the problem of finding a suitable commander. In London at this time on leave, was Major T.G.Torrie who was the Brigade Major of the Lucknow Cavalry Brigade. Torrie was a relative of Macdonogh and was extremely anxious to avoid returning to India thus 'Missing the War' he therefore asked his relation if he could help. Macdonogh obliged and appointed him the first Commandant of the Intelligence Corps. As Torrie was gleefully leaving the War Office he met a friend. Captain J.A. Dunnington-Jefferson a regular officer in the Royal Fusiliers also on home leave from India and also anxious to remain in Europe. When Torrie therefore asked him about his linguistic abilities Jefferson 'upgraded' his French and was forthwith appointed the first Adjutant of the Intelligence Corps.

On the 13th August 1914 under the command of Major Torrie the embryonic Intelligence Corps sailed to France. After a few days living in tents and enduring atrocious weather with knee high mud, Major Torrie dispersed his men to various headquarters telling them to 'Make themselves useful' he then left to join the 2nd Life Guards. Later he commanded the 7th East Lancashire Battalion and in 1916 was killed in action on the Somme. The departure of Torrie was the opportunity Wavell had been waiting for, he requested the now vacant post and was succesful. On the 20th September 1914 he was promoted temporary major and arrived in France to be the second Commandant of the Intelligence Corps.

For seven weeks Wavell tried to administer and organise a group he has described as 'An odd crowd of 30-40 officers with a smattering of languages, all hurriedly recruited mostly on their ability to ride a horse or motor cycle.' But his heart was not in the appointment and after some animated discussion with the Military Secretary's Branch he obtained his release and was posted to the prestigious appointment of Brigade Major of 9th Infantry Brigade then fighting the First Battle of Ypres. For some weeks after his departure the Corps had no designated Commandant but on 8th December 1914 the Adjutant, Captain

Dunnington-Jeffries was appointed Commandant and promoted major. He was to remain as Commandant until February 1916.

On arrival at their various headquarters the Intelligence Corps officers and men were used on a variety of tasks, examination of prisoners, liaison with neighbouring French units, carrying messages and organising passes and permits. Inevitably they became involved in the fighting and suffered casualties. 2nd Lieutenant A. Sang was attached to HQ 19th Brigade and while scouting ahead of the front line was shot in the head and killed, 2nd Lieutenant W.G. Fletcher was attached to the Royal Welsh Fusiliers and was killed, as was 2nd Lieutenant Seabrook who was attached to the 5th Cavalry Brigade. 2nd Lieutenant W.D. Drury was wounded and 2nd Lieutenants F.H. Bevan, C.A. Gladstone and H.W. Le Grand were taken prisoner. 2nd Lieutenant Julian Smith, a fluent French speaker was attached to the 9th Lancers.

On the 24th August the Battle of Mons was fought and the famous retreat began. Supporting the withdrawal were the 18pdrs guns of the 119 Field Battery, this battery became the prime target of the German artillery and began to suffer heavy casualties. It became necessary therefore to bring the guns back to a safer firing position but the surviving gunners were too few in number. Captain Francis Grenfell, who commanded a detachment of 9th Lancers, although already wounded, asked for volunteers and forty Lancers plus 2nd Lieutenant Julian Smith Intelligence Corps charged forward and manhandled the guns back to safety. Captain Grenfell was later awarded the Victoria Cross for this action. On the 6th September Julian Smith was wounded and died two days later, he is buried in the Cemetary at Nangis. In Canterbury Cathedral there is a fine memorial window erected to the memory of those in the 9th Lancers who lost their lives in the Great War which includes the name of ' 2nd Lieutenant J.M. Smith Intelligence Corps,

Throughout August and September more Intelligence Corps officers arrived in France and among these was 2nd Lieut F.E. Hotblack. Hotblack was commissioned on the 10th September 1914 and two days later crossed to France with 20 other temporary officers. In France he reported to Major Wavell and was sent to be part of the British Liaison Team at the HQ of General Castelnau's French Army subsequently, when the Tank Corps was formed, he was sent to be their first intelligence officer. Part of his duty in this post was to ensure that the tanks reached the correct objective, Hotblack decided the best way to do this was to walk in front of the tanks, if necessary marking the route with white tape. Not surprisingly given this raw courage in the face of severe machine gun fire Hotblack became the most decorated officer in the

Intelligence Corps earning two D.S.O.s, two M.C.s and four Mentions in Dispatches.

Two other officers in the second group were 2nd Lieutenant Sigmund Payne Best and 2nd Lieutenant John Lawrence Baird C.M.G. M.P. Payne Best was given a motorcycle and told to report to the Grand Hotel in Paris. From there he was ordered to Le Cateau where the retreat was beginning. During the retreat he made himself useful by carrying messages, bringing in stragglers and perhaps most important, helping senior officers find good billets. (In November 1939 Payne Best was involved in the celebrated 'Venlo Incident' where Payne Best tried to recruit Anti Nazi German officers and was 'kidnapped' by the German Secret Police) John Baird was aged forty and, was appointed to the Intelligence Corps because of his diplomatic background. He motored to Southampton and on arrival in France was tasked by Major Wavell to reconnoitre the flanks of the British Forces. He was given 'Three motors, four cyclists and a Roll Royce mounted with three Mitrailleuse to try and locate the Germans North and North West of St Omer'. In November 1914 he was part of the British Mission attached to the Belgium GHQ and after the War became 1st Viscount Stonehaven and Governor of Australia.

During this period the Intelligence Corps earned its first gallantry decoration. 2nd Lieutenant Rolleston West who had read Engineering at Cambridge and was therefore given a motorcycle rather than a horse was attached to 19 Brigade. On the 30th August he was told by Colonel Ward the Brigade Commander to pass a message to the Middlesex Regiment, which was fighting the rearguard action. He passed the message but on his return realised he had left his maps behind and decided to return and retrieve them, to his consternation he found that the charges laid to blow up the bridge across the river at Pontoise had failed to go off. He reported back to Colonel Ward who realised how potentially dangerous this could be as all the other bridges had been destroyed and that it was essential to destroy the Pontoise Bridge before the German cavalry reached it. Rolleston West and Lieutenant Pennycuik R.E. volunteered to drive back and blow the bridge. Pennycuik tucked new detonators into his breast pocket and, forcing their way through a tide of retreating refugees, successfully reached the bridge and blew it. Both Pennycuik and Rolleston West were awarded an immediate D.S.O.

Perhaps the group of Intelligence Corps soldiers who found a role more suited to their talents were the French speaking Metropolitan Special Branch officers. Given the broad task of 'counterespionage' they used their initiative and made contact with the French and Belgian

Gendarmerie to establish joint pass and permit systems. It was not an easy task as the civilian population, including a large number of refugees, constantly moved through the battle areas and a system of permits had to have the agreement of all the national law enforcement authorities. The policemen were also heavily involved in counter intelligence duties. Given the fear of spies the Government encouraged people to report suspicious activities. The result was a continuing flow of reports describing strange lights at night and suspicious individuals around barracks. All these reports had to be checked, and in one case a Frenchman was discovered telephoning directly to the Germans about British troop movements, for this treachery he had been paid fifty thousand francs.

In Sir John French's first Honours List published in the London Gazette dated 14th January 1915 there are 26 names under the heading 'Intelligence Corps' a remarkable record for such a small number of amateur soldiers. Major Torrie had told his men to 'Make themselves useful'. They had no intelligence training or unit cohesion, there was no clear role, no coordination of effort but they had the qualities of language and local knowledge, were mobile and were generally mature men with experience of the world. Their individual efforts, gallantry and initiative in the last months of 1914 established precedents that ensured the continuation of the Intelligence Corps for the rest of the war.

CHAPTER TWENTY-ONE

1915–1916

$\mathcal{B}$y the beginning of 1915 the frenetic movement battles of 1914 had stopped and the war became static. Both sides drew breath and began to re-organise for a long and painful war. On Christmas day 1914 the British Expeditionary Force in France was divided into the First and Second Armies and on the 11th July 1915 a Third Army was formed. A chain of command manned by operational staff officers was set in place at all levels, enabling commanders to make strategic and tactical decisions in a calm manner not pressurized by fluctuating and desperate operational situations. In spite of subsequent allegations of incompetence this staff system worked well.

Matching the establishment of this operational staff infrastructure an intelligence staff infrastructure was also put in place. This started at the battalion level where a regimental officer was selected, given intelligence training and appointed to be the Intelligence Officer. As well as briefing his own commander, he would be required to submit to a Brigade Intelligence Officer all information gathered by his unit. This information would be analysed and passed upwards from brigade through division, corps and army to General Haig at G.H.Q.

In addition to this traditional infrastructure of Regular Army Intelligence Officers there gradually developed the amorphous, intangible, unconventional and unprecedented structure of Non-Regular Intelligence Corps Officers. Commanders recognised the value of officers and men with specific capabilities to gain and analyse information, and had no wish to lose this capability, but the traditions of the British Army and the almost religious conviction of senior officers was that men with particular skills in intelligence acquisition were not a natural part of the army. Non-regular intelligence officers should be used, encouraged, respected and honoured - but not admitted into the family of the Regular Army. This conviction that fulltime intelligence officers and soldiers were only required in time of war, forced a distortion of the system to accommodate routine administrative and promotion requirments. For the soldiers came the obvious question of what cap badge they should wear? As there was no Intelligence Corps cap badge the chosen solution was to create a new battalion called '10th Battalion Royal Fusilier Intelligence (B)' and post the Intelligence Corps soldiers to this battalion. This simple solution became confused however, when a second '10th (Service) Battalion Royal Fusiliers' was also raised which was a routine, uncomplicated and subsequently very distinguished infantry battalion. Naturally the myth arose that the 10th (B) Battalion was a 'Spy Battalion' and had been given this title as a cover story for clandestine activities. More likely however it was a simple matter of administrative convenience. The Royal Fusiliers raised 53 battalions in the First Word War including Stockbrokers, Bankers Sportsmen and Public Schools Battalions and, as the Adjutant of the Intelligence Corps, John Dunnington-Jefferson was a Royal Fusilier officer, this may have been a factor.

For the Intelligence Corps officers who became staff officers there arose the question of how to recognise their status. It was not felt acceptable that they should be granted the privilege of the red tabs and red cap band worn by regular staff officers and the solution therefore was to give them green tabs and green cap bands. Throughout the whole war although these green tabbed officers continually won praise and honours, none were ever promoted above major. Senior intelligence appointments were always given to red hatted General Staff officers.

As the war progressed and each side introduced more and more sophisticated weapons and equipment so the need for specific intelligence skills developed. The extraction of information from prisoners required planning and language; air photography was proving extremely valuable, wireless and telephone intercepts were giving real time information; agents French, Belgium and British were penetrating deep into enemy lines and were producing critical information about enemy movements. Counter intelligence was also becoming more relevant, the Germans were infiltrating spies and saboteurs behind Allied lines; enemy propaganda had to be dealt with; censorship had to be instituted and the security of our own forces had to be protected. All this information had be passed, received, evaluated, coordinated and then distilled into conclusions about the enemy's strengths and intentions. Inevitably, therefore as each source of information was gradually developed and improved so did the requirement for the Intelligence Corp to expand.

Interrogation, called in 1915 'Examination of Prisoners' has always been a prime source of information. The capture of a frontline prisoner had great value but was a hated operation from the infantryman's point of view. It was a most dangerous task, usually carried out at night by a patrol armed with cudgels. Many young officers and soldiers died in the attempt to make a capture and so every effort was made to maximize the value from a prisoner. Experience showed that harsh treatment was counter-effective; a cup of tea with a shot of rum and a cigarette, then a discussion about the weather was the best way to induce a prisoner, who would naturally be in a state of shock to talk. It was of course impracticable for a German speaking Intelligence Corps officer to be in every forward battalion the procedure was therefore to get the prisoner back as quickly as possible to a divisional level prisoner of war cage. Experience showed that the cage should be sited next to the Casualty Clearing Station on the theory that a wounded soldier receiving treatment was much more likely to be receptive to a friendly approach. Two Intelligence Corps officers were found to be necessary at each divisional cage and their orders were to confine themselves to tactical information. Any prisoner judged to be of value would be sent back to the Corps Cage and a few special prisoners were sent back to an Army Cage.

Selected German speaking officers were also put inside the prisoner compounds to act as 'Stool Pigeons'. Two lessons were learned first, that this technique should only be used at divisional level as it was of little value putting a 'Stool Pigeon' in the Corps or Army Cages where the prisoners were no longer under stress and rapidly became suspicious; the second, and presumable as the result of an unfortunate incident, was that 'Stool Pigeons 'Should be thoroughly searched before entering the compound to ensure they were not carrying any incriminating material.' The Germans also used this technique and a German Air Force Officer said to be the Grand Duke of Mecklenburg Strelitz, who was educated at Eton and Oxford donned a Royal Flying Corps uniform and mingled with captured British pilots. He was not detected.

Given the successful results of prisoner interrogation it was decided to run courses for the British troops on how to behave if captured. The advice was simple and clear and in line with the 1899 Hague Convention - 'Only give your number, name and date of birth'. This policy survived the Second World War and was only adjusted after the Korean War when it became apparent that the Chinese interrogators were not interested in military information but wanted extended discussions to explain the benefits of socialism over capitalism. In this situation it was impossible to maintain a one-sentence response, especially as failure to chat resulted in extremely harsh treatment.

In October 1914 a young officer lent over the side of a frail wobbling aircraft at 800 feet and, disregarding the singing enemy machine gun bullets around him, took photos of the German front line. It is alleged that when these aerial photos were taken to a General he replied 'Take the damned toys away. I have fighting to do'. The value of 'Looking over the hill' however soon became apparent and gradually more and more effort was put into improving the technology of the cameras, developing the photos, analysing the information, writing comments and then sending the results to the commanders. In February 1915 Lt Colonel Charteris then GSO 1 at First Army Headquarters noted 'My table is covered with photographs taken from aeroplanes. We have just started this method of reconnaissance which will I think develop into something very important' He added pungently ' It is very necessary to check on the exaggerated reports and imagination of air observers. The photos cannot tell lies'. By March 1915 Charteris was able to report 'I now have two regular majors under me as well as three temporary officers devoted to studying air photographs'. By the summer of 1915 improved cameras had been developed to reduce the problems of vibration, Squadron Intelligence Sections had been established manned by Intelligence Corps officers and Royal Engineer draftsmen, dark rooms had been built and stereoscopic photos and mosaics were being produced which gave the exact locations of enemy positions and artillery.

For the Battle of the Somme 1st July 1916 the Squadron Intelligence Section assessed the aerial photos and their conclusions were reported directly by telephone to Corps Headquarters. By 1917 new cameras were able to identify the smallest objects on the battlefield including the types of shells in munition dumps, strongpoints by identifying paths made by men walking between positions and, by studying shapes and shadows identifying the differences between ditches and ridges. All of positive help when producing maps of the battle area. By the end of 1917 there were nine Intelligence Corps officers and six clerks distributed to the Army Wings and Corps Squadrons of the Royal Flying Corps and in the spring of 1918 in anticipation of the major German offensive 10,440 photos were examined.

Major General Trenchard recognised the contribution of aerial photography –

> My Intelligence Department provided me with the most thorough information on all targets such as gas factories, aeroplane factories, engine factories, poison gas factories etc. Each target having a detailed and illustrated plan. Maps were prepared of every large target that was within each. These were supplemented in a large way by the aerial photographs made by reconnaissance machines.

The value of air photography had been proven but it was still considered a specialization for non-regular officers.

Listening to enemy conversations is a most satisfactory source of information. Early in the war officers tried to do this by sneaking out at night through the wire, finding a shell hole and waiting. It was not expected that any overhead conversations would warn of an impending attack, but by identifying the dialects of various German units it might be possible to identify changes in formations. In 1915 when the static phase of the war began, given the complexity and unreliability of valves, most infantry units relied on telephone communications rather than wireless. At this time the British became very concerned that the Germans seemed to be getting advance notice of impending attacks and were successfully causing casualties by heavy artillery bombardments on reserve and forming up areas, On one occasion the day after the Glasgow Highlanders moved into the front line, the Germans broadcast a welcoming song – 'Will you stop your tickling Jock'

The reason for this success was discovered by the French who captured a strange looking electrical device which they had the foresight to remove, examine and not destroy. It proved to be an instrument that, through induction and coils of wire could intercept telephone conversations up to 3000 yards. It proved a most valuable find and very soon the British had developed a similar device known as the 'Interceptor Telephone'. The apparatus consisted of two ground aerials laid out on the ground in a V shape leading back to a three-electro valve listening set that amplified the alternating currents. It was a great success not only in translating German conversations but also in warning British units that their calls were being detected. Laying the ground lines was however a very hazardous operation as they had to be sited very close to the German wire. In March 1918 when the Germans launched their offensive the German-speaking corporal called Corporal Vince Shirley Intelligence Corps who had changed his name from Fritz Schurhoff in 1914 and was in charge of one of these listening teams picked up a rifle and joined a nearby platoon. For his actions he was awarded the Military Medal.

Wireless interception, which started in a very small way with only one listening station in 1914 gradually, increased in importance. It gave two benefits first to locate enemy gun positions and headquarters so that counter bombardment plans could be planned and second to enable conversations to be monitored. By 1916 a line of 'Compass Stations' had been established well back from the battle area and every enemy station that came on the air was plotted and the unit identified. At the strategic level, listening and direction finding stations were established at Devizes, Aberdeen, Peterborough, Westgate and London. The one on the roof of the War Office was described as 'A heavy wooden frame aerial attached to a scaffolding pole and rotated manually by a motor car wheel and brute force.' The bearings of approaching aircraft were usually received within ninety seconds of the original transmission and officers with headsets and microphones sitting round plotting tables were able to pass the coordinates of targets directly to Home Commands. Zeppelins were an easy target, as they flew slowly and were in constant radio contact with their weather base. One young pilot, Lieutenant W. Leefe-Robinson won the Victoria Cross for shooting down a zeppelin in full view of thousands of delighted Londoners.

Having identified the wireless station as well as the benefits of direction finding, the problems of understanding the conversation became more complex as the Germans began to use daily changing ciphers. The men and women who engaged in this erudite and sensitive task have a very special place in the history of military intelligence and their legacy continued with the success of the Bletchley and the Enigma Machine in the Second World War.

Since biblical times spies and agents has been a productive if perilous source of information. Given the broad definition that spies are men or women, who clandestinely entered enemy territory in order to gain information or commit acts of sabotage and agents are civilians living in enemy territory who pass information back across the line, both sources were exploited in World War 1.

The problem facing the Intelligence Authorities was how to get the spy into enemy territory. The first attempt was to form a French-speaking group of men known as the 'Suicide Club'. The aim was to have this group poised and ready to follow up a cavalry attack and, when the attack halted, would remain hidden and then emerge to mingle with the population. It was not a success. There were no cavalry attacks until 1918 and the group had a frustrating war. The second attempt was to land the spies by aeroplane. This was also not a great success. The Germans soon realised the connection between solo aeroplanes flying on moonlight nights in remote areas and the landing of spies. The spies, who were forced to carry pigeons or heavy radios were caught and executed and, after the loss of a number of pilots, General Trenchard commanding the Royal Flying Corps decided that the risks in landing agents in fields in the dark was too dangerous and he placed severe restriction on these flights. He ordered that aircraft could not penetrate more than fifteen miles behind the enemy lines and flights could only be made in certain phases of the moon. The next attempt was to put the spy in a wicker cage suspended under a balloon and then rely on the wind to take him to a selected area behind the German lines. It was more succesful than the aeroplane, but reliance on wind to be kindly to military operations is always problematical and officers were often deposited miles from the intended target.

Because of the difficulties of getting spies into France, great effort was made to recruit agents who were civilians and could legitimately live in enemy occupied territory. To contact these people an office was established in Folkestone, which was the terminal for ferryboats from neutral Holland, and here screening was carried out for potential agents. It was successful. Hundreds of Belgian and French citizens were willing to risk their lives and use their ingenuity to collect information and help the Allies. However over 600 were arrested and eighty-seven were executed. The main difficulty lay in getting the information back to Britain. Agents who could legitimately cross the border used messages written on rice paper, which were then concealed in walking sticks, stems of tobacco pipes, bars of chocolate or various human orifices. Messages were also written on silk as this did not rustle when searched. Secret writing was used but at the end of the war both the British and German authorities confidently asserted that there was no secret writing that they could not read and the letter could be read or amended and then sent on to the intended recipient. Semen distilled with water was tried as ink, but was not satisfactory as it had a distinctive odour.

Simple procedures had more success. Messages were put into turnips and the turnip thrown over the electric wire at agreed spots. At one border point an agent agreed to wash the dirty linen of the German guards, a message would be put into the washing that was sent across the border to be washed and then returned to the sentries' satisfaction. One of the most succesful agent operations involved a lady named Madame Rischard. At the beginning of the war Madame Rischard, who lived in Luxemburg, had gone to live in Switzerland but then wished to return home. Her husband was the Senior Railway Doctor to the Luxembourg State Railway and Madame Rischard wanted to re-join him. This necessitated getting a visa and Madame Rischard made several unsuccessful attempts to do this, ultimately on one visit to the Visa Office, to her surprise, was met by a British Officer in uniform, Captain the Hon G. Bruce. He made a direct approach 'Become an Agent and help the Allies and we will get you the visa to return home'. Madame Rischard refused, not because of fear of detection but from a feeling that such action was morally unacceptable. Eventually she confided her worry to her Priest at confession who told her it was her duty to help her country. She therefore agreed and was sent to a special school at 41 Rue St Roch in Paris. This school had been established by Captain Stanley Woolrych, who had joined the Intelligence Corps in October 1914 and had earned a Mention in Dispatches for searching dead German soldiers for identification documents in No Mans Land. In the schoolroom in Rue St Roch Woolrych placed tailors dummies dressed in German uniforms and drawings of trains. At this school Madam Rischard was taught the various types of uniforms, insignia and equipment of the German Army and, more important, how to deduce information from the movement of military trains e.g. it took fifty two trains to move a division.

On her return to Luxemburg she first recruited her initially reluctant husband and then stationmasters along the track so that after identifying a military train she could track its direction. So important was this information that it was decided to send an officer to Luxemburg to help analyse the information and improve communications. Captain Albert Baschwitz Meau, a Belgian officer, was selected to do this and was sent off by balloon which, to every ones delight, landed near Madame Rischard. The system for passing the information was simple and effective. A newspaper was published in Luxembourg, which was on sale in Switzerland, Madam Rischard would write innocuous articles in this paper using an agreed code, the paper was then sent to Switzerland, then forwarded to the Rue St Roch where it was decoded. Details of the troop railway movement before the last major offensive of the Germans in the Spring of 1918 was of immense value and after breakfast each day General Charteris would take the 'Railway Map' to General Haig showing the movement of German divisions across the whole front. It is satisfying that at the end of the war Madame Rischard was awarded the C.B.E. and Captain Baschwitz the D.S.O.

CHAPTER TWENTY-TWO

Intelligence and Security and Intelligence Aquisition

ince the concept of an intelligence corps was formulated in the South African War 'Intelligence and Security' had been linked together. Intelligence covering all aspects of gaining information about the enemy, security with the aim of preventing the enemy discovering details of our own forces. Security was sub divided into two functions, first under the title of Counter Espionage it involved aggressive actions to detect, frustrate or kill enemy agents, second, the more passive role of taking protective measures such as creating control zones and installing locks, lights, passes, permits and document controls.

In London, MO5 working closely with the Metropolitan Police had fulfilled both these functions in a most succesful way and in 1914 had destroyed the German spy network. But when the Army went overseas, as the 1904 recommendations pointed out, the necessary functions of security protection could not be undertaken by civilian organizations and it was necessary for the army to carry out this role. It was for this reason that the Mobilization Plans included the establishment of an 'Intelligence Police Element' as part of the proposed Intelligence Corps.

When the twenty-four french speaking Scotland Yard detectives were transferred to the Intelligence Corps and arrived in France in 1914 they were not part of any formed unit and had little direction, so they made themselves useful by acting as messengers, guarding headquarters and talking to French officials. As the war became more static however they began to fulfil the function that had generated their inclusion in the Mobilization Plan. Although they were detectives and were called 'Police', from the very beginning there was a fundamental difference between the 'Intelligence Police' and the 'Military Police.' The instruction to the Intelligence Police clearly stated that 'They should not make enquiries respecting larcenies and cases of desertion and it is not part of their duties to detect the illicit sale of spirits to troops or drinking during prohibited hours or to interfere with the morality and discipline of the British Military.' Their role was to prevent unauthorised persons gaining access to headquarters, camps and offices, but more important 'To prevent the collection and transmission to the enemy of information bearing on military operations, the detection of enemy agents and the control of the movements of suspects and undesirables.'

Under this broad directive one of their main duties was the complicated function of 'Port and Travel Control' After many conferences with their Allies a special passport was issued by the French Authorities which was necessary before entering France and the British initiated a pass that had to be obtained before permission was granted to visit their war area; One complication was that wives were not allowed to go into the War Area, but this did not apply to 'Lady Friends.' When the French were questioned about this and asked whether casual acquaintances or intimate friends did not tend to disturb work, the reply received was 'You English look at these things so strangely, with us it is not a distraction only an aperitif.'

Closer to the Front Line the country was divided into Zones based on Army boundaries. Within each Zone Intelligence Police Stations were established each containing two Intelligence Policemen. These policemen were not required to wear uniform and had great freedom of action, their duty was to be aware of anything unusual happening in their area. It meant close liaison with the French police, and establishing a rapport with a broad range of people who would be willing to tell them of any suspicious person or activity. In the Battle Zone the Intelligence Police had a combat role alongside the infantry. When a trench system was captured they would be required to seize papers, maps and radios and carry out quick interrogations. When villages were re-occupied they would compile lists of the inhabitants, arrest collaborators, identify deserters and post proclamations.

In all of these matters they would work closely with the Military Police, but each had their own objectives. The Military Police chain command was through 'A' Branch which was a Staff Branch dealing with court-martials and discipline, the chain of command for the Intelligence Police was through 'I(b)' a department of the Intelligence Staff. During the First World War as the Army reorganised and expanded, consideration was given to the amalgamation of the Military Police and the Intelligence Corps but the recommendations of 1904 remained intact, and the two Corps, although they worked closely together and often shared social facilities, remained separate organizations.

In 1920 S.T. Felstead in his book *German Spies at Bay* stated that 'Censorship probably detected most of the German spy network in the UK at the beginning of the war and the detection of later attempts to establish networks.' In 1914 the Censor Department had a staff of a dozen and its purpose was to examine mails sent from the UK to Germany and other countries bordering Germany. By 1915 the value of censorship had been realized and by 1917 approximately fifteen million messages were examined every month. In the UK, censorship was divided into three departments, press, private letters and parcels, and commercial wireless and cables. Of these, private letters and parcels was the largest and most important employing nearly 5000 people. Given the need for foreign languages men were recruited into the Intelligence Corps who could speak 'Uncommon Languages' including Chinese, Arabic, Lettish and Maltese.

Mail between neutral countries was examined on the grounds that German intelligence activity flourished in Scandinavia and Holland and letters from Gothenburg, Stockholm and Flushing were found to contain letters to the German Intelligence HQ in Wilhelmstrasse, Berlin. This censorship was possible because mails from America and Scandinavia were sent in ships that first stopped at British ports such as Falmouth, here the mail sacks would be clandestinely removed, sent to London by train and examined by the censorship staff then returned to Dover where the same ship would collect them.

Unit censorship was not a covert operation and was carried out by unit officers, a task they found both boring and intriguing. It was 'Not permitted to send letters criticising operations, superior officers, allied troops or any statement calculated to bring the Army or individuals into disrepute.' Given such a wide mandate it is not surprising that decisions by unit officers as to what might bring the Army into disrepute varied from unit to unit. One letter writer who quoted the Kipling line of poetry 'When the Captains and the Kings Depart' had the line struck out with the explanation that 'The Kings movements must not be referred to'. There was however universal amazement that the men in the trenches could write such passionate letters to their girl back in Blighty knowing that the intimate suggestions would be read by an officer in their battalion.

Two other intelligence related activities developed as the war progressed, neither of which were previously felt to be appropriate for the Regular Army. In August 1914 the British Government discovered that the Germans had set up a Propaganda Agency and David Lloyd George, then Chancellor of the Exchequer, was asked to do the same. He selected his fellow Liberal M.P. Mr Charles Masterman, who was a succesful writer to head this new organization and Masterman asked twenty-five leading writers to a meeting to discuss how it could be done. The group included Arthur Conan Doyle, John Masefield, G.K. Chesterton, John Galsworthy, Thomas Hardy and Rudyard Kipling.

One of the first pamphlets the Group produced was a 'Report on German Outrages' which gave lurid prominence to alleged outrages committed by the Germans against Belgium hospitals and women. It was most succesful and in the mood of the time generated great anger against Germany and great sympathy for 'Poor Belgium.' John Buchan, author of the spy novel 'The 39 Steps' was made a 2nd Lieutenant in the Intelligence Corps and charged with production. By 1918 the importance of propaganda, which had significant political implications not only on the Germans but also on our Allies meant that the Government decided to create a Department of Information and appoint Lord Beaverbrook, Editor of the Daily Express to be Minister of Information. Charles Masterman became Director of Publications and John Buchan, now an Intelligence Corps Lieutenant Colonel, was made Director of Intelligence. It is interesting that on his appointment he requested to wear the Red Tabs of the General Staff and not the Green Tabs of an Intelligence Staff Officer, as 'It would facilitate my work in London'. The request was refused.

Deception was another new commitment for the Army. Officers were selected for their ability to devise 'Machiavellian' ruses to deceive the enemy. In 1915 a major scheme was launched to deceive the Germans into thinking that the British did not intend to attack at Neuve Chapelle but farther to the North. Rather like the Deception Operation which involved General Patton before D Day, false reports were published in the papers, false messages were transmitted by radio, letters were sent by Belgium refugees in Britain to their relatives hinting that an attack was coming in another sector and dummy troop movements away from Neuve Chapelle took place.

Another sophisticated unit, which also required Intelligence Corps officers, was the unit formed to 'turn' German agents. It was a skill that required much patience and psychology but was succesful as, given the choice of death in the Tower or working for the British, many captured agents found the latter choice more acceptable. One German agent code-named Maquis who was captured in 1915 was 'turned' and for the rest of the war planted false information. An Indian National who had been recruited by the Germans was also 'turned' and was sent to Switzerland where he assumed the role of secretary to an Indian Rajah. Here he gained the trust of the Germans who eventually confided in him the names of a Pro-German Cell in India.

In August 1914 one of the officers who volunteered for service was Alec Waley. General Kirke wrote of him 'Although beyond military age and with no previous military experience whatever, he was one of the first to present himself to the War Office and beg to be allowed to serve in any capacity.' His persistence was rewarded and he was appointed a 2nd Lieutenant in the Intelligence Corps. Waley took part in the Retreat from Mons showing courage and initiative and, following the precedent set by Lieut E. Abadie in the Boer War, was selected to take charge of a new unit, the 'Pigeon Carrier Service' The French had given the British fifteen pigeons and 2nd Lieutenant Waley would put the pigeons in a cage on the back of his motorcycle, find his way to a forward battalion then pass the birds over to a handler. Communication from forward units back to their headquarters was either by telephone or runner, telephones were constantly cut and runners suffered severe casualties. Pigeons thus became a life saving method when calling for artillery support or reinforcements. Although in France plump pigeons did not have the threat from hawks as they did in South Africa, they did have the same vulnerability from hungry soldiers.

As well as providing means of communication for our own troops, pigeons were used extensively to bring back information from behind enemy lines. The pigeons were placed in wicker baskets attached to balloons and, when the wind was judged to be in the right direction, the balloon would sail over the German lines where a clockwork device would operate to release the pigeons. Attached to the leg of the bird would be a sheet of instructions headed 'Pour La Patrie.' 'Vivent Les Allies.' 'Demand de Renseignements'. The recipient would fill in details of German locations and units, put it in aluminium capsule and release the bird. It was surprisingly effective, pigeons released at 1100hrs in the evening were often back in lofts carried on the back of lorries at GHQ by 0900 hrs next day. The estimate of success was hoped to be 5% the actual return rate was 40%. The Germans were never able to control this traffic, although they gave eight days leave to every soldier who shot a pigeon and executed any civilian discovered with a pigeon. If they did capture a pigeon however they would send back a false message hoping to deceive the British. By the end of the war there were 20,000 birds in the Pigeon Service and 380 soldiers. Waley now a major in the Intelligence Corps was awarded the M.C.

CHAPTER TWENTY-THREE

1917

By 1917 the Intelligence Organization in France had settled down and a mass of information was being collected. To help handle this flow of information 'Central Collecting Centres' were established which analysed the information and coordinated information sources. Extracts from an Intelligence Order issued on the 16th May 1917 before the Battle of Messines dealing with collection methods shows the remarkable progress that had been made –

1. INTELLIGENCE COLLECTION METHODS

The transport of PoW to Advanced Collecting Stations where they will be searched and subjected to initial tactical questioning before being sent to a PoW Collecting Station where intelligence officers will conduct a more thorough examination.

The study of captured maps and documents by intelligence officers at Corps PoW cages and tactical information to be transmitted immediately to front line units.

Intelligence collected as a result of penetration of the enemy's lines by reconnaissance patrols.

Intelligence gathered by observation posts.

Reports by observers with the Royal Flying Corps which will be dropped at advanced positions near divisional HQs. After landing the observer will report directly to the intelligence officer in his Squadron HQ.

Aerial photography should take place several times a day and oblique photos should be used in conjunction with panorama photos from the ground.

Flash spotting and sound ranging systems to be confirmed by aerial photography.

Signal and wireless interception of the enemy's ground wireless stations, enemy aircraft transmissions operating with his artillery. The use of Compass Stations to locate enemy wireless sets and artillery positions and listening sets at the front line to listen to the enemy's trench conversations.

Intelligence emanating from the enemy's rear areas consisting of reports from agents, refugees, repatriated prisoners and documents retrieved from prisoners.

2. DISSEMINATION OF INTELLIGENCE

Messages are considered the most positive and rapid means of transmitting information to higher and lower formations.

Daily Intelligence Summaries are to be issued by Division, Corps and Army Intelligence Staffs at noon and during the evening.

Intelligence Staffs are to participate twice daily in conferences to discuss intelligence and artillery intelligence.

Use Standard Trench Maps at the scale of 1:10,000 and 1:20,000 and Special Attack Maps at a scale of 1:5000 for Platoon Commanders and Royal Artillery and Royal Flying Corps Observers.

3. COUNTER ESPIONAGE

Reports from the Intelligence Police and the Provost Marshall on the actions of the inhabitants both military and civil in their respective areas.

By 1917 the Intelligence Corps Organization had also be regularised. There was a Headquarters Company at G.H.Q with the Commandant of the Intelligence Corps, his Adjutant, 109 officers and 119 soldiers; an Intelligence Company with each Army plus a Lines of Communication Company. There were also Royal Flying Corps, Tank Corps and Wireless Intelligence Corps Sections. The Tank Section included Captain F.E. Hotblack and the Wireless Section included nineteen Women's Auxiliary Army Corps (W.A.A.C) known to the troops as 'HushWaacs'.

A very important fact was that at G.H.Q. it was the Senior General Staff Officer (Intelligence) who 'Controlled' the Intelligence Corps, the Commandant of the Corps was 'Responsible for administration, training and discipline and was to keep in close touch with the requirments of the General Staff (Intelligence) and to provide suitable personnel at short notice for special duties.' This situation whereby members of the Intelligence Corps were 'commanded' by their own officers but 'controlled and tasked' by staff officers was unique in the Army and remained the case until the 1970s.

The accepted philosophy was that Intelligence Corps officers were excellent at developing sources, collating the results and turning information into intelligence, but that the final and critical stage of analysing what all this intelligence meant and briefing the commander should remain with a General Staff Officer. In 1917 at GHQ there were three red-tabbed General Staff Officer (Intelligence) and twenty-three Intelligence Corps officers. The senior General Staff Officer in 1916 and 1917 was Brigadier General Staff (Intelligence) John Charteris.

Brigadier General John Charteris has become one of the most controversial Intelligence Officers in the history of British Military Intelligence. He was a Sapper, served on the North West Frontier, passed the Staff College at Quetta, and had held the unusual appointment of 'War Correspondent' with the Bulgarian Army. In 1914 when Brigadier Macdonogh was promoted, and returned to London as Director of Military Intelligence and General Haig was appointed to command the First Army, Charteris became Lieutenant Colonel and Head of Intelligence at Army Headquarters, and when Haig replaced Sir John French as Commander in Chief and went to GHQ, Charteris went with him and was promoted Brigadier General 'Head of Intelligence.' It was a meteoric rise and meant Charteris became the senior intelligence officer of the largest army Britain had ever sent overseas.

Under his direction the intelligence infrastructure grew from the muddled, uncoordinated, undirected organization of August 1914 to an organization where all possible sources of information were improved and exploited and a system of reporting enabled him to receive daily reports from every division, corps and army. It was his task to distil all this intelligence into a daily briefing for General Haig and in November 1917 after the Battle of Cambrai when he gave the wrong advice, he was sacked. By this time Charteris had achieved the complete confidence of General Haig, his briefings were concise, well presented and given with flair and conviction, but there is overwhelming evidence that they were too optimistic. Charteris was a large man, genial, enthusiastic and articulate. He spoke with confidence and his conclusions suited General Haig. Charteris felt that his General was under so much pressure that it was not his role to add to the pressure by continually giving bad news. By this time Haig believed that the only way to defeat Germany was by 'attrition' and Charteris supported him in this belief. After the Battle of the Somme, Charteris took Haig to see a German PoW cage, but had secretly arranged that all the fit soldiers would be taken out of sight, Haig therefore believed the reports of the poor morale and physical condition of the German Army. On one occasion when Charteris was sick and Major Marshall Cornwall had to take his place he subsequently wrote 'I soon discovered that the views held by Charteris and reported by him to Sir Douglas Haig regarding Germany's manpower reserves, morale and economic resources differed widely from the estimates made by the Director of Military Intelligence at the War Office, Colonel Cox head of MI 3 and the combined best intelligence brains at the disposal of the country.' Lloyd George was equally damming 'General Charteris, who was an embodiment of the Military Intelligence which he directed, glowed with victory. For him the news was all good. If there were any elements that might have caused doubt in more discriminating minds, General Charteris had not discerned them and if he had he was proof against their maleficent influence.' Before the battle of Cambrai which was to be the first major tank battle of the war, intelligence reports showed that a number of fresh German divisions had arrived from the Russian Front but as this would upset Haig's plan Charteris, in spite of the evidence produced by his staff, refused to believe the facts and directed that the fresh German divisions should not be marked on the intelligence maps.

The case of General Charteris is still discussed in Schools of Military Intelligence. An intelligence officer has to gain the confidence of his commander, if he continually is a bearer of depressing news it might protect his reputation but if he calls 'Wolf' too frequently he loses his credibility. If he is too optimistic in his attempt to be the bearer of good news however, he can end up like General Charteris who was moved to Salonika to interrogate Bulgarian prisoners.

CHAPTER TWENTY-FOUR

1918–1929

*A*t the eleventh hour of the eleventh day of the eleventh month of 1918 the 'War to end all Wars' ended. Soldiers got out of their trenches and cheered, and the 3000 men of the Intelligence Corps now had only one aim – to return to civilian life. This aim was supported by the Regular Army. By this time Intelligence Corps units were established in all the other areas of conflict – East Africa, West Africa, Italy, Egypt, Greece, Salonika, Turkey and Russia. The same system was in use i.e. regular staff officers in intelligence staff appointments, supported by teams of non-regulars with specialist skills. There was no Intelligence Corps unit in the United Kingdom as the Corps was seen to be an organization only to be deployed overseas in active operations.

The Intelligence Corps officers went home but one element remained, the Counter Espionage Section. It soon became apparent that many in the German Army bitterly opposed the armistice and that the German Secret Service was busily engaged in seditious activities including the promotion of communist ideology and trying to create dissension between the Allies. A security unit named the Field Security Police was created and were required to monitor political meetings, provide protective security, liaise with the French and Belgian authorities and carry out the vetting of civilian contractors and civil labour. They also undertook intelligence investigations and document translations. The soldiers wore civilian clothes drew three shillings day extra pay and, if they had to wear uniform, used the cap badge of the Royal Fusilier, they were forbidden to admit they belonged to the Intelligence Corps.

When the Treaty of Locarno was signed in 1925 and the GHQ moved to Wiesbaden there was reluctance to use the sensitive word 'Intelligence' and so the Intelligence Corps publicly became the 'Civil Affairs and Security Branch' which was thought to be more politically acceptable. In September 1929 agreement was finally reached on the withdrawal from Germany and so the bags were packed and the classified documents destroyed. The Intelligence Corps were evacuated in stages and on the 13th December 1929 the final party consisting of two officers and one soldier took the sign down from outside their office and left by car. The Intelligence Corps ceased to exist. In 1907 David Henderson had predicted that the formation of an Intelligence Corps would help 'The growth of an esprit- de- Corps which may be invaluable.' He was right, but it took one hundred years to prove he was right.

A number of senior officers when reviewing the Intelligence Organization after the war did recommend that it would be wise to have an intelligence unit formed in peacetime ready for war, but this idea was rejected. As a compromise it was suggested that on demobilization, temporary officers of the Intelligence Corps should be invited to become voluntary members of the 'Regular Army Reserve of Officers' and held on what was called The 'General List (Intelligence)', about one hundred officers agreed to do this. All the regular officers returned to their regiments.

In the War Office the decision was made to continue the Military Intelligence Directorate and, although considerably reduced in size, was staffed by officers of high calibre. Lord Ismay who served in the Directorate later commented that 'Of the dozen or so lieutenant colonels and majors who served under me, not one failed to reach the rank of major general.' The Directorate produced handbooks on foreign armies, which contained details of their armed forces and their capabilities, plus notes on topography, communications and climate.

In 1919 the country was experiencing a certain amount of labour unrest and the government expressed the fear that some form of 'Domestic revolution' might occur. Sir Basil Thomson, Head of the Special Branch approached Field Marshal Sir Douglas Haig and suggested that 'Army Intelligence and Special Branch should operate together.' During the war the Field Marshal had been an enthusiastic and appreciative supporter of 'Army Intelligence' but his comments concerning his response to Sir Basil epitomised the feeling of the Army to an Intelligence Corps in peacetime 'As regards troops, I said that I would not authorise any men being used as spies. Officers must act straightforwardly and as Englishmen. Espionage amongst our own men was hateful to us Army men - Thomson's machinery for getting information must work independently of the Army and its leaders.' Although the Government had reservations about using the Army in the United Kingdom, the disbandment of the Intelligence Corps was not a political decision it was a decision made by the Army itself. Why?

Bibliography

Chapter 1
Battles of the English Civil War
West Kent Yeomanry 1794-1909
Cromwell's Master Spy
The letter books of Samuel Luke 1644-45

A. Woolrych
    Lt Col J. F. Edmeades
D. L, Hobman
H. G. Tibbutt

Chapter 2
Marlborough and the Rise of the British Army
Marlborough his Life and Times
Marlborough
The Life and Times of John, Duke of Marlborough

Life of Marlborough
The Monmouth Episode

C. T. Atkinson
Winston S. Churchill
Sir John Fortescue
Royal United Service
    Institution Lecture 1895
General Viscount Wolseley
B. Little

Chapter 3
The Battlefields of England
Culloden
Mad is He
General Wolfe
James Wolfe Man and Soldier
Wolfe and North America
The Traitor and the Spy
The Capture of Major Andre

A. H. Burne
J. Prebble
D. Grinnell-Milne
E. Salmon
W. T. Waugh
Lt Col F. E. Whitton
J. T. Flexner
O. Hufeland

Chapter 4
The Subaltern
Military Forces of the Crown
Napoleon and the Invasion of England

The Yeomanry of Devon
The Anatomy of Glory

G. R. Gleig
C. Clode
H. F. B. Wheeler and
    A. M. Bradley
Benson Freeman
H. Lachonque

Chapter 5
Wellington's Headquarters Studies in the Napoleonic
    War Years of Victory
Years of Victory

S. G. P. Ward
Sir Charles Oma
A. Bryant

Chapter 6
Illustrated History of England
The Story of the Guides

Trevelyan
G. J. Younghusband

Chapter 7
Thomas Best Jervis

W. P. Jervis

Chapter 8
Mrs. Duberly's Campaigns
General Orders Army of the East 1854-55
Crimea Despatches

E. E. Tisdall
Official Publication
Captain Sayer (Topographical Branch)

Chapter 9
The Sebastopol Enquiry - Whom Shall we Hang? Anonymous

Chapter 10
The War Office Past and Present Captain O. Wheeler
The Early Years of the Ordnance Survey Colonel Sir Charles Close

Chapter 11
The Siege of Paris Robert Baldick
The Life of Major General Sir Charles Wilson Colonel C. E. Watson

Chapter 12
The Life of General Sir Redvers Buller Colonel C. H. Melville
Sir Frederick Maurice Lt Col F. Maurice
The Staff and Staff College Major A. R. Godwin-Austen
A Guardsman's Memories Lord Edward Gleichen
An Account of the British Wars with Persia Major M. S. Bell
The Drums of Kumasi A. Lloyd
Narrative of the Ashanti War Captain H. Brackenbury RA
The Washing of the Spears D. R. Morris

Chapter 13
A Soldier's Sailoring Major General A. B. Tulloch
Recollection of 40 years Service Major General A. B.Tulloch
From Korti to Khartoum Colonel C. Wilson
General Gordon's Khartoum Journal Lord Eiton
Kitchener - Portrait of an Imperialist P. Magnus
The Life of Sir J. M. Grierson D. S. MacDiarmid
The River War Winston S. Churchill
Wingate of the Sudan Sir R. Wingate, Bart
Life of Major General Sir John Ardagh Susan, Countess of Malmesbury

Chapter 14
The River Column Major General Sir Henry Brackenbury
Lord Cardwll at the War Office General Robert Biddulph
Field Marshal Sir W. Robertson Lt Col W. C. Issac
Sixty Years of a Soldiers Life Sir A. E. Turner
Secret Service Sir George Aston
From Private to Field Marshal Field Marshal Sir W. Robertson, Bart

Chapters 15, 16, 17, 18, 19
With the Inniskilling Dragoons Lt Col Watkins-Yardley
With Rimington L. March Phillips
Buller's Campaign J. Symons
Anti Commando Mr. Simpson and General I. Hamilton
On the Heels of De Wet The Intelligence Officer
The Last of the Gentlemen's Wars Major General J. F. C. Fuller
Baden-Powell W. Hillcourt
Real Soldiers of Fortune R. H. Davis
48 Years Service General H. Smith Dorrien
Secret Service in South Africa D. Blackburn and W. Caddell
Good Bye Dolly Gray R. Kruger
Kekewich in Kimberley Lt Col W. O'Meara

The Official History of the War in South Africa   Major General Sir F. Maurice
With the Flag to Pretoria   H. W. Wilson
The Times History of the War in South Africa   Dr. J. H. Breytenbach
Commandant Danie Theron   Colonel J. K. Dunlop
The Development of the British Army 1899-1914   J. Eastwood
General E. Ironside   Brigadier General W. H. H. Waters
Secret and Confidential   General C. Cockerill
What Fools We Were   Major General Sir C. E. Callwell
Field Marshal Sir Henry Wilson   John Bulloch
MIS   Colonel R. Meinertzhagen
Army Diary

Chapters 19-24
At G.H.Q.   John Charteris
Forearmed, The History of the Intelligence Corps   Anthony Clayton
British Military Intelligence 1870-1914   Thomas G. Ferguson
British Military Intelligence   Jock Haswell
The Intelligence Corps 1914 to 1929   A.F. Judge
Armour Against Fate   Michael Occleshaw
The Venlo Incident   S. Payne-Best
Men of Intelligence   Sir Kenneth Strong

All Chapters

History of the Corps of Royal Engineers (Vols 1-4)
In addition to the above published sources, the following Public Record Office papers have
    been consulted:
        Depot of Military Knowledge: WO 1/630, WO 43/17
        English Corps of Guides: WO 4/171, WO 6/138, WO 40/10
        Peninsula Corps of Guides: WO 1/257, WO 28/192, WO 28/194
        Field Intelligence Department: WO 108/75, WO 108/18
        Captain Collins Report: WO 33/32

From the Royal United Service Institution:
    The Raglan Papers and Papers of Lieutenant S. L. Barry 10th Hussars.
From Typescript Histories:
    The Development of the Intelligence Department   Maj or E. L. Wall
    A History of the Development of the Directorate   Lt Col W. R.V.Isaac
        of Military Intelligence
From Kent County Archives – Courtesy Mr. F. Hall County Archivist:
    The Sackville and Harris Papers
From Devon County Archives – Courtesy Mr. A. M. Wherry, Assistant Archivist:
Papers 1262M/L97 and L99
From East Sussex County Record Office – Courtesy C. G. Holland County Archivist:
Papers LCV/2/EW1 and LCV/EW3

Index